Vietnamization

Vietnam: America in the War Years

Series Editor: David L. Anderson
California State University, Monterey Bay

The Vietnam War and the tumultuous internal upheavals in America that coincided with it marked a watershed era in U.S. history. These events profoundly challenged America's heroic self-image. During the 1950s the United States defined Southeast Asia as an area of vital strategic importance. In the 1960s this view produced a costly American military campaign that continued into the early 1970s. The Vietnam War ended with an unprecedented U.S. failure to achieve its stated objectives. Simultaneous with this frustrating military intervention and the domestic debate that it produced were other tensions created by student activism on campuses, the black struggle for civil rights, and the women's liberation movement. The books in this series explore the complex and controversial issues of the period from the mid-1950s to the mid-1970s in brief and engaging volumes. To facilitate continued and informed debate on these contested subjects, each book examines a military, political, or diplomatic issue; the role of a key individual; or one of the domestic changes in America during the war.

Titles in the Series

Eugene M. Blang, *Allies at Odds: America, Europe, and Vietnam, 1961-1968*
Seth Jacobs, *Cold War Mandarin: Ngo Dinh Diem and the Origins of America's War in Vietnam*
Mitchell K. Hall, *Crossroads: American Popular Culture and the Vietnam Generation*
Walter LaFeber, *The Deadly Bet: LBJ, Vietnam, and the 1968 Election*
Joseph A. Fry, *Debating Vietnam: Fulbright, Stennis, and Their Senate Hearings*
Ronald B. Frankum, Jr., *Like Rolling Thunder: The Air War in Vietnam, 1964–1975*
David F. Schmitz, *Richard Nixon and the Vietnam War: The End of the American Century*
David F. Schmitz, *The Tet Offensive: Politics, War, and Public Opinion*
Melvin Small, *Antiwarriors: The Vietnam War and the Battle for America's Hearts and Minds*
Edward K. Spann, *Democracy's Children: The Young Rebels of the 1960s and the Power of Ideals*

Vietnamization

Politics, Strategy, Legacy

David L. Anderson

ROWMAN & LITTLEFIELD
Lanham • Boulder • New York • London

Published by Rowman & Littlefield
An imprint of The Rowman & Littlefield Publishing Group, Inc.
4501 Forbes Boulevard, Suite 200, Lanham, Maryland 20706
www.rowman.com

6 Tinworth Street, London SE11 5AL

British Library Cataloguing in Publication Information Available

Library of Congress Cataloging-in-Publication Data

Names: Anderson, David L.
Title: Vietnamization : Politics, strategy, legacy
ISBN: 978-1-5381-2936-4 (cloth)
ISBN: 978-1-5381-2937-1 (electronic)

Contents

Preface   vii

Abbreviations   xi

Introduction: Pacification, Counterinsurgency, and Vietnamization   1

1   Vietnamization Before Nixon   9

2   Nixon Announces Vietnamization   21

3   MACV Implements Vietnamization   31

4   Buying Time for Vietnamization: Cambodia 1970   45

5   Vietnamization: A Signal Sergeant's Quality Assurance Report   57

6   Vietnamization Tested: Lam Son 719 and the Easter Offensive   73

7   Vietnamization's Final, Failed Test, 1973–1975   93

8   Vietnamization and the End of the Republic of Vietnam: An Assessment   105

9   Vietnamization's Postwar Counterinsurgency Legacy   125

Notes   143

Bibliography   157

Index   163

About the Author   173

Preface

As a sergeant in the US Army Signal Corps in Vietnam in 1970, I observed and played a role in what Washington labeled *Vietnamization*, although at the time my need-to-know was too restricted for me to appreciate fully the broader aspects of what was happening around me. My attention then was narrowly and immediately concentrated on my responsibilities to the mission to which I was assigned and on getting through each day safely so that I could return home in one piece and continue my education, which the Selective Service System had delayed. I had no idea at the time that my life and career would ultimately lead me to writing and teaching about the war for the next four decades.

The origins of this book then are both professional and personal. I had the good fortune to return from my Vietnam service physically and psychologically healthy. Perhaps I acquired something of a survivor syndrome in the sense that I had to give some meaning to what I had witnessed, and for which other Americans lost their lives or physical and mental well-being. I eventually found my scholarly interests attracted to questions about why the United States intervened militarily in Vietnam's internal conflict, why that intervention lasted as long as it did, and how and why this large-scale American effort ended in frustration and failure to achieve its stated objectives. I also felt a need to continue over four decades to share through my writing and teaching what I thought were important lessons, or at least significant questions, about American foreign policy suggested by the war.

Although I felt then—and still do—that my own military service was honorable, I came to believe and have written that US decisions to enter the Vietnam conflict and persist for years in that action were some of the worst public policy decisions the nation had ever made. Thankfully, US national interests were able to survive those mistakes, but the toll the country paid for the error was much too high. One Vietnam War should have been enough.[1] I believed in the years after US forces left Vietnam that such mistakes would not soon be repeated. I was mistaken, however, because in 2003 the United States once again embarked upon another war of choice, this time in Iraq. To this day, Iraq burdens Americans with the role they played in destabilizing the greater Middle East and creating a tinderbox for a wildfire of global terrorism and alienation that may persist longer than the faded Cold War animosities behind the Vietnam War.

I had the honor and privilege over the past few years of my career to teach courses at the Naval Postgraduate School in Monterey, California, to mid-career military officers of all US services and some allied military forces. Many of my students had had numerous deployments in Iraq and Afghanistan. My course on American National Security Policy concentrated primarily on policies and strategies since September 11, 2001. As a historian, I taught this course from more of a historical methodology than from the behaviorist, economic, and other models employed by the international relations specialists on the faculty. Since I sought to provide my students historical perspectives on current policy making, I often turned to cases from the Vietnam War to pose questions about American challenges in the Middle East since 9/11.

The pages that follow explore Vietnamization as one of the links between the American experience in Vietnam and subsequent policy discussions of how the United States with its power and technology can aid emerging governments in becoming self-sufficient in their own defense against armed internal enemies. Long-term US military engagements began in Afghanistan and Iraq in 2001 and 2003. The deployment of American forces into hostilities in Afghanistan has now replaced Vietnam as America's longest war. Comparative analysis of these quagmires—to use a well-worn term—provides students of national defense strategy with valuable insights. The merits of comparing and contrasting the Vietnam War and the Iraq War in particular have been hotly contested, but top US military planners—for example, Gen. Colin Powell and Gen. David Petraeus—made overt reference to Vietnam in framing their policy recommendations years after the Vietnam War ended.[2] Political and military leaders make frequent use of historical precedents in the framing and analysis of policies, but the historical record itself must be carefully and accurately applied.

This book begins with an introduction on the general challenge of how to protect an endangered and underdeveloped ally while helping or even pressuring that partner to create a political structure that is self-sustaining, a process known as *pacification*. Chapters 1 through 3 are a historical narrative of the Nixon administration's fashioning of Vietnamization, a concept that was not particularly new when Nixon announced it in 1969. This description places Vietnamization in the policy context of pacification and counterinsurgency theory, and introduces some of the scholarship on strategy and tactics in Vietnam. Chapters 4 through 7 explore how Vietnamization fared as a policy once the United States had committed to it.

Chapter 5 recalls my own firsthand observations of Vietnamization in action, and other evidence from oral histories and memoirs provide insights in several chapters. James William Gibson terms memoirs, literature, and oral histories as "warrior knowledge," and asks "How can a major war like Vietnam be absorbed in the historical record without listening to those who fought it?"[3] In the introduction of his book, *Losing Binh Dinh: The Failure of Pacification and Vietnamization, 1969–1971,* Kevin Boylan explains his "key province approach." He says that most historians of the war take a top-down view. In particular, he criticized the Olympian perspective of the so-called revisionists, or those who argue that the US involvement in Vietnam was necessary for global communist containment and could have been won if properly conducted.[4] Counterinsurgencies are decentralized and noncontiguous, and thus he sees value in localized study of the conflict. While a panoramic observer writes without providing a context for individual episodes, a single-province approach can provide the missing setting. Boylan uses Binh Dinh to test revisionist theory that the United States was winning the war at the local level, and he finds that argument lacking.

I was a high-frequency radio operator, ad hoc interpreter, and quality assurance NCO in Vietnam, and I use a "key operation approach" as part of my analysis of Vietnamization from my personal observations in the context of communications-electronics. The army considers signal operators to be combat support, along with engineers and military police. It classifies combat as infantry, artillery, armor, aviation, and cavalry. There are also combat services that include maintenance, medical, ordnance, quartermaster, and transportation, as well as other specialized skills, including intelligence, special forces, and civil affairs. In a fashion similar to studies by Boylan of Binh Dinh or Eric Bergerud of Hau Nghia, I detail in chapter 5 a portion of a large canvass.[5] One military function, like one province, does not tell the entire story, but operational or functional analysis can be applied countrywide and not simply to one place. For the South Vietnamese armed forces alone to be able to contest and defeat the army of North Vietnam, it required not just combat readiness but also effective combat support and services to use the modern military technology that the United States could provide. All areas— combat and combat support—also required social and economic resources that were in short supply in the Republic of Vietnam in the South.

Chapter 8 is an assessment of the effectiveness of Vietnamization as a strategy and a consideration of its timing. Some retrospective analyses of Washington's failure in Southeast Asia have argued that 1969 was too late for US leaders to start Vietnamization in earnest or that it was working but not sustained long enough. In other words, the authors of these studies pose anguishing "if only" alternative scenarios. Excellent research by other historians refutes these "win" theses. This chapter compares the competing contentions and finds that, despite the confidence of the writers who believe there was an American solution to South Vietnam's inherent political bankruptcy, their critics are correct—the RVN from its inception was an artificial state with little historical foundation upon which to survive on its own.

Finally, chapter 9 briefly sketches some key strategies used in Iraq and Afghanistan, and analyzes counterinsurgency and pacification approaches that continued to rely upon perceptions—including what might have been—of Vietnamization and judgments of its value. Failing to evaluate candidly the Vietnam experience, Washington immersed US forces in new quagmires. Even after complete or partial troop withdrawals from Iraq and Afghanistan, US policy analysts found themselves struggling with "unpalatable choices" or "least bad options" created in part by the US intervention in local, violent conflicts.[6] Understanding Vietnamization is a key to knowing what went wrong with past American policies and what might improve future American strategic performance.

For consistency, a few editing conventions are followed in this book. Vietnamese place names, with the exception of Hanoi and Saigon, are separated into two or more syllables, such as Da Nang, following Vietnamese style. Vietnamese proper names and other words are printed without the original diacritical marks that indicate pronunciation in this polytonal language. With the exception of Ho Chi Minh—whose name is a pseudonym, and who is known historically as Ho—Vietnamese are referred to in the common style of either using the full name or the given name—for example, Nguyen Van Thieu is known as Thieu—since there are so few family names in Vietnam. The four military tactical zones in South Vietnam are identified throughout the text as I Corps, II Corps, III Corps, and IV Corps, although these designations formally changed to Military Regions on July 1, 1970—that is, MR 1, MR 2, MR 3, and MR 4. Since the military vernacular depends so heavily on acronyms and specialized abbreviations, a list of those most frequently used is provided for translation into civilian parlance.

Abbreviations

APC Accelerated Pacification Campaign
ARVN Army of the Republic of Vietnam
CIA Central Intelligence Agency
COIN Counterinsurgency
CORDS Civilian Operations and Revolutionary Development Support
CPA Coalition Provisional Authority in Iraq
CRIMP Consolidated RVN Improvement Plan
DRV Democratic Republic of Vietnam
FRUS *Foreign Relations of the United States*
GVN Government of South Vietnam
HES Hamlet Evaluation System
ICS, SEA Integrated Communications System, Southeast Asia
IMP Improvement and Modernization Program
JCS Joint Chiefs of Staff
JGS Joint General Staff of the RVNAF
MAAG Military Assistance Advisory Group
MACV Military Assistance Command, Vietnam
NLF National Liberation Front
NSC National Security Council
NSDM National Security Decision Memorandum
NSSM National Security Study Memorandum
NVA North Vietnamese Army
OJT On-the-Job Training
ORLL Operational Report—Lessons Learned
PAVN People's Army of Vietnam
PF Popular Forces of the RVN
PPP Public Papers of the Presidents of the United States

PRC People's Republic of China
PRG Provisional Revolutionary Government
PROVN Program for Pacification and Long-Term Development of Vietnam
RF Regional Forces of the RVN
RVN Republic of Vietnam
RVNAF Republic of Vietnam Armed Forces
SEATO Southeast Asia Treaty Organization
USMC US Marine Corps
VC Viet Cong, or Vietnamese Communist(s)
VCI Viet Cong Infrastructure
VNAF Republic of Vietnam Air Force
VNN Republic of Vietnam Navy

Introduction

Pacification, Counterinsurgency, and Vietnamization

Pacification and *counterinsurgency* are synonymous terms. They describe action taken by a government to defeat insurgency or rebellion against it and to create conditions under which the people of a country become more favorably inclined toward, or even develop allegiance to, the government.[1] Central to this process is that the government must make itself either loved or feared by the people, as Niccolò Machiavelli advised the rulers of Florence in 1513. In the case of the Democratic Republic of Vietnam (the DRV, or North Vietnam as it was known during the American war in Indochina), the Politburo in Hanoi mobilized loyalty to the state through a combination of patriotic revolutionary nationalism that derived from anticolonialist emotions and police-state methods that squashed dissent and forced political discipline in the North.

Vietnamization and counterinsurgency are interconnected concepts but not synonymous. For the Republic of Vietnam (the RVN, or South Vietnam) to be capable of sustaining itself militarily, politically, and economically against armed insurgency from the DRV—that is, to Vietnamize its own defense—it had to achieve legitimacy and effectiveness among the Vietnamese—the goal of pacification. The classic counterinsurgency (COIN) formula found in military doctrine has three steps: clear, hold, and build. To be successful, counterinsurgency has to remove the military threat to the population, defend the people from renewed military threat, and then create institutions and practices that the population accepts as legitimate and able to provide for basic needs, including public safety, income, health care, and education. The first two steps are clearly military and can be performed by the threatened state, an external ally, or combined operations of the two. A

1

powerful ally can improve the host state's military capability through materiel modernization and supply, basic and advanced training, tactical advice,
and reinforcement of the host's strength with allied forces (ground, air, and
sea). In practice, these two steps characterized Vietnamization. The third
step—build—represents the true COIN challenge.[2]

For a state to be self-sustaining against an armed insurgency, it must be
able to defend itself militarily, including the domestic resources necessary to
create a modern armed force, but must also simultaneously earn the allegiance and trust of the population through viable economic and social structures and processes. Although the political leaders in South Vietnam were
Vietnamese nationalists, they lacked the patriotic appeal of the regime in
Hanoi that could rightfully claim to have defeated the French. When Saigon
turned to coercive measures to force public support—a method also used by
the DRV—it often fostered opposition, rather than obedience. Southern authorities were in a "catch-22" dilemma because in many places the armed
insurgents actually governed a particular village or district, and the police or
military power used to "reassert lawful government" alienated the local population from the Saigon regime.[3]

Strategic insights to be gained from the American war in Vietnam, such
as the efficacy of counterinsurgency warfare, hinge in large part on the point
in time from which that war is examined. The United States began aiding
France in its Indochina War in 1950 and dramatically escalated its own direct
military participation in the country in 1965. The twentieth-century origins of
conflict within Vietnam, however, are deeply rooted in Vietnamese history
and the experience of French colonization. After centuries of internal struggle among Vietnamese over power in their own country, the French arrived
in the 1850s and disrupted this internal dynamic. By the end of the nineteenth
century, French power had broken the authority of both the Vietnamese
monarchy in Hue and the village leaders throughout the country who had
managed local affairs. A complex social and political crisis ensued as Vietnamese with various traditional and modern backgrounds resisted the French
intrusion and offered indigenous alternatives to colonial control. After Japanese expansion into Indochina in the 1940s broke French power in the region, Vietnamese nationalists of several types seized the opportunity to take
back their country. The First Indochina War from 1947 to 1954 brought
success to the Viet Minh, a communist-led front headed by Ho Chi Minh,
that defeated Paris's attempt to regain control. The Viet Minh created the
DRV, with its capital in Hanoi.

When the fighting ended, however, the DRV could claim control only of
the area north of the 17th parallel, a temporary cease-fire line established in
July 1954 at an international conference in Geneva, Switzerland. The French
Expeditionary Corps had de jure authority south of the line pending a national election that the conferees had proposed for 1956 to decide the political

administration of the entire country. Vietnamese officials in what now became known informally as South Vietnam immediately set to work to build an alternate regime to that in Hanoi. The leaders of this effort were a mix of Southerners who had either worked with the French in the past or who did not share Ho Chi Minh's communist vision for the country. There were also various families, criminal gangs, religious groups, business owners, and others who believed their own power and interests were threatened by the prospect of a Northern, communist-led government. Out of this mix, Ngo Dinh Diem and his brothers emerged as the most likely challengers to the Viet Minh, but this traditionalist, Catholic, anti-French family had many rivals and outright opponents in the South other than the Viet Minh.

While this drama emerged within Vietnam, the global Cold War erupted as the United States and the Soviet Union became bitter ideological and strategic enemies. With world politics defined simply in terms of a win–lose conflict between Moscow and its Marxist-Leninist followers in places like Beijing and Hanoi on the one hand and Washington and its allies in places like Paris and London on the other, divided Vietnam became a Cold War salient. When the conference at Geneva closed, the future of Vietnam was at a crossroads. One path was a postcolonial route that many people in the so-called Third World were taking as the world moved away from the century of European imperialism and as these new nations declared their independence. The other route for these former colonial subjects was to follow a course laid out by Washington and Moscow as these big powers enticed or pressed underdeveloped nations into their big power rivalry for global hegemony. This second option is what political scientists describe as "direct partisan intervention by outside powers to end a civil war."[4] Vietnam in 1954 was going through a conflict over who would rule at home—that is, a civil war—but US officials defined it in terms of global politics in which "partisan interveners [Americans] aim to establish, protect, or reestablish allied regimes."[5]

For US policymakers and policy historians, how Washington chose to define the options in Vietnam has been profound. At its most fundamental level, the Eisenhower administration's decision at the time was to identify South Vietnam as a Cold War bastion and to move to secure a pro-American regime in Saigon as vital to US national interests. Washington officials were aware from the beginning that the Communists in Hanoi had legitimate claims as nationalist heroes who had wrested much of their country from the grip of French colonialism. These Americans made the judgment, however, that the prudent course for the US strategy to contain global communist power was to keep Hanoi from controlling all of Vietnam and even all of Indochina through some sort of domino effect famously articulated at the time by President Eisenhower. Washington led the creation of the Southeast Asia Treaty Organization with an implied commitment to shore up South

Vietnam and bordering nations against communist-led aggression. In October 1955 Diem created the RVN, and six months later the final, remaining French forces left; the national elections proposed for 1956 never occurred. Without international ratification, a de facto two-state solution had emerged.

Washington's strategic decision to recognize the RVN as a sovereign state and to accept it as an ally posed a tactical burden for US planners at the time, and throughout the American war in Vietnam, and continues today to plague understanding of the war. It created an oversimplified distinction between the internal and external dimensions of military and political conflict in South Vietnam. If the danger to the survival of a friendly government in Saigon was external threat from Hanoi backed by Beijing and Moscow, then the strategy was border defense against international aggression. If the menace to the RVN under President Ngo Dinh Diem and later President Nguyen Van Thieu was political and social mobilization against them from nationalists in the South who welcomed unity with the North or who opposed the RVN administration for self-centered reasons, then the strategy was pacification of the rural and urban population in support of Saigon. In reality, both dangers existed simultaneously and had to be considered together, but finding an integrated approach bedeviled American military and political strategists until the end of the RVN in 1975.

There is general acceptance among historians and analysts that the United States failed in its objective to sustain a friendly government in Saigon, but scholars part ways on why America failed. The orthodox or majority school of Vietnam War historiography begins with the decision in the 1950s to make the American effort there part of the Cold War. Robert Schulzinger put it succinctly when he wrote, "Had American leaders not thought that all international events were connected to the Cold War there would have been no American war in Vietnam."[6] This historical interpretation of US policy labels it as "flawed containment"—that is, the United States decided to make Vietnam a bastion of containment when 1) there was no Soviet army threatening the country, 2) the communist leaders in Hanoi had historic distrust of the Chinese, and 3) thousands of Vietnamese viewed American intervention as a continuation of Western colonialism and the enabler of a government in Saigon that could not build its own domestic legitimacy. The United States made a tragic miscalculation in entering a long and costly war that continued until a point was reached at which the American public and Congress demanded Washington to fashion a face-saving way out. The exit strategy was Vietnamization, negotiations, and return of US prisoners of war—a program that the Nixon administration portrayed as honorable. In reality, it only provided for an interval of time that would insulate the United States and its president from blame before the collapse of the defective Saigon government.

A revisionist interpretation by some historians and military memoirists who served in Vietnam accepts the Cold War as a strategic imperative and views the decisions that led to American involvement as defense of US national interests. From that starting assumption, the point of analysis becomes not whether intervention was merited in the first place, but how the United States conducted its war effort. Since this approach accepts the US military presence in South Vietnam as a "necessary war," the question becomes whether that application of American power and purpose was used correctly.[7] In the search to find a way not taken, theories have been advanced about how the application of more US air and ground power earlier in the war or more diplomatic flexibility or more economic assistance to Saigon could have led to a US "victory" in the war. These scenarios are largely counterfactual or merely broad generalizations drawn from a few documented successes, and they do not clearly define what victory would have actually looked like. Since they ease the angst of dealing with a loss and the damage to national pride, however, these "win" scenarios have had staying power. Their appeal is so great that some observers suggest they should be considered the new orthodoxy. Since most writers continue to use the term *orthodox* for the flawed-origins argument and *revisionist* for the flawed-tactics argument, those definitions of the terms are used in this analysis.[8]

Like the orthodox school, the revisionist argument often comes down to an analysis of Vietnamization, since that policy became the context for shaping the Paris agreement of January 1973 that enabled Washington to withdraw its few forces still remaining in the RVN. Reflecting on the victory of the People's Army of Vietnam (PAVN, or North Vietnamese Army) over the RVN Armed Forces (RVNAF) in 1975, revisionist accounts often speculate on a counterfactual scenario that Vietnamization may have been the long-sought approach, but was too little, too late. In March 1968 Gen. Creighton Abrams assumed command of the US Military Assistance Command, Vietnam (MACV). His principal biographer, Lewis Sorley, argues that Abrams, along with Ambassador Ellsworth Bunker and William Colby, the CIA officer who directed the pacification program, "raced to render the South Vietnamese capable of defending themselves before the last American forces were withdrawn . . . [and] came very close to achieving the elusive goal of a viable nation and lasting peace."[9] A number of revisionists assert outright that Vietnamization worked; RVNAF leadership problems had been solved; and South Vietnam was fully capable of standing on its own as long as it remained supported by US airpower and American financial and material assistance. This belief leads them to the conclusion that the only reason Saigon ultimately fell was the failure of the US Congress to maintain the requisite level of support. A "stab-in-the-back" argument developed that weak-willed politicians in Washington abandoned America's allies.[10]

Sorley's critics, such as James Willbanks, Gregory Daddis, and Kevin Boylan, respond that from the 1950s through the 1960s the security of the Saigon government was too precarious to allow the luxury of reform. Not having built adequate popular support, the Saigon regime had a military that had became too dependent on American aid and technology, and was too politicized by 1969 to transform into an effective force within the timetable Nixon had imposed on MACV. The issue of unlimited congressional largesse arose only because the RVN over the two decades of its life never achieved self-sufficiency. Moreover, Daddis adds that the PAVN and its Southern adherents, the Viet Cong (VC), posed a conventional military threat to the Saigon regime that, combined with the RVN's resistance to correcting glaring administrative deficiencies, required Abrams to conduct both security and pacification efforts simultaneously in the same manner as his predecessor, Gen. William Westmoreland.[11]

To cut through this orthodox–revisionist argument, it is helpful to understand that the Second Indochina War—that is, the war from the time the French left in 1955 until Hanoi unified the country through conventional military assault in 1975—was simultaneously a clash between North Vietnam and South Vietnam as well as an armed insurgency within South Vietnam itself. The line between these conflicts was so blurred as to be essentially nonexistent, but how US officials perceived and defined that line was central to American strategy and tactics. Also, American strategists believed that the fighting in Vietnam required only limited resources, and this limited-war assumption narrowed US options. The amount of effort expended in Vietnam was constrained because American leaders deemed other containment fronts in Europe or Latin America more important, and because Pentagon planners assessed that the communist enemy in Hanoi was not strong enough to withstand even a portion of the power at Washington's disposal. Further, American involvement was not a simple morality play of good versus evil, as both Cold War advocates of the war and antiwar critics of US force claimed. As the Buffalo Springfield 1966 song lyric by Stephen Stills sardonically put it, "Singing songs and carrying signs, most say hooray for our side."[12] The DRV was a heroic defender against the evils of Western imperialism, but it was also a brutal police state that ruled within its borders with political executions, imprisonment, heavy doses of ideological education, and social regimentation. The RVN was corrupt, and it, too, relied upon secret police, political prisons, assassinations, and manipulation of democratic forms. Compared to the North, however, South Vietnam was a more open society with courageous journalists, antigovernment candidates in elections, and free enterprise opportunities.

A look at Vietnamization as it developed and was practiced makes clear several points in this fog of war over interpretations. Vietnamization did not work and likely could not work for several reasons. The decision by the

Politburo in Hanoi to conduct a violent and relentless assault on the security of the people and institutions of the RVN made creating and growing effective government in the South nearly impossible. Security had always to be paramount, even if it meant the delay of or disregard for nurturing fragile social and economic institutions. One of the first, if not often *the* first, tasks of every general who commanded US forces in South Vietnam was military security to protect pacification. Before the major escalation of American forces in 1965, there was not enough time and resources to both secure the South and train the RVN in good civil and military practices. Once the war had been Americanized, a type of neocolonial mentality set in that the US forces fought the war for the RVN, and training and fostering the South's military organizations and civilian agencies still took second place.

With the first US military and civil involvement in Vietnam in the 1950s, Americans saw the challenge not as counterinsurgency (because the Viet Minh Communists were still consolidating their authority in the North) but as providing security and enabling reform in the South. The Viet Minh had forced France to cede political control to them as the DRV, and the Geneva Conference of 1954 provided international recognition of DRV authority north of the 17th parallel. South of that line, physical control and governance remained to be determined. In keeping with the grand strategy of containment of global communism, Washington took steps to keep the South safe from DRV expansion. A debate among US officials in South Vietnam began almost immediately over which effort should take precedence—security or reform. Lt. Gen. John W. "Iron Mike" O'Daniel, head of the US Military Assistance Advisory Group (MAAG) in 1954–1955, argued that the RVN needed first to provide security for its population and its borders against threats from Hanoi. MAAG largely aimed its training at developing the military and paramilitary capacity of the South's armed forces, which was a form of Vietnamization. US diplomats countered that the government in Saigon, whose leaders had just declared the Republic of Vietnam in October 1955, needed to become more democratic with a broader popular base to survive, which is a prescription for pacification. As an ally, not a colony, South Vietnam had to compete with other global demands for US resources. Although relatively generous, US aid could not provide simultaneous military assistance and domestic development. Similarly, Saigon had to marshal its own limited resources and focus its political will in one area or the other.[13]

By the late 1960s, a half-million US troops had been deployed throughout the South, as the PAVN and VC increasingly threatened to overwhelm the RVN and its military. Pacification, or *civic action*, the term then in vogue, often worked where American units were present and provided security. Saigon's authority quickly dissipated, however, when the Americans moved to another area of operations and the VC insurgents moved back into the vicinity. This process kept reoccurring even after MACV and the RVN began an Accelerated Pacification Campaign (APC) from November 1, 1968, to January 31, 1969, and attempted to exploit damage done to the Viet Cong Infrastructure (VCI, the Communists' clandestine political operatives) during the North's Tet Offensive early in 1968. In Hau Nghia province west of Saigon, for example, a civilian American member of the provincial advisory team wrote that the APC "goes forward, but it is only occupation, not pacification."[14] The senior adviser, a lieutenant colonel, added that "The essential, first occupation and the provision of security, is well under way, [but] the frequent mortarings, occasional assassinations and infrequent minings initiated by the VC serve to shake the people's confidence in GVN [Government of Vietnam] presence as much as our military successes build it up."[15] Despite this assessment, and with domestic political pressure mounting in the United States to relieve the burden of the war, President Nixon began withdrawing American forces from Hau Nghia—first, to participate in cross-border operations in Cambodia in the spring of 1970, and then, out of South Vietnam entirely later that year.

The RVNAF demonstrated repeatedly over time an inability to ensure its own adequate security for pacification. Both institutional military weakness and lack of popular allegiance to either the Ngo Dinh Diem or Nguyen Van Thieu governments handicapped Saigon's forces. When Nixon formally announced the turn to Vietnamization in 1969—or, more accurately, the return to the pre-1965 supply and advisory mission—the fragility of the RVN remained. Military self-defense was undeveloped. Corruption and politicization of the RVNAF officer corps had always been present, and had grown worse while US forces took primary responsibility for the war. Neglect of the welfare of Army of the Republic of Vietnam (ARVN) enlisted men had fomented morale and desertion problems. The economic base of the South—historically, farming and fishing—had not been developed because of the colonial century, and the dearth of resources and education hampered the potential for economic self-sufficiency. Although some South Vietnamese identified with the Thieu government as a matter of survival, there was little enthusiasm among the populace for the Saigon regime. Thieu continually guarded against a possible coup, which only heightened distrust and weakened the growth of effective self-government in the RVN. The term *nation building* was often used to describe the American purpose in South Vietnam, but after two decades of effort, the goal of a state in the South that was capable of self-defense, self-government, and economic self-development remained a distant objective.

Chapter One

Vietnamization Before Nixon

Heralded by the Nixon administration as a strategic innovation, *Vietnamization* was the general idea that the United States would increasingly transfer responsibility for combat operations in the Republic of Vietnam (RVN) from American troops to strengthened South Vietnamese forces while withdrawing US military units from the country. It was an operational term often attributed to Nixon's secretary of defense, Melvin Laird, but it was not a new concept in 1969.

EISENHOWER, KENNEDY, AND THE POLICY OF HELPING SOUTH VIETNAM HELP ITSELF

In the 1950s, the Eisenhower administration sought to create an RVN military that could defend its own country, and it kept the number of American armed forces personnel in the South under 1,000. In September 1950, shortly after the United States recognized the French-created State of Vietnam in Saigon as a rival to the Democratic Republic of Vietnam (DRV), the first uniformed US military unit of 342 officers and enlisted men arrived in Vietnam as the Military Assistance Advisory Group (MAAG), Indochina, to observe the use of American military equipment and supplies going to French and allied Vietnamese units. Although US matériel aid to the French war effort increased over time, by the spring of 1954, with the Viet Minh siege at Dien Bien Phu prompting Paris to engage in serious ceasefire talks, the chief of France's general staff, Gen. Paul Ely, requested the assistance of Americans in the training of Saigon's soldiers in what was called the Vietnamese National Army (VNA). Despite Pentagon concerns about overcommitment, Lt. Gen. John W. O'Daniel, the MAAG chief, interpreted his unit's orders to perform "end use checks of American equipment" as permission to do training.[1]

After the Geneva Conference, MAAG, Indochina, became MAAG, Vietnam, with a separate unit for Cambodia, and Lt. Gen. Samuel T. "Hanging Sam" Williams succeeded O'Daniel as commander. Seeking ways to improve the Army of the Republic of Vietnam—usually referred to as ARVN, and drawn from the old VNA—Washington created the Temporary Equipment Recovery Mission of 350 men in 1956. Only seven of these soldiers cataloged equipment recovery; the remainder set up training for the Vietnamese in logistics management. By the end of 1956, there were 740 American personnel under Williams's command advising Saigon on the development of its military forces.[2]

Neither Lt. Gen. O'Daniel nor Lt. Gen. Williams believed that the Communists in Vietnam were capable of mounting an insurgency that would threaten the survival of the Saigon government, and there was little serious guerrilla activity in the mid-1950s. Consequently, they focused their training on improving the South's ability to defend against conventional attack from the North and paid little attention to counterguerrilla warfare. They occupied themselves and their advisers with the enormous challenge of building the RVN Armed Forces (RVNAF) into a stable military organization in an unstable country. Their approach was representative of most US military thinking in the 1950s. American diplomatic representatives in Saigon worried, however, that the government of Ngo Dinh Diem was vulnerable to internal political enemies and needed to expand its popular base through evidence of economic progress and political openness. *Counterinsurgency* (COIN) was a term little used in the 1950s, but in discussions among US officials there were precursors of what in the future would be deliberations over how to combine and reconcile military security and pacification.[3]

When John Kennedy inherited ownership of US policy in Vietnam from Eisenhower, Diem's government faced an expanding armed insurrection. The Lao Dong, or Vietnamese Communist Party, had formed the National Liberation Front (NLF) in December 1960 in South Vietnam, with the aim of overthrowing the Saigon regime by a combination of political and military tactics. Although the NLF included discontented non-Communists in its ranks, US and South Vietnamese officials quickly labeled it the Viet Cong (VC), or Vietnamese Communists.

Although the new president was a Cold War strategist who thought in global, big-power terms, he personally turned discussions of US policy in Vietnam to consideration of counterinsurgency theory. Kennedy worried about Soviet leader Nikita Khrushchev's boasts that the USSR would aid "wars of national liberation" in the postcolonial world against Western capitalist aggression. Influenced by the writings of Gen. Maxwell Taylor, Kennedy was searching for a limited war—or small war—option to nuclear confrontation, and desired a way to counter communist revolutionary warfare on the ground. A regular reader, the Harvard-educated chief executive told others that he was impressed by the novel *The Ugly American* by William J. Lederer and Eugene Burdick. This fictional account, drawn from actual encounters in Southeast Asia between arrogant American officials and local patriotic activists, in part inspired the Peace Corps, a Kennedy program to counter a point made in the novel that "the Red world is far better at public relations than the free world."[4] Kennedy also became intrigued by the ideas of Sir Robert Thompson, a British counterinsurgency advocate who had been an architect of successful efforts to suppress communist rebels in Malaya.[5]

At his first National Security Council meeting on February 1, 1961, Kennedy ordered the creation of a Limited War Task Force to study counterinsurgency strategy. He followed up by going personally to Fort Bragg, North Carolina, to learn about and endorse training of the US Army Special Forces in guerrilla warfare in underdeveloped countries. The president authorized the distinctive Green Beret headgear of the army's special operators, and in September 1961 the army activated the 5th Special Forces Group (Airborne), tasked to train RVNAF personnel in COIN methods. There had been only limited academic study of COIN in contrast to the many volumes available on nuclear war strategy, but Lt. Gen. Lionel W. McGarr, the current MAAG chief, responded to the growing violence in the South by authoring a handbook, *Tactics and Techniques of Counterinsurgent Operations*. It described ARVN training designed "to ultimately separate the people from the insurgents and induce them to support the local government." It formed the basis for Kennedy's Counterinsurgency Plan, "for a carefully integrated political, military, economic, paramilitary, and police campaign to eliminate the Viet Cong and establish firm government control."[6]

In addition to McGarr, Kennedy readily accepted advice in developing a COIN approach from Brig. Gen. Edward Lansdale, Walt W. Rostow, and Roger Hilsman. Lansdale had experience in advising the Philippine government against left-wing rebels and had met frequently with Ngo Dinh Diem during the start-up of his government in Saigon. Rostow was an MIT economist who specialized in modernization theory and headed the State Department's Policy Planning Council, and Hilsman was assistant secretary of state for Far Eastern affairs. Under their influence, Kennedy's plan laid out tactics that would remain in various forms in US Vietnam policy from then until the Nixon and Ford administrations. It called for providing security for the Southern population against VC guerrilla attacks, and also creating government programs that would help build popular support for the Saigon regime. Senior leaders in the US military—known as the "Never Again Club"—opposed this thinking because they remembered that Washington had trained South Korea for internal defense only to see its forces almost destroyed by a conventional assault from North Korea.[7]

Although concerned about the political and social structure of the RVN, Rostow and others had only a limited perception of conditions in Vietnam. They assumed that the armed insurgents were the product of external instigation and infiltration. They thought wars of national liberation were imposed from outside—their most frequently named suspect was China—and from the top down. The chairman of the State Department's Vietnam Interdepartmental Working Group, Paul Kattenburg, expressed discomfort with this premise. He believed it was disingenuous to term Saigon's opponents "insurgents" rather than "revolutionaries," because it obscured the possibility that they were "champions of a popular movement."[8] They had not necessarily been thrust upon peace-loving rice farmers, but might actually represent the discontent of local people facing repression from RVN officials.[9]

Second-guessers after the American war in Vietnam had failed in the 1970s claimed that the United States had started too late to Vietnamize or build a regime in South Vietnam that could stand on its own. Rostow, however, recalled that in 1961, "my nightmare was . . . that we wouldn't deal with it [guerrilla warfare] early enough."[10] He and others talked about reform, but could not take their eyes off of China looming large near a long and open Cambodian and Laotian frontier across which it could travel into South Vietnam. The planners did not believe they had much time to secure the South from failure.

Lansdale's counterinsurgency ideas about modernizing Saigon's government to sustain itself were not much different than Rostow's, but his personal commitment to Diem undermined his effectiveness as an agent of reform. Especially after the Kennedy administration accepted a neutral government in Laos to lessen US tensions with the USSR over that country, Diem resisted American efforts to broaden his base and reduce reliance on his family and narrow circle of supporters. US Ambassador Elbridge Durbrow in Saigon clashed with Lansdale and Williams specifically over their patience with the RVN president. The diplomat thought it was wrong to pin the high stakes of US Cold War security on a flawed leader like Diem.[11]

Unable to modify Diem's behavior, Washington turned to an increase in American military support of the South, both to convince the RVN president that the United States was on his side, as well as to send a warning to Hanoi, Beijing, and Moscow of US determination. To help protect the Saigon government from the mounting, violent VC pressure, Washington increased the flow of arms, military technology, and military advisers to the RVN, in what historian John Prados terms a "move toward early Vietnamization."[12] The White House ordered the armed forces, State Department, and Central Intelligence Agency to offer "special training" at all ranks "in the planning and conduct of counter-insurgency programs," and "to engage in research projects designed to improve the US capability for guiding underdeveloped countries through the modernization barrier and countering subversive insurgency."[13] In 1962, Washington phased out MAAG and replaced it with Military Assistance Command, Vietnam (MACV). When Kennedy died in 1963, the number of US military personnel in the South had reached 16,000, many of whom were US Army Special Forces trainers and advisers.[14]

While Kennedy wanted counterinsurgency warfare, he began to doubt that the RVN could be defended without large-scale use of American forces. Rostow pushed for American troops in South Vietnam as a "trip wire" to deter Chinese intervention with the threat of greater US involvement. Diem wanted more military support and less political interference, and was not receptive to change. Despite Saigon's political ineptitude, Kennedy believed in 1962 that COIN was working. The principal evidence was the strategic hamlet program. Inspired by Robert Thompson and championed by Hilsman, these fenced and armed villages were supposed to bring security to the rural population and thereby lead them to accept the noncommunist government.

Situating the hamlets in areas where they wanted political control and not reform, Diem and his brother Ngo Dinh Nhu hid true conditions within the hamlets and told US officials what they wanted the Americans to hear. Secretary of Defense Robert McNamara later acknowledged that he had overrelied on statistics and field reports that gave a false sense of progress—reports that led Kennedy to consider scaling back US involvement in South Vietnam. In an ARVN coup, soldiers murdered Diem and Nhu in November 1963, and an assassin killed Kennedy three weeks later. There are some indications that Kennedy may have thought that the RVN had developed as a state about as far as the United States could expect, and that the US contribution to that effort had peaked.[15] Even if there were limits to how far American assistance to Saigon might go, however, Kennedy remained publicly and thus politically committed to staying loyal to the survival of South Vietnam. On September 13, 1963, he declared in language that could have been that of Richard Nixon a decade later that "we want the war to be won, the Communists to be contained, and the Americans to go home. . . . But we are not there to see a war lost."[16]

LYNDON JOHNSON AND THE AMERICANIZATION OF THE WAR IN VIETNAM

The new president, Lyndon Johnson, was generally more of a hawk than Kennedy, and had been wary of talk of withdrawing 1,000 US troops. In Johnson's first session on Vietnam with his top advisers—the same group upon whom Kennedy had relied—the head of the Central Intelligence Agency detected a change in "tone" in the new commander in chief: "Johnson definitely feels that we place too much emphasis on social reforms; he has very little tolerance with our spending so much time being 'do-gooders.'"[17]

Still, Johnson's political instincts were similar to Kennedy's, believing that Washington should strike a balance between withdrawal and escalation by providing military training and political mentoring to the South Vietnamese so they could manage their own destiny. [18]

Johnson supplied more instructors and advisers to help the RVN improve its defenses, and in 1964 he added American airpower as a deterrent to the North. Selective bombing of northern targets occurred after the Gulf of Tonkin incident in August 1964—a minor and ambiguous naval skirmish involving US Navy and DRV vessels off the coast of North Vietnam. This event gave the president a pretext for air-mailing to Hanoi a threat of increased pressure. He secured from Congress the Gulf of Tonkin Resolution that gave him authority "to take all necessary measures to repel any armed attack against the forces of the United States and to prevent further armed aggression." [19]

As these events were occurring, Johnson was also launching his presidential election campaign. He wanted to appear to be a firm leader but also to reassure voters that he was not planning on sending US troops to Vietnam. In language that anticipated Richard Nixon's later explanation of Vietnamization, Johnson declared in a campaign speech in Akron, Ohio, in October 1964:

> But we are not about to send American boys 9 or 10,000 miles away from home to do what Asian boys ought to be doing for themselves. President Eisenhower said in 1954 to the Government of Viet-Nam, "President Diem, we want to help you help yourselves. We will give you advice, we will provide leadership, we will help you with material things, with your weapons and the things that you do not have, to protect your independence. . . ." We have now some 18,000 men in Viet-Nam, officers and men, advising, counseling, leading them. [20]

Following Johnson's election victory in November, he moved toward further escalation of American force. At first, he would not concede that American ground forces would ultimately take a leading role. There was an element of sincerity in his expressed desire that the US effort remain solely one of advice and support, but by December 1964 he was telling Ambassador Maxwell Taylor in Saigon that "I myself am ready to substantially increase the number of Americans in Vietnam, if it is necessary to provide this kind of [effective] fighting force against the Viet Cong." [21] In February 1965, National Security Adviser McGeorge Bundy dramatically reported to Johnson that "the situation in Vietnam is deteriorating, and without new US action defeat appears inevitable—probably not in a matter of weeks or perhaps even months, but within the next year or so. . . . There is still time to turn it around, but not much." [22] Within days, Washington launched Operation Rolling Thunder, a graduated aerial bombardment of targets in the DRV, and in

March deployed a force of 3,500 marines to begin active security patrols around key bases.

The American training and equipping of the RVNAF was not, however, producing a Saigon force able to defend itself. Despite repeated, so-called studies and various urgings from MACV and the US embassy, the Saigon government lacked the public support to get effective conscription legislation and enforcement to meet manpower needs. A porous draft and personnel drain caused by persistent desertions due to poor pay and conditions in the army kept the South's forces under strength throughout the entire course of the war. The increased level of enemy activity made it impossible for US advisers to regroup ARVN units for training. Operational requirements for infantry meant that each ARVN corps headquarters was often unable to release even a single battalion for formal training. US field advisers reported that the low rate of training was one of the principal causes of the low level of combat effectiveness. [23]

With Rolling Thunder and the marine deployment, a line had been crossed. VC attacks supported by People's Army of Vietnam (PAVN) infiltration into the South posed an existential threat to the RVN. With the ARVN experiencing heavy losses and on the brink of disintegration, Gen. William C. Westmoreland, the MACV commander, advised that there was "no solution . . . other than to put our own finger in the dike." [24] The Joint Chiefs of Staff recommended sending at least three divisions to begin offensive operations against the enemy. The Johnson administration's first large-unit deployment of entire US combat divisions came in July 1965, and this surge to 100,000 in the number of Americans in the RVN is accurately referred to as the Americanization of the war. Washington gave MACV a two-part task: First, US infantry and airmobile divisions began conducting large-scale offensive operations "independent of or in conjunction with GVN [Government of Vietnam] forces" as necessary, with RVNAF troops providing population security and smaller operations. Through province- and district-level advisory teams, the second part was to help the RVN develop viable government structures to exercise effective control throughout the country. [25]

Johnson's description of his decision to escalate the American war had a striking parallel with COIN theory. In his memoirs, he wrote that "in the summer of 1965 I came to the painful conclusion that an independent South Vietnam could survive only if the United States and other nations went to its aid with their own fighting forces." He added that from that time until the end of his presidency, his goals were "defeating aggression, building a nation, and searching for peace." [26] This strategic outline parallels the COIN formula of clear, hold, and build. There is more consistency in US policy in Vietnam from the 1960s into the 1970s than historical surveys of the war often acknowledge.

Even more ominous for the future course of American policy in Vietnam than an implicit scaling up of COIN tactics to a strategic model for large-scale war was how little attention Washington seemed to be paying to why the Saigon regime was floundering. Johnson had not even informed Nguyen Van Thieu, the RVN's new head of state, before ordering the US troop escalation. What kind of state was the United States trying to defend and build against insurgents? South Vietnam was in political disarray, and a massive insertion of US troops and firepower was not going to create good government by fiat. Washington was embarking, in the words of historian Brian VanDeMark, on a "massive military effort on a foundation of political quicksand." He notes that neither before nor after 1954 had South Vietnam been a political entity. Divisions within Vietnam dating back centuries and magnified by decades of colonialism had left factionalism, rivalry, and chronic political disorder. If Saigon could not marshal the political will required for effective government, the daunting and likely unworkable task of the United States was to try "to save a people in spite of themselves."[27]

After the surge in the summer of 1965, the number of US military personnel in the RVN continued to rise steadily, and reached 485,600 by the end of 1967. Over the same time, RVNAF strength rose to 643,000. Following the Tet Offensive in early 1968, President Johnson rejected MACV requests for another 206,000 ground troops and began slowing the increase of forces. Several factors influenced his decision. The American deployment of forces to Vietnam had gone on longer and proven vastly more expensive in lives and treasure than he and his advisers had anticipated. Public opposition to these costs with no apparent benefit to the United States was evident in the increasing number of antiwar demonstrations, growing congressional criticism, and eroding support in public opinion polls. The peak US force level came shortly after Richard Nixon took office in January 1969, reaching 543,400 in April 1969, and reflected the escalation that Johnson had started in 1965, but began to reconsider in his last months in office.[28]

WESTMORELAND, ABRAMS, AND THE DEBATE OVER A "BETTER WAR" STRATEGY

From 1964 to 1967, Gen. Creighton W. Abrams, serving as US Army Vice Chief of Staff, worked under Chief of Staff Gen. Harold K. Johnson to create the US expeditionary force sent to Vietnam to meet the manpower needs required to Americanize the defense of South Vietnam. Working together, generals Abrams and Johnson fashioned an army with a large number of draftees and inexperienced commissioned and noncommissioned officers. In 1966, they also conducted a study known as "A Program for Pacification and Long-Term Development of Vietnam," or PROVN. Although the program was not adopted at the time, Abrams took from it the idea of "one war"—that military operations, pacification, and upgrading the RVNAF should be integrated to gain the population security required for Saigon to prevail in this conflict. In an interview, Abrams asserted that the way to deal effectively with the enemy was to counter the threat on different levels: "The enemy's operational pattern is his understanding that this is just one, repeat one, war."[29] It was not about large units, pacification, or territorial security, but it was all of these simultaneously. To speak of guerrilla war and conventional war was, in Abrams's view, a false dichotomy.[30]

The one-war description has sometimes been cited to argue that Abrams had a "better war" concept in Vietnam than Gen. Westmoreland, who commanded MACV from 1964 until replaced by Abrams in 1968. The contrast between the two officers and their approaches has been overstated. PROVN was not unique in army history, and was not critical of Westmoreland. The study was done before Westmoreland launched large-unit operations in the RVN, and Abrams's PROVN-inspired strategy actually was a continuation of integrated tactics started by Westmoreland. Every senior US commander in Vietnam from Williams in the 1950s to Westmoreland a decade later agreed with what Westmoreland put explicitly into one of his first directives in 1965: "The war in Vietnam is a political as well as a military war. It is political because the ultimate goal is to regain the loyalty and cooperation of the people, and to create conditions which permit the people to go about their normal lives in peace and security."[31]

The aim was to destroy the VC and to strengthen the RVN's military, administration, and public services. Westmoreland's 1966 battle plan (pre-PROVN) was a variation on the "oil spot" approach of Lt. Gen. McGarr from 1960 to 1963, which combined military and political operations to clear the enemy from areas, remove the Viet Cong Infrastructure (VCI), and work with Saigon to establish government services—the classic COIN formula. In his next battle plan, Westmoreland wrote that "the Revolutionary Development program, designed to restore local government, provide and maintain public security and win the support of the people to the Government of Vietnam, offers the only real hope for bringing this conflict to a successful conclusion."[32] Pacification was his goal, but he had to face the reality on the ground of a large and dangerous enemy force and a weak ally. "The enemy had committed big units," Westmoreland noted in his memoirs, "and I ignored them at my peril."[33] He had to marshal his resources to "stem the tide" of the threat before he could concentrate on pacification.

US forces had to provide the shield while the RVN got its house in order. American troops were best equipped for offensive operations against a large enemy, while the ARVN had the benefit of language and cultural identity to work on pacification. PROVN authors wanted US forces more involved in pacification, but agreed with Westmoreland's logic that, in the report's words, "Rural Construction can progress significantly only in conjunction with the effective neutralization of major enemy forces."[34] The document further stated that "the primary role" of US forces was to fully engage the PAVN and VC main force units.[35] The PROVN outline was vague on how long the division of labor between US and ARVN soldiers—that is, offensive operations versus pacification—would continue, but estimated five years, or until at least 1971.[36]

Authors such as Lewis Sorley, Phillip Davidson, and Max Boot have offered a road-not-taken argument that Westmoreland's large-unit operations did not employ counterinsurgency or pacification. They make an "if only" claim of a better outcome for the United States if Westmoreland had concentrated less on security and more on reform. Actually, counterinsurgency thinking permeated US operations in Vietnam from the Kennedy administration onward. President Johnson deployed conventional military units to meet Westmoreland's request for American firepower to protect counterinsurgency operations, as well as to destroy main-force PAVN units infiltrating the RVN. Historian Kevin Boylan has documented that corruption and inefficiency endemic in the Southern government and its armed forces meant that pacification was only successful when protected by US combat units.[37]

In May 1967, Abrams reported to Vietnam as Westmoreland's deputy commander with the primary responsibility of upgrading the ARVN. Over the next six months, he traveled to every ARVN command throughout the country and worked to improve the training, support, and advice that they were receiving. When the Tet Offensive suddenly erupted in January 1968, many of these same ARVN units responded well in the face of the enemy, and Abrams received considerable credit for their performance. From a forward MACV headquarters at Phu Bai, Abrams personally directed the joint US-ARVN counterattack that retook the city of Hue during the Tet fighting.[38]

Hanoi's Tet Offensive prompted the Johnson administration to undertake a long-overdue reexamination of US strategy in Vietnam. The war had gone on longer, required more American troops, and cost more than Washington had foreseen in 1965 when the United States had moved from military advising to Americanizing the war. The United States had for years sought to develop the RVNAF, and immediately began to increase that effort after Tet. Johnson's new secretary of defense was Clark Clifford, who took the position in January just prior to the PAVN and VC offensive. He was concerned about the president's political viability and saw right away the negative political impact of US casualties. He began looking for ways to reduce US losses and have the RVNAF assume more of the fighting. ARVN Maj. Gen. Nguyen Duy Hinh wrote later, "The 1968 Tet Offensive can fairly be said to have generated the Vietnamization program. . . . By the time President Nixon announced it in June 1969, the task of Vietnamization had become an accelerated process."[39]

Johnson made the change in command in Vietnam from Westmoreland to Abrams on June 10, 1968, and the new MACV commander in tandem with Clifford began what he called "Vietnamizing," which meant trying to use more South Vietnamese soldiers in the fighting of the war and ending the steady stream of US troops into the country to defend South Vietnam.[40] Historian Gregory Daddis has warned, however, about emphasizing the significance of this change of command over the more powerful fact that the commander-in-chief position itself was about to change. The new president, Richard Nixon, would soon make Vietnamization the name for his policy in Vietnam, and it would take a course over which Abrams would have little control.[41]

As Americans went to the polls in November 1968 to elect a new president, the voters had clearly soured on the war. Johnson had voluntarily withdrawn as a candidate for reelection. The resulting campaign for his successor was tumultuous and often agonizing among a host of Democratic aspirants. Antiwar senator Eugene McCarthy of Minnesota saw his candidacy overtaken by the popular senator from New York, Robert Kennedy. President Kennedy's younger brother was also critical of the war, but fell victim to an assassin in June. Johnson's vice president, Hubert H. Humphrey, finally secured the Democratic nomination amid sometimes violent antiwar protests at the party's convention in Chicago. Humphrey wanted changes to the US conduct of the war, such as putting an end to the bombing of North Vietnam, but he entered the contest under the shadow of his past loyalty to Johnson.[42]

On the Republican side, President Dwight Eisenhower's two-term vice president, Richard Nixon, came back from what observers had thought was political oblivion to gain his party's nomination for president. Nixon took political advantage of the mood of unease in the nation, but the war was not the only issue on voters' minds. Law and order was a huge concern as racial and economic tensions had sparked horrifying riots in American cities. The assassination of civil rights icon Martin Luther King Jr. in April and the presidential candidacy of civil rights opponent Governor George Wallace of Alabama further churned the political pot. Although considered a moderate Republican, Nixon campaigned as a conservative on law enforcement and race relations and as an opponent of the Johnson-Humphrey Great Society spending on social programs.

On the hot topic of the war, Nixon pledged to moderate and conservative voters to maintain the fight against communism in Southeast Asia. For Americans of all stripes seeking relief from the burden of the war, he allowed them to believe that he had a secret plan to end American involvement in the fighting. On the stump, he hinted that Americans could be phased out of Vietnam, but he gave no indication as to how. He claimed the war was winnable and that "an honorable end to war" was possible, but he remained adamant that he would not simply pull out American forces in a manner that would reward communist aggression and damage American credibility.[43] A shrewd politician, Nixon waged a campaign that left his policy options in Vietnam open to fashion a face-saving way out of the war with minimal damage to his political leadership and America's international stature.[44]

In the final days before the election, Johnson announced a bombing halt as a step toward restarting negotiations in Paris. Humphrey had been promising that he would follow this course if elected, and the prospects of a diplomatic breakthrough suddenly presented the possibility that the vice president might prevail with the voters. Nixon made covert contacts with President Nguyen Van Thieu and secured a public statement from him that he would not participate in any talks at that time. Nixon let Thieu believe he would be better served by the Republican Nixon than the Democrat Humphrey, who clearly wanted a negotiated American withdrawal. Johnson and Humphrey discovered the ploy before election day and privately asked Nixon about actions that Johnson considered to be "treason."[45] In an outright lie to Johnson, Nixon denied any contacts with Thieu, and Humphrey made a political calculation not to make the charge public. Whether this eleventh-hour drama determined the outcome of the election is unknowable, but Nixon's secretive and duplicitous moves forecast methods he would follow in the White House. His assurances to Thieu disguised his own disregard for the Vietnamese leadership, to whom he would soon shift sole military and political responsibility for the outcome of the war as he abandoned Americanization and embraced Vietnamization.

Chapter Two

Nixon Announces Vietnamization

Richard Nixon defeated Hubert Humphrey by a very close margin. Although a clear victor in the electoral vote, Nixon gained only 43.4 percent of the popular vote to Humphrey's 42.7 percent. George Wallace received 13.5 percent. A narrow plurality of Americans had chosen Nixon based in large part on the hope that with some vague and unarticulated secret plan, he would start getting Americans out of the violence of Vietnam. Historians have found no evidence that candidate Nixon had a secret plan—Vietnamization or otherwise—but on January 21, 1969, the day after his inauguration, he began "browsing" for one, as veteran diplomat Philip Habib termed it.[1] The president's national security adviser, Henry Kissinger, addressed National Security Study Memorandum 1 (NSSM 1) to the Departments of State and Defense and the CIA, "to develop an agreed evaluation of the situation in Vietnam as a basis for making policy decisions."[2] This document consisted of twenty-nine questions and numerous sub-questions under headings that included negotiations, Republic of Vietnam Armed Forces (RVNAF) and enemy strengths and weaknesses, pacification, South Vietnamese government (GVN) politics, and current operations.

MELVIN LAIRD OUTMANEUVERS HENRY KISSINGER

As Kissinger recorded in his memoirs, the new administration found itself "between the hammer of antiwar pressure and anvil of Hanoi."[3] It was clear that the American public would likely support negotiations with Hanoi for a staged withdrawal of US and People's Army of Vietnam (PAVN) forces from South Vietnam. Kissinger had great faith in diplomacy, but Hanoi's position in tentative peace talks that Lyndon Johnson had begun in Paris in the spring of 1968 was for total, unilateral withdrawal of US troops from the

South and the replacement of Thieu's "puppet" regime in Saigon with a coalition government. Diplomatic negotiations by their very nature take time, and Hanoi seemed in no hurry.[4]

Keenly aware of how the public's desire for a quick exit had politically burdened Johnson and the Democratic candidates, the new president told his aide H. R. Haldeman, "I'm going to end the war fast."[5] Nixon believed there would be no positive movement in negotiations until "maximum pressure" on the DRV had brought about military progress for the US-RVN alliance.

Secretary of Defense Melvin Laird took a third position. He was skeptical about both negotiations and possible military victory, and was acutely aware that domestic support for the United States staying in Vietnam was almost gone. In addition, he realized that the financial costs of the war were weakening US global military readiness. Laird's favored approach was "all-out advocacy of Vietnamization," which meant keeping a hard line in negotiations but rapidly withdrawing US forces and strengthening the RVNAF. Kissinger claimed to have "great hope for negotiations" and real doubts about either military victory or Vietnamization.[6]

Few Americans, not even antiwar Americans, were comfortable with a "cut and run" exit of simply leaving Vietnam after almost two decades of support and sacrifice for Saigon. The three major Democratic candidates in 1968—Eugene McCarthy, Robert Kennedy, and Hubert Humphrey—had proposed some type of negotiations. Kissinger believed the DRV was smart enough to see the benefit of negotiation to achieve its goals without continued costly warfare. Nixon thought that the DRV had a breaking point and that it would flinch under punishing US military pressure. Laird doubted the efficacy of both force and negotiation and hence favored Vietnamization as an orderly withdrawal. Not only domestic pressure in America but also the continuing, stubborn resistance of Hanoi to military force or negotiation left Vietnamization as the default option, regardless of clear signs that the long-term prospects for Saigon on its own were not good. Hanoi always understood that the political and military courses of the war were inseparable.[7]

At the beginning of his administration, Nixon was playing Laird and Kissinger against each other. The national security adviser was closer in view to Nixon than Laird in the belief that a combination of force and diplomacy was the most effective approach. Kissinger's twenty-nine questions were in part a bureaucratic move to tie up the Defense Department while he built his rapport with the president. A veteran member of Congress from Wisconsin, Laird was a master at political maneuver—a "Midwest Machiavelli," according to the *Milwaukee Journal*—and up to the challenge presented by Dr. Kissinger, the Harvard professor who was new to the political big leagues.[8]

From March 6 to 12, 1969, Laird traveled to Saigon with the chairman of the Joint Chiefs of Staff (JCS) Gen. Earle Wheeler to assess a broad range of conditions, and for "frank" discussions with President Thieu. He also stopped at US Pacific Headquarters in Hawaii to confer with Adm. John McCain, the commander in chief of Pacific forces. His first-ever meeting with the RVN president was stormy. As described by his biographer Dale Van Atta, Laird went into the meeting "unhampered by the subtlety that others might use in dealing with Asians." The secretary informed Thieu, according to Van Atta, that RVN military leaders "had to realize that they were going to take a more responsible role and it wasn't going to be Americanized any longer." "With a hint of authority in his voice," Thieu countered that this relationship was not what he had been promised by President Johnson. Laird proceeded to give Thieu a "civics lesson" on US elections. This description of the encounter conveys a dark tone of neocolonial patronizing in Laird's approach to an ally whose interests the United States claimed to be defending.[9]

Upon his return to Washington, Laird reported to Kissinger that, with an improvement in RVNAF performance, "we should be able to retain this posture [of keeping pressure on the enemy] with a simultaneous diminution in the US share of the total military effort. . . . I believe it is essential that we decide how to initiate the removal from Southeast Asia of some US military personnel."[10] He also outlined "Termination ('T' Day) Planning"—a contingency plan for the orderly and systematic withdrawal of US personnel and equipment either upon cessation of hostilities or the transfer of effort to the RVNAF as it became more efficient. He made clear, however, that progress had been slow in the modernization of the RVNAF, and that the effort required acceleration.[11]

While this Vietnamization planning was getting under way, Nixon decided to begin secret bombing of Cambodia as a signal to Hanoi, Saigon, Beijing, and Moscow that the United States was not weak and that diplomatic talks should be conducted in earnest. In an operation labeled Menu—beginning with a mission named Breakfast and keeping available the names Lunch, Supper, Dessert, and Snack—bombings began on March 17. Kissinger had pushed Nixon to bomb in Cambodia, something he knew Nixon wanted to do. Abrams reported that there were good targets in Cambodia, and that he knew the location of Hanoi's Central Office for South Vietnam (COSVN), located in Cambodia. The planning was kept secret from Secretary of State William Rogers; Laird; the chief US negotiator in Paris, Ambassador Henry Cabot Lodge; and Ambassador Ellsworth Bunker in Saigon. When he learned of the plan, Laird opposed it, realizing there would be public outrage when it became known. For that reason, Kissinger instructed the air force colonel in charge of the targets to create fake reports that the strikes were in South Vietnam, not Cambodia. Communist leaders knew, of course, exactly where the bombs were hitting.[12]

Even before taking the oath of office, Nixon had shared privately with H. R. Haldeman his idea of how to achieve results in Vietnam where Johnson had failed: "I call it the Madman Theory, Bob. I want the North Vietnamese to believe I've reached the point where I might do *anything* to stop the war. We'll slip the word to them that, 'for God's sake, you know, Nixon is obsessed about communism. We can't restrain him when he's angry—and he has his hand on the nuclear button'—and Ho Chi Minh himself will be in Paris in two days begging for peace."[13] The gambler Nixon may have been bluffing, but his eagerness to push the envelope of options was real. Even with Vietnamization under active discussion, Nixon kept open through October the idea of a massive, punishing blow against North Vietnam—code-named Duck Hook—as an active policy choice.[14]

On March 28, 1969, the National Security Council (NSC) discussed Laird's report from his visit to Saigon and other studies of the status of the war. Lt. Gen. Andrew Goodpaster, deputy commander of MACV, reported that Abrams's headquarters was close to "de-Americanizing" the war. The president agreed with this assessment, as did Laird, but the secretary of defense thought the word choice sounded negative: "What we need is a term [like] 'Vietnamizing' to put the emphasis on the right issue."[15] Following the meeting, National Security Decision Memorandum 9 (NSDM 9) directed the study of a timetable under two scenarios: mutual withdrawal of US and DRV forces, or "Vietnamizing the war."[16]

Laird had outmaneuvered Kissinger when Nixon agreed to the Vietnamization concept, and the national security adviser was angry because he believed removing US troops took away one of the most important bargaining levers in the Paris negotiations. Kissinger appealed to Nixon not to de-escalate while US diplomats were arguing for mutual withdrawals. In April, the national security adviser circulated more study memoranda (NSSM 36 and NSSM 37) requiring timetables and specific data in an effort to delay the start of unilateral withdrawal. The president thought that Kissinger did not adequately appreciate domestic politics or understand that a reduction of US personnel in the RVN would help administration supporters in the 1970 midterm elections. Nixon held to the belief that his determination could outlast that of the Politburo as long as the United States continued to pile on military pressure, such as the Breakfast bombings.[17]

In a nationally televised address on May 14, Nixon revealed that the United States was ready to accept a National Liberation Front (NLF) role in the political life of the South, and that it would agree to simultaneous North Vietnamese and US troop withdrawals from the South. Previously the United States had insisted on PAVN withdrawal preceding US withdrawal. Wanting to believe that negotiations would work, Kissinger claimed the speech had been "cleared" with Saigon, but Bui Diem, the RVN's ambassador in Washington, charged that it came as a shock to his government: "The game of imposition and attempted finesse that would become the Nixon administration trademark in dealing with its ally had begun with a bang."[18]

In response to NSDM 9, NSSM 36, and NSSM 37, the JCS prepared a withdrawal outline for Laird's consideration, and the secretary again visited Vietnam. On June 2, Laird submitted through Kissinger a report for the president recommending an initial withdrawal increment of 20,000 to 25,000 in July, but keeping the remaining schedule flexible. From his own observations, Laird was disappointed in RVNAF progress in assuming the "burden of the war," but he believed that the Southern government's strength was improving. The unknowns were RVNAF leadership, motivation of forces, psychological reaction of the South Vietnamese to US redeployment, and the organizational structure of the Saigon regime. Laird cautioned that "we should strive for a sensitive balance between too much, too soon, and too little, too late."[19] The RVN had to know that Washington remained serious about its commitment to the independence and survival of South Vietnam. Those Americans most vocal against the war would probably not be silenced by this small beginning move, in Laird's estimation, but "important elements of the US public would be encouraged."[20] This assessment indicated that Laird saw Vietnamization as a way to buy time for the administration in responding to domestic political pressure to de-escalate the American war effort.

Laird's report also contained various redeployment "packages" developed by the Pentagon. These long-term plans aimed "to Vietnamize the War during the period 1970–1972." US withdrawals without reduction of North Vietnamese forces in the South could risk collapse of the Saigon government. The size and timing of the American troop departures were critical, Laird stressed, and thus he emphasized that "we will exert a major effort to expand, train, and modernize the RVNAF, and do whatever else may be required to transfer progressively to the South Vietnamese greatly increased responsibility for all aspects of the war."[21]

After getting State and CIA comments on the Department of Defense proposals, Kissinger submitted them to the president for approval. In this final form, the plan was first to remove 50,000 to 100,000 troops in 1969. The second part considered varying timetables from eighteen to forty-two months, with "residual American troops" ranging from 260,000 to 306,000 at the end of forty-two months. If 290,000 troops were withdrawn in forty-two months, Laird foresaw possible interruption of the pacification progress. "A much faster withdrawal could result in more serious problems for pacification and allied military capabilities," Kissinger estimated, "as well as possible adverse effects on the GVN, in the absence of reciprocal North Vietnamese withdrawals."[22]

Under Abrams's "one-war" concept, MACV's Accelerated Pacification Campaign was considered a companion to Vietnamization, and with some irony the general acknowledged the key to pacification was "to provide meaningful, continuing security for the Vietnamese people."[23] Despite the image of "one war," Abrams's approach was sequential as COIN doctrine had always been—secure, hold, and build. The first step in MACV's plan was "maximum security for rural areas" in which Saigon could then provide law and order and build the local economies. [24] As all US military commanders in Vietnam had repeatedly cautioned, security had to come first, because without it all other pacification programs were doomed to failure. Vietnamization in practice meant that security was to be provided by the RVN's problematic national, territorial, and local forces.

Thus, there was a contradiction between pacification and Vietnamization. If security responsibility were turned over too quickly to RVNAF—which would be a Vietnamization leap—the pacification progress would be threatened. MACV's intention to increase the size of the RVNAF put its tacticians at odds with Robert Komer, head of American pacification efforts at MACV. Military strength planners wanted to transfer regional South Vietnamese forces to regular Army of the Republic of Vietnam (ARVN) maneuver units, but Komer argued territorials were needed in the villages for security to launch the Accelerated Pacification Campaign in order "to expand Saigon's control of the countryside." [25]

NIXON'S ANNOUNCEMENTS AT MIDWAY AND GUAM

Having decided upon Vietnamization but still attracted to Duck Hook as a secret option, Nixon scheduled a meeting with President Thieu at Midway Island on June 8. Nixon had hinted to Thieu that there would be a summit meeting if he were elected, but this offer was the first move Washington had made in that direction. South Vietnamese leaders viewed the chosen location as a "desolate and gooney-bird ridden place" in the middle of the Pacific, and Thieu and his ambassador to Washington, Bui Diem, could not help but note that Soviet officials—regardless of what they privately thought of Hanoi— had always made a big show and given the red-carpet treatment to DRV leaders invited to Moscow. Saigon believed that the Nixon administration wanted to hide its meeting with Thieu because Kissinger was afraid the RVN president "would produce an awkward scene." Diem bitterly complained:

> Our meetings were relegated to such places . . . almost as if we were regarded
> as lepers by those in whom we had placed our security and with whom we had
> shed so much blood. Circumstances forced us to swallow such things, but we
> did not forget them. With a continuous history of two thousand years, Vietna
> mese—whether Communists or non-Communists—have a low tolerance for
> humiliation, and such indignities created permanent scars. [26]

Nixon's honeymoon with the American public was ending, in Bui Diem's opinion, and the American president was announcing troop withdrawal for political purposes. "Thieu was not happy about the move toward Vietnamiza-tion," Diem recorded, but he was accepting the inevitable.[27] Washington did not want a joint communiqué at Midway, and preferred that Saigon simply agree publicly to a US troop withdrawal. Saigon desired a declaration putting the Nixon administration on the record with a public affirmation that the United States would not accept a coalition government.

Nixon and Thieu met at Midway as planned on June 8, 1969, and in prepared remarks during a midday break in the talks, the US president an-nounced the withdrawal of 25,000 US forces, citing improved ARVN capa-bility. Nixon said the "replacement" would be completed by August, at which time further assessments would be made of ARVN troops replacing American units. In a joint statement at the end of the day, Nixon reaffirmed American support of Saigon. In this shared statement, Thieu reaffirmed an RVN position taken in the Paris talks that he would negotiate directly with the NLF, and both presidents expressed a common resolve in opposition to the idea of a coalition government in South Vietnam.[28]

The South Vietnamese government viewed Vietnamization and the Paris negotiations as a two-part White House strategy "to buy time from the on-slaught of domestic antiwar sentiment." Washington did not want Saigon creating problems, Ambassador Diem reasoned, and complained that the idea of troop withdrawals "had never been officially submitted to the South Viet-namese for their approval or for some counterproposal." Thieu had avoided a confrontation at Midway by offering to label the American move as a "rede-ployment" of forces rather than a withdrawal. He accepted private US assu-rances that he would be fully briefed on the progress of talks with Hanoi. At a press conference in Saigon upon return from Midway, Thieu emphasized the rejection of a coalition government and declared that all South Vietna-mese could be proud of their own strength. On the decrease in US troops, he claimed that "it was beneficial for the Vietnamese people to rely less on the Americans and more on themselves."[29]

There was little else that Thieu could say or do. Publicly, the Midway meeting papered over cracks in the Washington–Saigon alliance that re-mained unreported. Meeting with Chiang Kai-shek in Taiwan after leaving Midway, Thieu told his Chinese host: "You know when Nixon decides to withdraw, there is nothing I can do about it. Just as when Eisenhower, Ken-nedy, and Johnson decided to go in, there was very little my predecessors had to say about it."[30] Chiang could commiserate, having himself faced American pressure to compromise with Mao Zedong during China's civil war.

The NLF followed news stories of the planned Midway meeting and the public statements it produced with great interest. It saw Vietnamization for what it was—a move "to placate public opinion in the United States." It was also aware that it was not a new concept. It reminded the communist cadre of the *jaunissement* (yellowing) that the French had employed to reduce their own casualties and create an image of an independent anticommunist force. Vietnamization was more serious in their view than the "phony" French move, however, because the United States had vastly more capacity than France had possessed to support Saigon's forces after the withdrawal of US ground troops. As one NLF official put it, "all the corpses would henceforth be Vietnamese." He and his comrades feared that Vietnamization might "hamstring opposition" to the American war in the United States and the world while helping to sustain Thieu. The NLF decided that it needed its own propaganda ploy.[31]

Timed to coincide with publication of the joint US-RVN statement, the NLF made an announcement of its own. On June 8, a gathering of hundreds of antigovernment activists in Tay Ninh proclaimed the founding of the Provisional Revolutionary Government (PRG) of the Republic of South Vietnam. A film crew was on hand to record the event, and film clips and press releases immediately followed, publicizing the birth of a rival regime in South Vietnam. The Soviet Union and other communist countries quickly extended recognition to the PRG and opened embassies in their capitals for what they termed the "official" representatives of the South Vietnamese people. By creating this interim administrative structure, the NLF had performed a bit of "guerrilla diplomacy" that made it more difficult for Washington to entice Moscow for the sake of big-power relations to put leverage on the DRV and NLF to make diplomatic concessions.[32]

As a follow-up to Midway, Bui Diem floated to Secretary of State Rogers Thieu's notion of "long haul/low cost." The idea was that a smaller American presence in the RVN would help ensure long-term US support because the cost would be less. There were problems with this argument. It was increasingly doubtful that the American public would support any level of assistance to Saigon. In addition, Rogers was not in on the Nixon-Kissinger policy loop, and American policy was whatever the two of them determined it to be.[33] Later, as negotiations dragged on, Kissinger did at one point in September suggest to Nixon that "the enemy might fear that Vietnamization, by gradually reducing US presence and lowering casualties, could maintain American public opinion while the GVN is successively strengthened."[34] Ambassador Bunker had reported from Saigon on intelligence that officials in the DRV were fuming about the "perfidious trick of the Nixon Administration" to take away the antiwar pressure they were counting on to force the White House into concessions.[35] Kissinger did not indicate, however, that he had confidence Vietnamization would move Hanoi toward any concessions.

Under the cover of deep secrecy, Kissinger took steps on June 14 to open a back channel for his own personal bilateral negotiations with Hanoi. Clearly, the Nixon administration was prepared to seek some settlement with the Politburo without coordination with, or even the knowledge of, Saigon. Kissinger had previously communicated outside the State Department—and without the knowledge of the secretary of state—directly with Soviet ambassador Anatoly Dobrynin in Washington. That approach had gained nothing from the DRV, which was able to use the Moscow–Beijing rivalry to its advantage to limit diplomatic pressure from its socialist allies. Consequently, on July 15 the White House sent a letter to North Vietnam addressed to Ho Chi Minh via Jean Sainteny, a former French official long connected with Hanoi's leaders. Signed by Nixon, the letter indicated that Washington was prepared for substantive negotiations, but gave a November 1 deadline for response, after which there would be military actions of "great consequence."[36]

Addressed to the dying Ho Chi Minh, who had not been in active leadership for years, the letter showed the administration's lack of knowledge about Hanoi and frankly confused the Politburo. The United States was offering to negotiate while it was bombing Cambodia and announcing strengthening of the RVN. Nixon and Kissinger were underestimating the strength and willpower of their opponents, and seemed to think that the combination of force and diplomacy were in Washington's favor. The real leader of the government in Hanoi, Le Duan—who had not trusted negotiations since the DRV got what he thought was a bad bargain at Geneva in 1954—decided to allow a direct meeting to learn more about this new team in Washington.[37]

Kissinger held his first secret meeting with DRV officials in Paris on August 4, but his bargaining position was already weak. Johnson had stopped bombing the North in 1968, and now Nixon was beginning unilateral withdrawal of US ground forces. Hanoi was already getting what it wanted, and it now only had the removal of Thieu as its principal demand. Publicly, and even privately, Kissinger kept insisting—and would continue to insist—that Thieu remain in power, but he treated Thieu with disdain and kept the Saigon government totally out of the details of the peace process.[38]

Speaking with journalists in Guam on July 25 during a Pacific trip to greet the US *Apollo 11* astronauts, the president made a broad statement that reporters quickly labeled the "Nixon Doctrine." US policy would be to provide military and economic aid to Asian nations fighting armed insurrections, he explained, but those governments would be expected to provide their own soldiers to bear the burden of the fighting. "We will keep our treaty commitments [such as SEATO]," Nixon affirmed, "but, . . . as far as the problems of internal security are concerned, as far as the problems of military defense, except for the threat of a major power involving nuclear weapons, that the United States is going to encourage and has a right to expect that this problem will be increasingly handled by, and the responsibility for it taken by, the Asian nations themselves."[39]

Vietnamization was a policy, not a plan, and its timing and evolution were determined almost entirely by US domestic politics. Fewer American service personnel in Vietnam meant fewer American casualties and, the administration hoped, less public outcry against the war. Although Vietnamization was portrayed as evidence of progress in Saigon's ability to fight, it was actually central to Nixon's effort to reduce political pressure at home from his critics and supporters. While the program decreased the role of American troops, as peace advocates demanded, it also increased supplies to the RVNAF, which had the political benefit of reassuring domestic hawks that Washington's support of South Vietnam remained strong.

Chapter Three

MACV Implements Vietnamization

Washington had publicly proclaimed Vietnamization, but it now fell to MACV and the US embassy in Saigon to make it work on the ground. To be successful, Vietnamization had to be about more than simply substituting RVNAF troops for US units—or South Vietnamese blood for American blood. Efforts to strengthen Saigon's military forces were straightforward. As US troop levels dropped sharply in 1969 and 1970, MACV returned to the advisory model for US units that had existed before the United States began its large-scale deployments in 1965. MACV set up a host of special schools and training activities in an improvement and modernization program (IMP) for the expanded RVNAF.

As had always been true, however, nation building in South Vietnam required many nonmilitary improvements. The RVN needed rural pacification, strong political processes, public services, economic viability, and especially the ability to provide security for its citizens. These reform tasks—policing, land reform, inflation control, local elections, rooting out of Viet Cong Infrastructure, and increase of the rice harvest—were not ones that US military advice and equipment alone could provide. Vietnamization went hand in hand with pacification. Since 1967, MACV had within its organization the Office of Civil Operations and Revolutionary Development Support (CORDS). The 1969 CORDS pacification plan emphasized that the US program for South Vietnam had three "mutually supporting principles: self-defense, self-government, and self-development." This plan, according to Ambassador Ellsworth Bunker in Saigon, "explains why the Vietnamese refer to 'Vietnamization' as 'The Three Selfs.'"[1]

RVNAF IMPROVEMENT AND MODERNIZATION PLANS

Unlike T-Day (termination of hostilities day) planning in 1968 that had assumed withdrawal under some type of cease-fire arrangement, Vietnamization required military planners to assume that there would not be a political settlement, and that the RVNAF would have to continue to fight without any reduction in enemy force levels. When Gen. Creighton Abrams sent the twenty-nine questions of NSSM 1 to the senior US military advisers in each of the four corps tactical zones, the answers varied by region, but all of them reported that, against a combined VC-PAVN threat, "the South Vietnamese could do little more than hold their own and judged [RVNAF] offensive capabilities marginal at best."[2] Lt. Gen. Walter T. Kerwin Jr. in III Corps suggested in particular the greater use of women in the services and the posting of ARVN soldiers nearer to home to reduce desertions and better connect the army to the people. MACV had identified these same problems and suggestions for years. The American officers cited continuing need for air, artillery, and logistical support and requirements for additional training. Tellingly, the advisers estimated that "it would take five years to make such changes," and doubted the RVN's ability to survive unless American ground forces were withdrawn slowly and US combat support services remained as long as possible.[3]

When Secretary of Defense Melvin Laird and Gen. Earle Wheeler visited the RVN in March 1969, Abrams noted areas in which the RVNAF was making progress, but argued that the rate of any improvement had to be measured against the level of enemy threat and government progress in pacification. The secretary acknowledged these indicators of withdrawal feasibility but ordered Abrams to prepare a schedule with specific force-reduction target dates. Laird calculated that the American public would expect a withdrawal plan "in three, six, or nine months, but probably within the next three to four months."[4] The commander of MACV expressed personal opposition to unilateral US withdrawal based upon his corps advisers' assessments, and CIA and Pentagon analysts in Washington were more negative than Abrams in their predictions that Saigon could not survive alone the VC threat, even without PAVN pressure. Despite these warnings, the Nixon administration issued NSSM 36, setting the timetable for Vietnamization to be completed by December 1972. It had ordered the US command in Vietnam to turn over almost the entire ground-war effort to the RVNAF, whether or not Saigon was ready in time.[5]

As implementation of Vietnamization began at MACV's sprawling headquarters at Saigon's Tan Son Nhut Airport ("Pentagon East"), Abrams sensed correctly that the initial targets were estimates and that Washington would likely speed up the redeployment process. Even more critical to those planners on the scene than the overall number was the type of US personnel that would remain. The plan had three phases: During the first stage, over the course of twelve to eighteen months, more than 200,000 American combat forces would be withdrawn, but during phase two, over a period to be determined, the RVNAF would still need a residual American contingent of 200,000 combat support troops, including artillery, engineer, signal, helicopter, fixed-wing aircraft, and advisory. Of particular importance to the effectiveness of RVN forces would be engineer battalions to maintain the roads to reduce dependence on aerial resupply, and signal battalions to operate and maintain the highly sophisticated communication system until Saigon could develop its own network. The final phase would be to leave a small number of American advisers and security personnel once the RVN had the capacity to provide its own defense.[6]

MACV viewed the residual support element during phase two as central to Vietnamization. It anticipated that protecting combat support units from cuts would be basically impossible if MACV was going to meet the redeployment directives coming from the White House. MACV's Vietnamization plan was in essence a procedure to draw down combat and support forces in proportional numbers, in what Abrams termed a "cut-and-try" approach to meet deadlines, while maintaining some balanced military capability as long as possible.[7] Ironically, North Vietnamese strategists might have been perceiving Vietnamization in terms similar to Abrams. CIA analysts estimated that Hanoi remained confident of victory but could see the remaining US force "as a formidable obstacle . . . by virtue of its essential combat support makeup."[8] The intelligence analysts reasoned that Hanoi might calculate that US support troops would incur fewer casualties than combat units and reduce antiwar pressure in the United States, thus enabling Washington to sustain Saigon long enough to give "the South Vietnamese populace and the communist cadres [VC]" the impression that Vietnamization was succeeding. Consequently, the CIA concluded that the enemy would "seek out opportunities to inflict setbacks" on Vietnamization programs and would "devote increasing resources to countering the pacification effort."[9]

President Thieu was more keenly aware of the existential danger to his nation than Nixon, Kissinger, and Laird seemed to be. He had not been included in the planning for Vietnamization, but, after being presented with a fait accompli at Midway, he grasped the opportunity to get American support for an increase in the size of the RVNAF and upgrades in armored vehicles, artillery, and aircraft supplied to his forces. The dollar amount of US aid to the RVN defense budget had not increased in two years, and funds were especially needed to improve the poor living conditions of ARVN soldiers and their dependents. Abrams rejected the equipment and funding requests as unnecessary as long as a US force remained in the RVN, but he did support an increase in the size of the armed forces and police, as long as these were light infantry units that could be easily and cheaply trained and equipped.

Adm. John S. McCain, Commander in Chief, Pacific (CINCPAC), endorsed Abrams's reasoning, and added that Thieu's request did not match his forces' technical abilities nor address the leadership and desertion issues within the South's military. [10]

Laird approved a larger Vietnamese force in August, but kept pressing US commanders to come up with a revised RVNAF IMP that would create a South Vietnamese force that could "maintain at least current security levels" while reducing American troops to a "support force" of 190,000 to 260,000 by July 1971, and to a small advisory force by July 1973. It was clear that the large residual force that MACV desired was not what the White House envisioned. The JCS shared MACV's concern, and even proposed that "certain out-of-country and offshore support forces would also be needed." This proposal meant approaching specifically Thailand and South Korea, but the chiefs conceded the uncertainty of negotiating such assistance. [11]

Under administration pressure, MACV revised its estimates and projected that RVNAF improvements, RVN population control, and VC threats would be at a level by July 1970 that could enable Laird's requests to be met. In December, MACV presented Laird with what was labeled Phase III RVNAF IMP, increasing South Vietnamese forces to 1,061,505 by mid-1973. The secretary's staff thought MACV was still undervaluing the RVN's capabilities to justify continuing US support forces. Laird traveled to Saigon in February 1970 and met with Abrams, Bunker, and Thieu. Upon his return to Washington, he ordered the JCS to come up with an even stronger program. The final outcome was the Consolidated RVNAF Improvement and Modernization Plan (CRIMP) that set the RVN force level at 1.1 million and gave heavier artillery and fighter interceptor aircraft to Saigon. Better food and housing for the ARVN was also part of the package. Laird approved the first two years of the program, reserving action on the third year until the military situation in Vietnam and the financial situation in the United States were clear. [12]

After a year of pulling and tugging between civilian leaders in Washington and military leaders in Saigon for control of Vietnamization, Washington's political leaders were in charge of the process. Americans in both places understood the weaknesses in the RVN, especially that there were incompetent and corrupt officers in the RVNAF that undercut the credibility of Vietnamization. American politics would no longer support an open-ended commitment to South Vietnam. Laird characterized Vietnamization as "a critical test case for the Nixon Doctrine," and he insisted that the RVNAF be completely self-sufficient with no residual US force. [13] This decision was at the presidential level, and meant that the success or failure of US policy in Vietnam would now rest with the South Vietnamese themselves.

Vietnamization was a political policy decided by Washington, not an MACV military strategy. Abrams was not directed to develop a plan to win the war, but rather to manage a US exit that would leave the RVN capable of sustaining itself without overt American assistance. US forces were pulling out whether they were winning or losing. There would be no glorious victories. The big question remaining was whether the South could be "pacified" before the Americans left.[14]

ABRAMS'S "ONE-WAR" CONCEPT

Upon replacing Westmoreland in March 1968 as the top US general in Vietnam, Abrams had begun implementing the "one-war" concept from the PROVN study. Sometimes termed "Abrams's War," his approach cut back on heavy use of artillery against villages and on large-unit rural sweeps that often hurt civilians. He employed small-unit patrols to interrupt enemy supplies and to provide more local security. These steps were intended to help the RVN compete politically and more effectively with the NLF. It was a complex effort that required time to implement and a capable ally, neither of which Abrams had. Vietnamization meant that MACV had to prepare Saigon's forces to counter a joint VC-PAVN threat on their own without US combat support, by 1973 or sooner.[15]

In pursuit of this goal, Abrams achieved considerable success in expanding and modernizing the weapons available to the RVNAF. The ARVN benefited the most from CRIMP, but the territorial forces, the RVN Navy (VNN), and RVN Air Force (VNAF) also made gains. Long-range artillery pieces, antiaircraft weapons, tanks, armored vehicles, machine guns, mortars, radios, jeeps, and trucks poured in. This equipment allowed for an increase of the ARVN by 450,000 to create a new infantry division and many additional combat battalions and brigades. The VNAF got F-5A fighter-bombers, large C-123 and C-7 cargo planes, and troop-carrying and attack helicopters handed down from departing American units. The VNN received over 500 brown-water patrol boats, seagoing cargo and patrol vessels, and more sailors, doubling its strength up to 40,000.[16]

In 1968 MACV had introduced the System for Evaluating Effectiveness of RVNAF (SEER) that it now employed to evaluate Vietnamization. SEER produced an impressive amount of raw data on enemy killed and weapons captured that seemed to show that the RVNAF was improving in "effectiveness" and "efficiency," but subjective evaluations from US advisers were ambiguous. The data system was not able, for example, to match performance measures with unit mission or type and level of enemy activity. There were too many variables to make generalizations possible, and the jury remained out on RVNAF progress toward self-sufficiency. MACV was, in fact, collecting a Niagara of data, including the Territorial Forces Evaluation System and the Hamlet Evaluation System (HES). The "one-war" concept demanded the measurement of political and military activity in many areas. Abrams was a hard-charging armor officer who railed that "the chart *itself* becomes the whole damn war, instead of the *people* and the *real* things," but he accepted "all these guidelines and objectives and so on—you can't fault them, and they ought to be *part* of it."[17] William Colby, the director of CORDS, acknowledged that HES was imperfect, but insisted that it "is really not much in doubt [that] security *did* expand during 1969."[18] Admirers of Abrams cite the statistics as evidence of pacification progress, but Gregory Daddis, in a detailed study of these reports, has termed them "a churning pool of unreliable data."[19]

One American senior officer who served three tours in South Vietnam as an adviser did not think highly of HES, as he shared in a later interview. He recalled that, while he was a major on his second tour and stationed near An Khe after Tet, "the youngest full colonel I have ever seen" and "a computer nerd" questioned his honest answer on an HES questionnaire that there were VC within two hours of his location. In contrast to previous reports by others who had not answered the question honestly, his response caused the computer to downgrade the security evaluation of his area. The young colonel declared that the HES computer program enabled him "to predict what was going to happen anywhere in Vietnam at any time." "But Colonel," the adviser pushed back, "what you're dealing with are my guesses. My guesses become your facts." The army statistician's answer was "Well, we have a factor built in to take care of that."[20]

Outlining concrete mission objectives was a particular difficulty for Abrams's "one war," and for Vietnamization. In all four tactical zones, various kinds of pairing off and combined operations gave ARVN units battle experience. The results were mixed, with some areas such as I Corps performing well, in part because of a particularly good relationship between the senior US and ARVN commanders. Others were far less successful. An example was efforts in the Central Highlands (II Corps) to pair US and ARVN units in Binh Dinh province, a traditional VC stronghold. With American and South Korean forces supplementing ARVN artillery, South Vietnamese territorial forces were strengthened and trained for an area security operation code-named Washington Green. This military action alone did not dent the VC Infrastructure in the province. When the US 173rd Airborne Brigade—the Sky Soldiers—left II Corps in 1971, Binh Dinh came quickly under VC control. Lt. Gen. William R. Peers, the I Field Force commander in the Highlands, identified the contradiction in MACV's strategy. In his exit debriefing in 1969, he said it was unclear whether MACV wanted US advisers to concentrate on developing RVNAF regular forces or the South's territorial forces. As the official army history described the dilemma, "If the goal was pacification, then the greater emphasis on territorial security made sense; if the objective was Vietnamization, then other measures and arrangements were called for."[21]

In an in-depth analysis of MACV programs in Binh Dinh, Kevin Boylan has detailed specifically how Vietnamization and pacification clashed. While US forces operated in the province, there was a "fast and thin"—that is, superficial—disruption of VC activity. The inability of Saigon's regional forces (RFs) and popular forces (PFs) to maintain local security on their own revealed how dependent they were on American cover. The ARVN regulars, who were brought in to fill the void left by American withdrawal, were no longer available to pursue offensive operations against the PAVN. Northern commanders were then able to infiltrate 5,000 of their own regulars into the area and to provide fillers for VC units that had been weakened during the American presence. After Washington Green, Abrams never again used American combat units for pacification duty.[22]

Moreover, even when the Sky Soldiers were still patrolling, a hard-core Viet Cong Infrastructure had remained. MACV classified this VCI as "legal" assassins because they disguised themselves as innocent civilians. The Americans generally defeated any PAVN or organized VC units they encountered, but suffered dozens of casualties from mines and booby traps. In this environment, some of the American soldiers became "disrespectful, abusive, and even life-threatening" toward the locals. The colonel who headed the 173rd Airborne personnel office concluded that the presence of the American combat forces in the villages was a mistake because it "usually pisses off the population" and worked in a way that was contrary to winning hearts and minds.[23] At its base, however, the failure of pacification and Vietnamization in Binh Dinh was not from the behavior of the American soldiers but because of the weakness and ineffectiveness of the RVN and the strength and effectiveness of the enemy. A US Army historian later wrote that Washington Green "raised doubts in the minds of advisors about whether the regime by itself could cope with a resurgent Viet Cong movement."[24] Binh Dinh was only one province, but reports from throughout South Vietnam provided evidence that the communist infrastructure remained strong in many provinces after two years of Vietnamization.[25]

Vietnamization proceeded with planned US troop withdrawals during 1970, and the problems of too rapid an American exit appeared, as Abrams had warned. Peers's successor in II Corps, Lt. Gen. Arthur S. Collins Jr., reported that local South Vietnamese forces were "woefully weak because of lack of leadership at the regimental and battalion level."[26] The deputy senior adviser in the Highlands, Brig. Gen. Gordon J. Duquemin, was equally blunt. He said it was "patently ridiculous" to expect ARVN commanders to do something they did not want to do.[27] "Prodding constitutes our major contribution to the Vietnamization process," Duquemin lamented, forecasting that nothing substantive could be accomplished as long as incompetent Vietnamese commanders remained in place.[28] He suggested a complete overhaul of the RVN's officer personnel system. With the RVNAF rapidly expanding in size, the number of technically competent, strong, and experienced officers was too small. As one South Vietnamese general wrote after the war, "There was finally the will and determination to fight, which again depended on motivation and leadership, and without which there was no sense in upgrading mere physical capabilities."[29]

Many Vietnamese generals took exception to the word *Vietnamization* and its implications. Thieu's frustrations with Washington revealed during and after the Midway meeting were shared by his officers. They often noted that RVNAF casualties were five times higher than those incurred by US forces, and that South Vietnamese had been fighting Hanoi before the Americans arrived and would be fighting after the Americans left. In their view, the term *Vietnamization* played into the hands of communist propaganda that characterized the RVN military as puppets. They took pride in the performance of their troops in responding to the Tet Offensive and to the failure of the attack to spark a national revolt against Saigon. They readily acknowledged the benefits of American financial, material, and technological assistance, but also expressed confidence in their own abilities to fight. Whether or not this pride was fully justified, Thieu and his officers trusted almost to the very end in 1975 that the United States would not totally abandon them, and the cold realization that no more help was coming contributed to the chaos of the RVN's final hours.[30]

THE CHALLENGES OF COMBAT SUPPORT

Vietnamizing the battlefield through combined US-RVNAF operations was one headache for Abrams, and another was combat support. Before Washington ordered Vietnamization, MACV had been primarily concerned with supplying US forces with what they needed, and had left Saigon to depend primarily upon its own logistical units. There had also been no consistent MACV commitment to using American technical personnel to train Vietnamese specialists. Now directed by the White House to reduce both US combat and support personnel, a hasty solution had to be devised for the RVNAF to perform such complex operations as harbor operations, road and bridge construction, and long-range communication networks.

A US Army study of the Vietnamization program done by a former ARVN officer after the war pointed out its hasty implementation, beginning in 1969, in contrast to the Americanization period from 1965 to 1968, when "the US tended to do everything by itself." In this author's estimation, when Nixon began American troop withdrawal in rapid succession as "apparently dictated by domestic political needs," the RVN did not have enough time to adjust. He pointed in particular to military technology skills: "It is fairly easy to beef up the Army, but not easy to build up the Navy and Air Force. The training of specialists, operators, and repairmen to handle and maintain sophisticated equipment and armament, the education and training of pilots, ship captains, etc., all required time."[31]

Maj. Gen. Joseph M. Heiser Jr., who headed 1st Logistical Command, set up a buddy system for on-the-job training (OJT) of South Vietnamese in the management of maintenance and storage facilities for ordnance, food, fuel, and other necessities. Although the ARVN had operated its own logistics school for several years, lack of centralized guidance from MACV made the accelerated efforts unit by unit in many cases. This localized model was adopted by ports, transportation, aviation, communication, intelligence, and other functional organizations. These efforts strengthened RVNAF units in some areas, but much more development remained to be done as American support units began to depart the RVN. "While in the US Army there were five logistics soldiers to support every combat soldier," a career ARVN logistics officer who served for twenty years recalled, "in the RVNAF a single logistics soldier had to support eight combat soldiers, a 'ratio of 40:1 in favor of US Army logistics.'"[32]

Especially challenging were engineering, helicopter, and signal requirements. US engineering battalions from all services, with the help of private companies like Pacific Architects and Engineering and RMK-BRJ (whose projects included MACV headquarters), had built the bases and roads during the Americanization of the war. There had been little involvement of South Vietnamese engineers in these hurried projects, and there was a severe shortage of skilled laborers in Vietnam, as was true in most postcolonial countries. With limited time to transition to a self-sufficient RVN, Abrams decided against a large-scale Vietnamization of engineering. US units were to get the bases and roads in top shape before leaving so that RVN engineers and civilian contractors would only have to keep up maintenance. OJT efforts were begun to train ARVN soldiers in construction trade skills, such as earthmoving, welding, and concrete mixing, and the maintenance of heavy equipment, such as Rome plows and construction cranes. These hurried programs were largely unsuccessful, and in 1970 and 1971 private American contractors took on the task of training Vietnamese contractors and unskilled local workers for the needed jobs.[33]

MACV made a particularly concerted effort to Vietnamize combat support in rotary-wing (helicopter) operations. The American war in Vietnam has often been termed a "helicopter war" because US commanders turned extensively to use of these aircraft for troop movement, supply, medical evacuation, and command and control. Perhaps Westmoreland had relied too much on airmobile tactics, but by 1969 it was the American way of war in Vietnam that the VNAF and ARVN were about to inherit in its entirety.

Consequently, Abrams's MACV created an ambitious program to supply more aircraft and to train Vietnamese to fly and maintain this expanded fleet. In 1970–1971, the US military turned over helicopter support responsibility to the RVNAF.[34]

US combat support specialists witnessing this handover testified to serious shortcomings. An experienced American helicopter mechanic interviewed by *Newsweek* described his observation of

> serious maintenance deficiencies—oil and fuel leaks, engine filters and compressor blades caked with dirt, and missing rivets. [This sergeant first class] and other advisers revealed that Vietnamese never flushed engines with water and solvent, a routine item of maintenance required for every twenty-five hours of operation. Over US objections, many of the helicopters had nevertheless been rated fit to fly by the Vietnamese maintenance men. One chopper, with a torque so low that the advisers called it a "potential crash waiting to happen," had been rated unfit to fly early one day, but a Vietnamese technician blithely gave the chopper a "positive checkout." Taking the machine up, [the sergeant said], would [have been] "tantamount to suicide."[35]

Not surprisingly, the aviation and logistics challenges compounded each other. Many of the rotary and fixed-wing aircraft transferred to the RVNAF were often grounded due to lack of repair parts. The generous flow—some would say "dumping"—of materiel in the RVN in support of Vietnamization had created warehouses full of parts, but very few South Vietnamese had been trained in how to locate parts in a warehouse. In the words of an army adviser, "there was very little inventory control. Although the United States attempted to train some Vietnamese civilians, the RVNAF officers had no interest in that."[36]

It had long been recognized by MACV that the technically sophisticated fixed communication facilities installed by the United States in Vietnam would pose a challenge whenever and however US military deployment in the RVN ended. The system had grown at incredible speed from 1965 to 1968 as demands skyrocketed for high-speed and reliable communication for the hundreds of US and RVN units. State-of-the-art transmitting and switching facilities were both an opportunity and a necessity. Since the American war in Vietnam was not one of moving fronts but of long-term occupation and maneuver in confined areas of operation, transmitting towers, underground cables, and other multichannel fixed installations could be built in place of mobile vans and portable antennas, such as those used in World War II and Korea. The rugged topography of Vietnam's mountains and valleys and the dense triple-canopy forests in many areas mitigated against tactical line-of-sight high-frequency and microwave systems, requiring tropospheric scatter installations to broadcast over the horizon. The signal assets of combat divisions did not include the equipment or skills for long-distance communication. Combat commanders had short-range systems for their units to communicate with each other and with battalion headquarters and fire-support bases, but required units of the US Army 1st Signal Brigade to connect throughout the corps tactical zone and with headquarters in Saigon and beyond the RVN through the Integrated Communication System, Southeast Asia (ICS, SEA).[37]

In April 1969, as Vietnamization was getting under way, the army finally completed the integrated wideband communications system (IWCS) it had been building since 1965. With the installation of the microwave terminal at Dong Ha linking to Quang Tri, the IWCS had 67 links in South Vietnam and 33 links in Thailand, providing 470,000 circuits throughout Southeast Asia. The entire system was comprised of coastal cables and sophisticated automated telephone dialing centers, heavily used multichannel teletype systems, and data systems that carried a huge volume of traffic in everything from logistics management through the global supply chain to soldiers' payroll records kept at Fort Benjamin Harrison in Indianapolis. Although experimentation in satellite communication was in progress, "satcom," as it was called, was unreliable. Connections back to the United States for all echelons from MACV and the US embassy in Saigon down to the tactical commands in each corps zone connected to the world via an undersea cable from Vung Tau to Sattahip, Thailand.[38]

The 1st Signal Brigade had an ad hoc buddy system as early as 1966 between US and ARVN signal battalions, the latter supplied with World War II–era equipment, but the brigade had of necessity given priority to meeting American communication requirements over training of South Vietnamese. The brigade's mission was daunting, serving Vietnam and Thailand and linking American forces in Southeast Asia to the world. In March 1970, Maj. Gen. Thomas M. Rienzi, commander of the 1st Signal Brigade, ordered that units down to company level begin essential training of South Vietnamese buddy units, and wherever possible, to turn over sole responsibility for signal sites to the RVNAF. Complex systems such as dial telephone exchanges and high-gain tropospheric scatter antenna facilities required more extensive training at special signal schools, or with the private contractors who had designed and built the equipment. A South Vietnamese Signal School at Vung Tau began preparing ARVN soldiers in an eight-week course to be followed by up to nine months of on-the-job training at the high-level 361st and 369th Signal Battalions. Some of the best students were to become instructors, and some ARVN signal officers were given a crash English-language course. In 1971, with Vietnamization well under way, Maj. Gen. Rienzi acknowledged that "an understanding of English was necessary" for the "hard skills" required for communications electronics, and that "the language problem has been present throughout our experience in Vietnam and has never been really solved."[39]

The number of Signal Corps combat support personnel needed was daunting. At the peak of US force level, there were 24,000 signal soldiers in the 1st Signal Brigade and thousands more in field forces signal organizations. As one radio relay and carrier attendant stationed at Nha Trang in 1969 put it, "They just needed so many signal people to support the guys in Vietnam, there was a huge signal presence in Vietnam. They were all over the place."[40] He had civilian job experience with an electronics company and, after being drafted, had been trained at the Army Signal School at Fort Gordon, Georgia. He described his job at 459th Signal Battalion as "multiplexing telephone circuits onto radio shots and shooting them line of sight, thirty or forty miles, and then at the other end, breaking them down back to telephone lines."[41] He spent a year at this site and reported that the only Vietnamese he saw were some civilians who kept the backup generators in operation.

The challenge, which proved overwhelming, was to Vietnamize the communication system as quickly as possible. US signal officers interviewed about the program estimated, "If the current rate continues, it will take sixteen years to staff the ICS, SEA system with Vietnamese."[42] Even with students with prior technical educations, qualified instructors, and a well-established training center, the realistic estimate for the RVN's assuming control of ICS stations was eight to ten years. Since the PAVN was not downsizing and the war continued, these essential combat-support operations faced the same obstacle as combat operations. Although MACV went ahead and created a detailed signal Vietnamization plan, American unit withdrawals made it difficult to implement because the US Army could not commit large enough numbers of highly skilled personnel for long enough to accomplish Vietnamization without endangering the security requirements for effective pacification. In 1970, the Department of Defense awarded a bid to Federal Electric, an International Telephone and Telegraph subsidiary, to provide ARVN training. In his 1971 study of communications-electronics in Vietnam, Maj. Gen. Rienzi zeroed in on the paramount issue: "Training the Vietnamese to take over the systems we have built in their country has . . . been a matter of deep concern to all of us. . . . We must press ahead energetically in the training program in communications electronics in order to enable the South Vietnamese to unite their country."[43]

The US Army realized that in order to make the RVNAF effective, training was as important as expansion in size. Fighting experience and ability to perform under fire were critical, but so were tactical and technical skills. A modern military has to be professional in all aspects. It is part of the social, economic, and political environment from which it is derived, and it must manage to operate within that context. One of the greatest hurdles facing the training and improvement of the South's forces was a lack of qualified leadership at both the officer and noncommissioned officer levels. Reporting on both combat and combat-support operations, American advisers continually cited poor leadership as the chief reason for unit ineffectiveness. Unsatisfactory leaders were often not relieved because of lack of replacements. Rapid expansion of the RVNAF occurred without a strong base of qualified military and civilian leaders, and, as one analysis pointed out, "the shortage of able personnel to occupy civil administrative positions only made the military problem more severe."[44]

Vietnamization was not a strategy for defeating Hanoi militarily or for aiding Saigon in pacification efforts in the RVN. It was a politically driven initiative to lessen domestic political opposition to the administration, and it had all appearances of being a cover for ending Washington's commitment to the survival of the Thieu government. South Vietnamese military and political leaders were keenly aware of their need for continued US financial, material, and technical support. Abrams himself stoically soldiered on and kept trying to adapt to huge readiness gaps created by the American drawdown, but other senior military and political insiders detected a race to extract Americans from the conflict. Once begun, the exit was basically irreversible. As implemented, Vietnamization was a withdrawal of American personnel that outpaced and often ignored the need to provide the materiel and combat support South Vietnam would have to have in order to survive.[45]

Chapter Four

Buying Time for Vietnamization

Cambodia 1970

During 1969, the Nixon administration improvised a policy in Vietnam that was a combination of threat, negotiation, and Vietnamization. As part of his "madman" idea, Nixon let it be leaked to the press that the president might "go for broke" in an air and naval assault on North Vietnam, and he ordered secret preparation of the contingency plan called Duck Hook to carry out such attacks. In his letter to Ho Chi Minh in July, he threatened that the United States would use "great force" if there was no progress in Kissinger's negotiations in Paris with the DRV. Le Duan and the communist leadership called his bluff and did not flinch in their refusal to make negotiating concessions. The godfather of Vietnamization, Secretary of Defense Melvin Laird, warned Nixon that the antiwar movement, which had been quiet for a while, would erupt if the United States were to resume bombing of the North, mine the DRV harbors, or possibly even use tactical nuclear weapons—all moves the president had been contemplating.

NIXON CHOOSES TO "GO THE LONG ROAD"
WITH SUPPORT OF THE "SILENT MAJORITY"

In preparation for a National Security Council meeting on September 12, 1969, Kissinger advised the president that "we are headed toward autumn in an uncertain fashion."[1] In a background memorandum, Kissinger conveyed to Nixon his deep concern that "time runs more quickly against our strategy" than Hanoi's for several reasons, including that "withdrawal of US troops will become like salted peanuts to the American public: the more US troops come home, the more will be demanded."[2] In a formal "Vietnam Options" paper, the national security adviser outlined four courses of action: 1) continue the current pace of flexible Vietnamization coupled with negotiation; 2) accelerate negotiation; 3) accelerate Vietnamization; and 4) escalate militarily. Of these, the third option of accelerating Vietnamization required a fixed withdrawal schedule over two years, removing all US forces and ending with a declaration that Saigon was ready to stand on its own. The fourth approach of military escalation would completely stop US troop withdrawals and turn to major military force to blockade Haiphong Harbor, resume bombing of the North, "pressure" Hanoi's trade, and utilize remaining US ground forces backed by naval and air support. Kissinger believed that Nixon, frustrated with the current course, would reject choices one and three, the Vietnamization options, because the first would be too slow, and the third would be a surrender. The national security adviser was setting up a menu that discounted Vietnamization and favored combining options two and four in a mix of diplomacy and force. As he put it, "military escalation would be used as a *means* to a negotiated settlement, not as an *end*, since we have ruled out military victory."[3] At the NSC meeting the next day, the president postponed a decision on these four alternatives.[4]

A month later, on October 11, Nixon met with the Joint Chiefs of Staff and decided finally upon a course of action. He had reframed and narrowed Kissinger's four options into a new list of three: 1) "get out now"; 2) "negotiate a settlement"; and 3) "go the long road." In the days before this meeting, the military chiefs had shared their concerns that there were major operational hurdles for the escalation of force that Kissinger had outlined. As a result, Kissinger's number 4 was no longer on the table. The president refused to accept the "get out now" option on his list. He described it as a unilateral withdrawal, which he viewed as cutting and running. He preferred his second option, that of a negotiated settlement, but he realized an agreement was not currently available on terms he could accept. The timing was particularly bad for getting any diplomatic movement from Hanoi because Ho Chi Minh had died on September 2. Although only a figurehead by the time of his death, Uncle Ho was such a powerful international symbol of communist revolution that his passing required, at least temporarily, that Moscow, Beijing, and Hanoi demonstrate fraternal unity and keep some distance from the capitalist enemy in Washington. Consequently, Nixon turned to the "long road" choice on his list, which was not an immediate withdrawal, but set a specific target date for withdrawal. He informed Secretary Laird and the Joint Chiefs: "Go the long road, which also carries with it a risk of failing."[5]

The long-road option actually was an accelerated Vietnamization course over the next eighteen months—which Kissinger had tried to derail—and the pairing of the long road with the risk of failing suggests what scholars have called the "decent interval strategy." The Nixon administration's political calculus was to carry out a steady, unilateral withdrawal of US forces down to a small US advisory contingent by, or soon after, the 1972 presidential election. This step actually took shape under the prodding of Laird in the Phase III RVNAF IMP begun in November.

In later years, Laird claimed there was no decent interval, because Vietnamization could have worked as long as the United States had supplied material aid to the RVN.[6] Nixon realized, however, that the long-road approach was as problematic as escalation. He wanted to give the Thieu regime a decent chance at survival, but acknowledged that it might not survive once US military measures were no longer available. Politically, Nixon wanted to create space between the departure of US forces and Thieu's fall, but the RVNAF was not yet strong enough even for this scenario. The president told his generals and admirals, "If we hold the line politically, Vietnamization can work, provided we have time to do it deliberately. . . . The people will stand for support [of Saigon] but will not stand for a long, drawn-out ground action."[7] Later, when all US troops were out after 1973, the public and Congress would not even tolerate support.

Knowing that Vietnamization would require time and that the window of opportunity was short, Washington took several time-buying steps. Nixon had begun the secret bombing of Cambodia after only two months in office, both to underscore his go-for-broke threat and to relieve pressure on US and ARVN forces along the RVN–Cambodia border. Although the potential for domestic political reaction led Nixon reluctantly to give up the Duck Hook plan for massive air attacks on the North, he still tried to intimidate Hanoi and its principal supplier Moscow with a global nuclear alert over a two-week period in late October. Kept secret from the public, this JCS Readiness Test, as it was called, may have been a remnant of Duck Hook, and certainly was consistent with the madman posturing. It was dangerous, and even prompted Moscow to make some defensive preparations, but when it was ended on October 30, it had not generated any change in the diplomatic stance of Moscow or Hanoi.[8]

Writing after the war, both Nixon and Kissinger expressed regret that the administration did not take stronger military action against the DRV during its first months in office. In the fall deliberations over options, however, leaders of the Department of State, Department of Defense, MACV, and JCS had come out against Duck Hook. Opinion polls indicated that Laird's gradual withdrawal approach had public support that was buying political time for the president to increase aid to the RVN and to use American airpower against targets inside South Vietnam. Nixon was open to military escalation aimed at the North, but, like Laird, and unlike Kissinger, he was a political animal who recognized the limits set by what voters would tolerate.[9]

Frustrated that his military and diplomatic options were stalled, on November 3, 1969, Nixon made his "silent majority" speech, one of the most significant foreign policy addresses of his presidency. Veterans of the McCarthy and Kennedy campaigns and other antiwar groups had reappeared in force in a national Moratorium Day protest on October 15, with hundreds of thousands turning out in peaceful demonstrations. With another such event scheduled for November 15, the president went to the airwaves to gain public support for more time to make changes in the course of the war. He also wanted to convey to Hanoi that, despite the expressions of antiwar sentiment, the United States was not going to be deterred in its support of Saigon.[10]

The speech reviewed what the administration had done since he took office in January. Nixon noted that both Hanoi and Moscow had repeatedly rejected US offers to negotiate. He also recalled his statement at Guam—the Nixon Doctrine—that the United States would aid nations threatened by aggression with military and economic assistance, "but we shall look to the nation directly threatened to assume the primary responsibility of providing the manpower for its defense."[11] In that framework, he affirmed that US policy in Vietnam had changed: "In the previous administration, we Americanized the war in Vietnam. In this administration, we are Vietnamizing the search for peace."[12] He claimed that, by December 15, the Vietnamization program would have made possible the withdrawal of 20 percent of US combat forces. He emphasized that American casualties were, in the last two months, at the lowest point in three years. In the absence of response from the other side on negotiations, the president declared that he would continue "implementation of our plan for Vietnamization . . . a plan in which we will withdraw all of our forces from Vietnam on a schedule in accordance with our program, as the South Vietnamese become strong enough to defend their own freedom."[13]

Having set that goal, Nixon also made an appeal. He looked directly into the camera and admonished the viewers: "If a vocal minority [of protesters], however fervent its cause, prevails over reason and the will of the majority, this Nation has no future as a free society. . . . And so tonight—to you, the great silent majority of my fellow Americans—I ask for your support. . . . Let us understand: North Vietnam cannot defeat or humiliate the United States. Only Americans can do that."[14]

Nixon's plan for an honorable peace was no longer a secret: It was Vietnamization. Polls indicated a favorable public response to the speech, but these opinion samples also showed that 50 percent of Americans thought the war was a mistake.[15] The turnout for the November Moratorium was not as large as October, but was still impressive. In the days after the speech, Nixon continued to assuage public discontent with announcements of more troop withdrawals, an end of draft calls for the rest of the year, and finally, the start of a lottery system to determine the order in which men would be inducted to meet the declining number needed for service. The president had relieved some political pressure for the moment, but he had also turned a policy corner. He had publicly prioritized Vietnamization ahead of the stalled nego-tiations, and had made the definition of success not a political settlement but a conclusion that left Vietnam with a regime in Saigon strong enough to defend itself. Despite his assertions that he would not simply pull out, he was staging a graduated, unilateral withdrawal that would leave the RVN to de-termine its own fate without any US forces in the fight.

Despite the bold confidence of the Silent Majority speech, the president and his advisers were keenly aware that the RVNAF and the Saigon regime were far from able to defend alone their country from the joint threat of the PAVN and the VC. Nixon's preference for securing the South through more bombing of the North had been ruled out as politically unacceptable. Al-though reluctant to admit it, the president understood that the majority of Americans, both vocal and silent, wanted their country, and especially their sons, out of Vietnam as quickly as possible. Any escalation of the US mili-tary role would spark a sharp reaction against the White House and damage its ability to concentrate on what it considered higher international prior-ities—namely, arms control talks with Moscow and improved relations with Beijing that had been broken for twenty years. Despite Kissinger's faith in his flair for diplomacy, the leaders of the DRV, specifically General Secre-tary Le Duan and Foreign Minister Le Duc Tho, showed no signs of weaken-ing their adamant demand that the United States unilaterally withdraw its troops from the RVN and abandon its support of Thieu. By process of elimi-nation, Vietnamization had become the fallback position for Nixon's plan to end the American war in Vietnam. Writing after the war, he acknowledged that "our whole strategy depended on whether this program succeeded."[16]

As is often the case with announced policies, there was a public percep-tion of Vietnamization in the United States and an actual performance of the policy on the ground in Vietnam. Nixon had given the policy exposure in his televised address, and in the months that followed, most military actions would be viewed as tests of Vietnamization. The president had raised expec-tations, and a natural question for journalists, antiwar activists, and the gener-al public was whether it was working and whether it could succeed. The public discussion recognized that a limit had been reached in what had been a seemingly open-ended American military commitment. As Laird phrased it, Vietnamization had become "a critical test case for the Nixon Doctrine," which meant whether a government facing an insurgency could survive on its own with US material assistance alone.[17]

Hanoi, of course, was following closely the public policy discussions in the United States. During the Cold War, it was often said that all Moscow had to do to gain intelligence on American foreign policy was read the *New York Times*. Vietnam's communist leaders had reduced the level of military activity in the South as 1969 progressed and as they took the measure of the Nixon approach. The heavy fighting during the Tet Offensive and afterward

in 1968, as well as the Cambodian bombing and increased pacification program under the new administration, had taken a toll on the PAVN. Needing
some time to regroup, Le Duan was willing to depart from his aversion to
negotiations and allow the diplomats in Paris to talk. Although Kissinger
himself had serious doubts that the RVNAF could compete on its own with
the PAVN and VC—which denoted itself as the People's Liberation Armed
Forces—he entertained some hope that Vietnamization was making Hanoi
nervous in terms of the public support it was providing Nixon. [18]

In reality, Le Duc Tho was reporting to Hanoi from Paris that Vietnamization was simply a political cover for unilateral US withdrawal, and that
eventually US negotiators would drop demands for the mutual extraction of
forces. As Kissinger had feared, Laird's plan was weakening the US bargaining position. Hanoi judged that, if it could endure American bombing a while
longer, it could prevail. According to a history of the Paris talks published
later in Hanoi, Tho directly challenged Kissinger: "Before, there were over a
million US and puppet troops, and you failed. How can you succeed when
you let the puppet troops do the fighting? Now, with only US support, how
can you win?"[19] Historian Robert Brigham has argued that Kissinger, wanting to keep alive his desire for a negotiated settlement, may not have shared
with Nixon or Thieu a frank assessment of how unlikely the prospects were
of obtaining a diplomatic breakthrough with the DRV.[20]

For MACV planners in Vietnam, Washington's political decision to opt
for Vietnamization presented the challenge of crafting what was in military
terms a redeployment of forces. As entire US combat brigades boarded
planes and ships out of the country, with no simultaneous reduction of enemy
forces in the South, the security vacuums created had to be filled either by
shifting the positions and missions of ARVN troops and remaining US units,
or by creating new joint operations. This process occurred throughout the
South, but the area in which it first became urgent was III Corps—the area
around Saigon—and IV Corps—the Mekong Delta. As MACV was just getting new unit roles established in late 1969 and early 1970, a dramatic change
in leadership occurred in Phnom Penh, which made the RVN–Cambodian
border a threat to, and an opportunity for, Vietnamization.

FIGHTING IN CAMBODIA TO PROTECT VIETNAMIZATION

On March 18, 1970, a coup installed pro-American general Lon Nol as head
of the Cambodian government in place of that country's neutralist leader,
Prince Norodom Sihanouk. The sudden change happened in large measure
without prior planning, as disgruntled elements in Cambodia's military and
parliament took advantage of the prince's temporary absence from the country to make their move. US and RVN military leaders had long wanted

permission to cross into purportedly neutral Cambodia to attack PAVN and VC base areas and supply routes connected to North Vietnam via the Ho Chi Minh Trail, through Laos into Cambodia. Evidence is mixed on how much prior knowledge the US intelligence community had about Sihanouk's ouster, but Nixon, Kissinger, and Abrams quickly determined that an opportunity had come for an ARVN attack on enemy bases in Cambodia with US support. Laird and Secretary of State William Rogers were excluded from the military planning and opposed it when they discovered what was afoot. They warned that the American public would be outraged by an apparent expansion of the war across borders. They also could cite a State Department intelligence analysis that ARVN troops in Cambodia might bolster Lon Nol's weak army in fighting against Cambodian communists, known as the Khmer Rouge. On the other hand, the presence of Vietnamese soldiers in Cambodia could possibly help Khmer Rouge recruiting of villagers to oppose the American puppet forces of Saigon and Phenom Penh. [21]

Still frustrated by the inability to intimidate or persuade Hanoi into a settlement, Nixon ordered a cross-border operation with both American and South Vietnamese forces. For him it was a "big play," not unlike the madman approach, that would convey to the enemy his daring and determination. Facing the threat of Khmer Rouge expansion in eastern Cambodia, Lon Nol welcomed the operation, and Thieu was eager to deploy his forces into this previously off-limits zone. American officials in Washington and Saigon proceeded to carry out the president's wishes, but with varying amounts of enthusiasm. At first, Ambassador Bunker objected to abandoning the concept of neutrality, and Laird argued that any operation should be conducted strictly by the ARVN, without US troops.

Following the coup against Sihanouk, Nixon had asked Abrams for a military assessment, and the general responded that this was a good time to make a move in Cambodia to improve the security of US forces and to advance Vietnamization. Abrams contended that he needed to liquidate enemy sanctuaries "to assure the safety of his men and still meet the twelve-month withdrawal schedule." He forcefully claimed that "the destruction of enemy supplies . . . is one of the prerequisites for maintaining the pace of Vietnamization." [22] Adm. McCain also insisted that Cambodia had to be protected if Vietnamization was going to be successful. Abrams and McCain assessed that Saigon's forces would need at least American combat support, such as airlift and artillery. As ultimately executed on April 30, the move involved more than 44,000 troops, with slightly over half of them American. The ARVN took primary responsibility for the "Parrot's Beak" near Saigon, and US units attacked along the "Fishhook" slightly to the north. Both names derived from the map shape of the Cambodian frontier at those points. [23]

The dividing of the operational areas reflected, in part, the current status of Vietnamization as a work in progress. In June 1969, the first redeployment to meet Washington's timetable had been to withdraw the US 9th Infantry Division from the Mekong Delta. That move left the ARVN 7th Infantry Division with primary responsibility for the heavily populated region. This change provided high political visibility, which Nixon wanted, and was relatively cautious. Enemy activity in IV Corps had been light, and the delta was at the extreme end of the DRV supply line, along the Ho Chi Minh Trail. The ARVN 7th had little combat experience and was now spread thinly over a large area, but the largest US combat command in Vietnam still remained nearby, in III Corps.

Led by Lt. Gen. Julian Ewell, the US II Field Force was protecting the vital area surrounding Saigon, and included elements of five US divisions, three US brigades, and three ARVN divisions. The principal South Vietnamese officer in III Corps was the somewhat flamboyant but effective Gen. Do Cao Tri. In keeping with MACV's improvement and modernization plan, Ewell worked with Tri to pair US and ARVN forces in a buddy program known as *Dong Tien*, or Progress Together. He moved US forces out of the capital, leaving its defense to the ARVN, and then linked US and ARVN divisions west and north of Saigon in the provinces bordering on Cambodia. To give the ARVN much-needed experience and independence in finding and destroying the VC (the so-called "attrition mission"), its rifle companies were in the field day and night while Ewell promised Tri artillery, aviation, and communication support from his American partners. US infantry battalions were to work closely with territorial forces to help them improve village security, but the old problem of tension between Vietnamization and pacification remained. With American combat strength declining each month, Tri had to use more of his regulars to supplement the territorials' security role. The US officers and soldiers considered training to be a secondary role for which they themselves were not trained, and which seemed redundant to the work of advisory teams. The handoff from the US military to the RVNAF was just getting started and going through what Abrams had labeled "cut and try" adjustment when Washington decided to widen the joint mission into Cambodia.[24]

Although the public debate that quickly emerged in the United States had the White House referring to the Cambodian "incursion" and its critics speaking of the Cambodian "invasion," on the ground the deployment was most accurately described as a number of separate, although coordinated, cross-border battalion-sized operations. Consistent with the partnering efforts in III Corps, Tri's ARVN units took the lead in the Parrot's Beak. The Fishhook front was also in III Corps, but the ARVN Airborne force there was less prepared. Abrams assigned that sector to the US 1st Cavalry and 25th Infantry Divisions. Overall, the ARVN units actively engaged in Cambodia performed well, and the combined efforts of the US and ARVN forces managed to eliminate many of Hanoi's principal stockpiles along the border with minimal friendly casualties. Many ARVN units operated independently with-out US intervention, proved able to supply themselves, and exhibited good morale. Clear deficiencies remained, however. The RVN units, particularly in the Fishhook, required extensive American helicopter assistance, air sup-port, and heavy artillery fire. ARVN combat leadership also was largely in the hands of corps commanders like Tri (who tragically died in a helicopter crash during the fighting), with less capable division commanders and staff largely bypassed.[25]

Nixon informed a national television audience on April 30 that the opera-tion in Cambodia was "to clean out enemy sanctuaries," to attack what he described as the headquarters for all enemy operations in South Vietnam, "to protect our men in Viet-Nam, and to guarantee the continued success of Vietnamization programs."[26] He lied outright when he claimed that the Unit-ed States had respected Cambodian neutrality for five years. He maintained that the land deployment was not an escalation but part of the de-escalation of American involvement in Indochina, and he defiantly declared in closing that "I would rather be a one-term President and do what I believe is right than to be a two-term President at the cost of seeing America become a second-rate power and to see this nation accept the first defeat in its proud 190-year history."[27]

His political defensiveness proved merited, because the following days brought some of the most dramatic and costly antiwar protests of the entire war. Sixty percent of the public opposed the operation. The most tragic events came at Kent State University in Ohio, where four students were shot dead during protests, and at Jackson State University in Mississippi, where two students died. Spontaneous street demonstrations spread across the na-tion, culminating in a gathering of 75,000 people on May 9 outside the White House. Even before this backlash peaked, JCS Chairman Gen. Earle Wheeler was instructing Abrams to wrap up the American operations in Cambodia and pull back as soon as possible. President Thieu, however, kept some RVNAF units on the Cambodian side of the frontier until 1975.[28]

While many people in the United States were giving a grade of F to the entry of US combat forces into previously "neutral" Cambodia, as a military test of Vietnamization, the grade for the Cambodian move was probably C+. American troops were back inside South Vietnam by the end of June, and they had found and eliminated some enemy supplies, weapons caches, and bunker complexes. They never encountered a central headquarters for Ha-noi's war in the South. Nixon had claimed that the Central Office for South Vietnam (COSVN) was a physical command post, but it was actually a mobile staff that moved frequently along the Cambodian frontier with III Corps. The offensive forced Cambodian Khmer Rouge guerrillas away from the Vietnamese border, nearer to Phnom Penh, and into closer ties with the PAVN than the Khmer Rouge had previously desired. The incursion also prompted Hanoi to break off both secret and public negotiations with American representatives in Paris.[29]

The incursion into Cambodia was intended as a way to buy time for Vietnamization by degrading DRV supply and staging areas, thereby taking pressure off of the RVNAF as it attempted to simultaneously train and assume greater operational responsibility. Nixon had alluded to this goal in his April 30 speech, and later reaffirmed it in his book, *The Real War*. Nixon wrote that his principal purpose in going into Cambodia was to counter what he characterized as a DRV invasion of that neutral country, "so that Vietnamization and plans for the withdrawal of American troops could continue."[30]

Although weakened, PAVN bases and supply lines were back in operation in Cambodia within weeks of the departure of US forces. Some RVN units had performed well, reflecting progress in Vietnamization. One ARVN armor lieutenant remembered the Cambodian operation with pride:

> Of course, we needed airpower support, but American soldiers and advisers were not with us in Cambodia, and we still won the war in Cambodia. That's the pride of South Vietnam to answer those people who said that South Vietnam armed forces didn't want to fight or have capability to fight. . . . We never think we depend on American forces to fight for us. Among 4,000 armored cavalry officers, I never heard of one to desert the army, absolutely not. . . . I and all my friends always had a pride to fight and defend South Vietnam.[31]

Overall RVNAF forces showed serious weaknesses, however, in infantry, artillery, and field maintenance—including fuel shortages. In the words of Lt. Gen. Phillip Davidson, who had served as Abrams's chief of intelligence in 1969, the old problems remained: "lack of leadership, both civil and military, the static nature of the infantry divisions, the shortage of technicians, the politicization of the ARVN, the lack of discipline, and the convoluted command system."[32] More time was needed for Vietnamization, and meanwhile, US troop levels continued downward rapidly.

Doubts about what had been accomplished abounded. Secretary Laird questioned whether "wandering all over Cambodia" did much for "the real mission of providing local security for the population" in South Vietnam.[33] Nothing had changed in the basic social condition in the RVN: inflation, high taxation, corruption, urban stagnation, and government unresponsiveness. Worse for Abrams were voices in Washington claiming that the Cambodian operation had gone well, adding that the RVNAF must now take over for US forces, "ready or not." Saigon's forces were not ready, and MACV knew it. The military brass had long wanted to expand the war to Cambodia. It now had been tried and had not worked, and the public's patience was worn out. Despite accounts that have portrayed Abrams as fighting a "better war" that was being won by 1970, there is little evidence to support the claim.[34]

While US Army commanders were working in III and IV Corps and Cambodia to protect and implement Vietnamization, the III Marine Amphibious Force (III MAF) in I Corps was pursuing the Improvement and Modernization Plan directives from the Pentagon and Abrams. The official USMC history records that the marines made some progress in 1970 in equipping and training RVN regular, regional, and popular forces, but they had less success in getting Gen. Hoang Xuan Lam, the ARVN commander in I Corps, to assume responsibility for an independent tactical area of responsibility (TAOR) in Quang Nam, the province encompassing the key city of Da Nang, and where Lam's headquarters was located. Despite repeated pressure from Lt. Gen. Keith B. McCutcheon, the III MAF commander, Gen. Lam resisted. When the 7th Marine Division departed South Vietnam in October in accordance with the redeployment schedule, the 5th Marine Division had to add the 7th Division's TAOR to its own, while one of Lam's ARVN divisions accepted only a small area around An Hoa. The marines' assessment was, "[W]ith additional major Marine redeployments scheduled for early 1971, Americans and South Vietnamese alike were running out of time to finish the job."[35]

Lt. Gen. McCutcheon made numerous complaints about ARVN division- and corps-level performance. He charged that top commanders had "little appreciation for the time and space factors involved in an operation, nor of the logistic effort to support one."[36] The South Vietnamese had created the Quang Da Special Zone (QDSZ) as a loosely structured division-level command to guard Da Nang, but it never created its own supply, long-lines communication, and aviation support—serious ARVN deficiencies found throughout the South. The QDSZ was chronically short of competent high-ranking officers and had no commander at all for many weeks in 1970. The colonel in charge died in a plane crash on the way to Saigon to be promoted to brigadier general, and "military politics and bureaucratic inefficiency" in the capital left the post vacant, with no ARVN officer in the province with authority to coordinate with III MAF and the 1st Marine Division.[37]

Late in 1970, Sir Robert Thompson, the British counterinsurgency theorist, visited Quang Nam province and asserted that "it was quite clear that continued progress had been made in both Pacification and Vietnamization programmes during the year, so that the 1969 gains were expanded and consolidated." Lt. Gen. McCutcheon took exception to this rosy assessment: "Despite election turnout and improved ratings in the Hamlet Evaluation System, we must accept the fact that a large portion of the Quang Nam people are apathetic toward the GVN. . . . I doubt that many people, not directly involved in government or military business at a relatively high level, are aware of Vietnamization. Those who are aware of it almost certainly consider it a euphemism for US withdrawal."[38]

The United States was losing leverage with its drawdown. It was no longer conducting offensive operations, but rather supporting the South Vietnamese. Abrams was not able to shape strategy. He faced the same truth as other commanders, historian Gregory Daddis concludes—that there "were limits to what American power could achieve in a war that preceded US intervention and would continue long after foreign troops withdrew."[39] Nixon complained that Abrams was not creative, but in Vietnamization, the president had given the general an unrealistic mission.

Sgt. David Anderson in Phu Bai, March 1970. Author photo.

ARVN guards at Hoi An signal site, May 1970. Author photo.

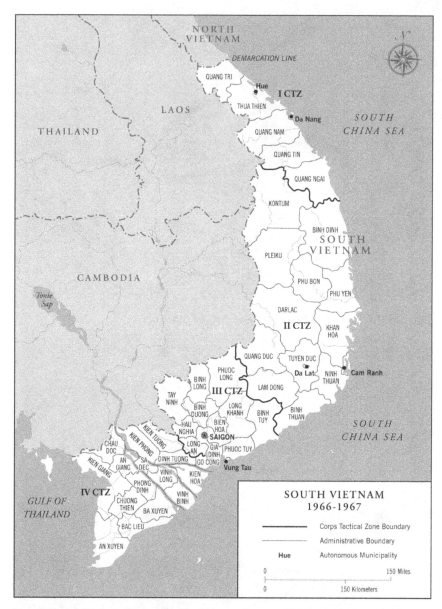

Map of South Vietnam Corps Tactical Zones. Source: US Army Center of Military History.

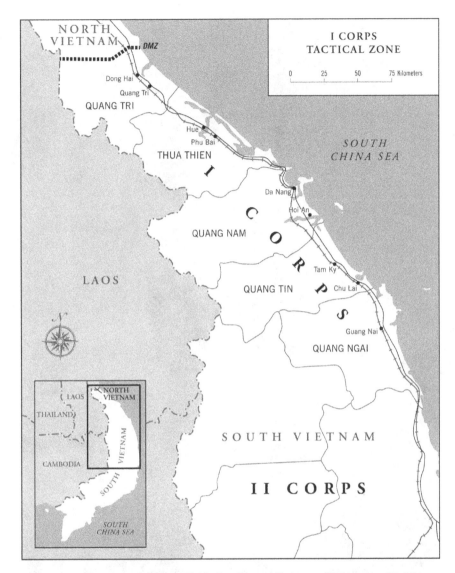

I Corps Tactical Zone. Source: US Marine Corps History and Museums Division.

Richard Nixon and Henry Kissinger confer in the White House, February 10, 1971. Source: Richard M. Nixon Library.

Richard Nixon and Nguyen Van Thieu make joint statement on Vietnamization at Midway Island, June 8, 1969. Source: Richard M. Nixon Library.

Infantrymen of the ARVN 1st Division dash from a helicopter in Quang Tri Province in 1969. Source: VA002367, Douglas Pike Photograph Collection, The Vietnam Center and Archive, Texas Tech University.

ARVN signal soldier repairs radios in 1973. Source: VA000141, Douglas Pike
Photograph Collection, The Vietnam Center and Archive, Texas Tech University.

Chapter Five

Vietnamization

A Signal Sergeant's Quality Assurance Report

As a policy, Vietnamization had yet to be conceived or announced when I received my diploma from Rice University and my I-A draft classification card on the same day—June 1, 1968. In the aftermath of the Tet Offensive, the American war in Vietnam was at its most violent phase, and US troop levels there were at their all-time high. I had been insulated from the harsh possibilities of military service in Vietnam by my student draft deferment, but now that prospect became very real. I had no way of knowing whether I would ever see the war myself, but as it turned out, I was about to have a front-row seat on the war and on Vietnamization in practice as a quality assurance NCO.

My specific experience was in combat support and military technology, an area that Gen. Creighton Abrams identified from the beginning as critical if the RVNAF was going to defend South Vietnam on its own. In the short time frame in which the Nixon administration attempted to implement Vietnamization, the effort's primary accomplishment was to put modern infantry weapons in the hands of a large number of young, conscripted Vietnamese soldiers. For a state to build an effective national defense force, however, tactical and technical training to utilize personnel and materiel effectively takes a great deal of time—even years—especially when the native government's social, economic, and political foundations themselves have been stunted by a century of colonialism and almost two decades of assault by violent internal enemies. From my vantage point in South Vietnam throughout most of 1970, these pernicious obstacles to the feasibility of rapid Vietnamization appeared insurmountable.

THE MAKING OF A SERGEANT

While I was a college student from 1964 to 1968, I opposed the Vietnam War—not from a radical perspective, but from a largely rational assessment that the war on the scale that it had attained was not in America's strategic interest. I majored in history and minored in political science, and had developed my views largely from my classes. The destructiveness of the war for both Vietnamese and Americans troubled my sensitivities, and I supported antiwar senator Eugene McCarthy in the 1968 presidential race. McCarthy argued essentially for a negotiated end to the war. I also came from what was known as the "oil patch" in West Texas, and had grown up with a family and regional Cold War patriotism that made the idea of resisting the draft a non-option. My father had held an occupational deferment in World War II, but my uncles had served in the Big War. There was in my background an unspoken expectation that when your country calls, you serve.

Not keen on going to Vietnam, I attempted what scholars call "military avoidance." I had been admitted to law school at the University of Texas, and a US Navy recruiter had gone through a rather complicated process of getting me into a Naval Judge Advocate General (JAG) program that would have delayed my service until after law school. About the time of my graduation, however, that coveted JAG billet had been pulled from the recruiter's file and given to the son of someone with political influence. The recruiter was livid but powerless.

As it turned out, I got a summer job at the Port of Houston working for the US Coast Guard merchant marine inspection office, and the captain in charge attempted to get me a billet in Houston upon completion of Coast Guard officer candidate school (OCS). I was rejected for Coast Guard OCS because of extreme nearsightedness. That same physical limitation also made OCS openings in the navy and air force unavailable to me in the summer of 1968, since my vision disqualified me from the only open slots—aviators or surface warfare officers. My remaining options were Marine Officer Candidate Course, Army OCS in a combat branch, voluntary enlistment in one of the services for at least three years, or the risk of the draft. A seasoned army recruiting sergeant advised me to go into the army as a draftee, if called, and to wait until after basic training to make a decision about going to Army OCS, which would be available to me anytime I chose. I found an apartment in Austin and began law school, and the first week there I received an induction notice. The Texas headquarters of Selective Service located in Austin said it would allow me to postpone my induction to the end of the semester, but not beyond, and UT Law School said they would keep my place open for me upon my completion of military service. Rather than further delaying the inevitable, I reported for induction on October 14, 1968.

My basic training was at Fort Bliss near El Paso—not far from where I had grown up in Hobbs, New Mexico, and Midland, Texas. During basic, while low-crawling in a cold rain under barbed wire during a nighttime, live-fire training exercise, I glanced over toward the private next to me and recalled: "You know, when I was a kid, I used to like to play army!" After Fort Bliss, I went to advanced individual training (AIT) at the Electronic Warfare School at Fort Huachuca, Arizona. The drill instructors at Fort Bliss had given me a card to turn in anytime I wanted to go to OCS, but I decided to hold onto it and see what Fort Huachuca had in store for me. As long as my options kept me out of being an infantryman, military occupation special-ty (MOS) 11B, I chose to remain a two-year draftee. My military obligation would be completed sooner, and I would be back in law school. Volunteering for OCS would have extended my active duty from two years to at least three years.

In Arizona along with about a half-dozen others in my training cycle (mostly college graduates), I completed the ten-week high-frequency radio operator course (05B) in five weeks. Our group of overachievers received orders to remain at Fort Huachuca as instructors. It was the spring of 1969, and with the growing controversy over the war, the army was having trouble getting junior NCOs to reenlist. Instructor cadre were needed. On November 14, 1969, after only thirteen months in service, I was promoted to sergeant E-5. I had also been selected as the post's "Soldier of the Month" right before my promotion. Naively, I thought I would complete my two-year conscrip-tion in southern Arizona.

By this time, I had also decided to enroll in a history PhD program in the fall of 1970, instead of going back to law school, and had begun the applica-tion process. As a history major at Rice, the history of US foreign relations had been among my favorite classes. Being in the military increased my interest in learning more about how my country had gotten into this mess in Vietnam. As an instructor, even in an army training center, I also had found that I really enjoyed teaching. The field of communications-electronics was something new, and there were no worries about classroom discipline. I could require a problem student simply to drop and give me ten push-ups.

Near the end of November 1969, the training company's first sergeant called me into the orderly room. He looked at me across his desk and said, "Congratulations, Sgt. Anderson—you're going to Vietnam." As far as I could tell, he was being sincere, not sarcastic, but I was totally blindsided. I soon discovered that most of my AIT classmates who had stayed as instruc-tors also were getting transfer orders. Most of us went to Vietnam, but one went to Germany. I found out years later that the Germany posting was a cover and that he purportedly had a number of temporary duty (TDY) mis-sions to Southeast Asia as a sharpshooter because he was a naturally talented marksman. One other member of our group stayed until May 1970, when the radio school closed. The army assigned him to an armored cavalry unit at Fort Meade, Maryland, whose primary mission was standby riot control for Washington, DC.

After spending the Christmas and New Year's holiday at home in Midland, I landed at Cam Ranh Bay on January 6, 1970. The flight from McChord Air Force Base (AFB) had taken more than eighteen hours in a DC-8 operated by the Flying Tigers. We made refueling stops at Anchorage and Yokota AFB near Tokyo. The very young infantryman seated next to me became increasingly nervous as we neared Vietnam. I tried to relax him by reminding him that we would be landing at a large military base and that our first experience would be just more army routine. As it happened, however, we taxied to a stop as rockets were hitting the field. We were hustled aboard a bus with wire mesh over the windows. Welcome to the war.

My travel orders said that I was to report to Company C, 43rd Signal Battalion at An Khe in the Central Highlands. That unit supported an infantry division that would participate in the Cambodian operations later in the spring. Since the orders made me an asset of the 1st Signal Brigade, the brigade's clerk at the 22nd Replacement Battalion—a buck sergeant like me—had the responsibility and authority to modify the original orders as needed in accord with the brigade's current requirements. I met with him and went over several postings that were then available. One of my Fort Huachuca buddies, who had preceded me to Vietnam, had encouraged me to seek out the sergeant, because the replacement clerk had managed to get him assigned to the Military Affiliate Radio System (MARS) station in Cam Ranh Bay (a very secure posting). This friend had almost gone AWOL upon getting his Vietnam orders. I had worked to persuade him not to do that, and as it turned out, his Vietnam service was not only relatively safe but was a rewarding job that helped soldiers communicate with their loved ones back home. There were forty-seven such stations scattered at bases throughout the RVN in 1970.[1]

CAM RANH BAY: THE LANGUAGE HURDLE OF VIETNAMIZATION

The replacement clerk changed my original orders, and I literally went up the hill from the replacement center to the 361st Signal Battalion. I thought good luck was with me because Cam Ranh was a large and secure combat base, except for an occasional rocket aimed at the airfield. In the evenings off duty, we wore civilian clothes, and there were a lot of creature comforts, with barracks, hot showers, mess halls, snack bars, clubs, and a big PX just two blocks from our unit. Just beyond our company area and over a tall, white sand dune was the beautiful South China Sea.

There was a problem, however. My MOS was 05B4H, which translated into high-frequency radio operator, NCO, instructor. Not included in the MOS designator but also in my occupational profile was that I was a college graduate, had qualified as a high-speed code intercept operator, was a French linguist (based upon both army testing and my six semesters of college French), and had a secret-cryptology clearance because one of my jobs at Fort Huachuca had been to instruct field-grade officers in encrypted voice communication. This résumé did not match the unit to which I was assigned. The 361st was a long-lines outfit that operated tropospheric scatter microwave facilities, and the Table of Organization and Equipment (TOE) of this highly sophisticated electronic installation that could transmit almost two hundred miles did not include any slots for 05B high-frequency radio operators.

Since I was an instructor, the battalion personnel officer first assigned me to the "school house," which was shorthand for the building that housed the in-country training provided to replacements on the equipment and procedures utilized by this long-lines site. It quickly became apparent that I did not know much about tropospheric scatter communication, and the commander moved me to a desk in the operations office (S-3). The operations sergeant was M.Sgt. Robbins, who was on his third straight tour in Vietnam, all at the same job. We called him "Grandpa" behind his back—a term of respect, because it sure looked like he ran the whole battalion. He was thrilled to have me, mainly because I was a college graduate who could type and could compose a complete sentence. I soon discovered that all of the men in the office except M.Sgt. Robbins were college graduates. At the desk next to mine was a friend I had gone to high school with in Hobbs, and who himself had been drafted out of graduate school at Emory University. M.Sgt. Robbins immediately put me to work as the author of various monthly and quarterly reports, but he soon realized that I had an even more valuable and much needed talent—French language ability.

The unit had no linguist on its TOE, but Vietnamization had created an urgent need for one. The battalion operations officer was a West Point–educated major, and he had an ARVN captain as a counterpart. The 1st Signal Brigade had placed this ARVN officer in the battalion S-3 to learn to manage this integrated wideband communication site. The difficulty with this plan was that the US major spoke English, had studied Portuguese at West Point, and knew no Vietnamese. The South Vietnamese captain spoke Vietnamese and French but no English. With no training as an interpreter, and frankly, only basic conversational French, it became my job to facilitate communication between the two officers. In effect, Vietnamization in the 361st Signal Battalion in 1970 meant that a US Signal Corps officer was instructing and mentoring an ARVN officer to take over command of a highly technical IWCS facility through the hand gestures and college French of a sergeant whose expertise was tactical, not long-range communication, and whose French was better suited to translating Molière than to conveying electronic and military concepts. Needless to say, the mentoring process was slow and only marginally effective, and not, I am sure, what Washington had envisioned Vietnamization to be. At least we were communicating, but the brigade commander later pointed out in his lessons-learned study that the language barrier hampered training.

As bad as the situation was for efforts to Vietnamize the 361st Signal Battalion across a serious language divide, the jury-rigged process received a further setback with my sudden transfer out. I do not know what happened after I left the unit, but there was no apparent way for the operations office to fill the Vietnamization gap that my departure created. First Signal Brigade headquarters at Long Binh had refused to issue permanent orders assigning me to the 361st because my MOS was not authorized for that type of unit. The battalion personnel officer, an experienced female warrant officer, informed me that the brigade was sending me to 12th Signal Group headquarters at Phu Bai for assignment to its headquarters detachment, or one of the signal battalions under its organization in I Corps, the five northern provinces of the RVN.

PHU BAI: THE TECHNOLOGY HURDLE OF VIETNAMIZATION

On February 9, I got off a C-130 at the Phu Bai airport, where I was met by a specialist 4 (spec.4) who drove me to the combat base in a jeep and deposited me at the transient hooch at Headquarters, Headquarters Detachment (HHD), 12th Signal Group. I turned in my personnel folder to the S-1 personnel office, kept my duffel bag packed, and waited assignment. I had been told before leaving Cam Ranh that I would likely stay in Phu Bai or go to Da Nang, but I could be assigned to any one of the many radio telephone/teletype sites the brigade operated throughout the northern provinces of South Vietnam in support of the 101st Airborne Division (Airmobile); 1st Brigade, 5th Infantry Division (Mechanized); 3rd Marine Amphibious Force; 1st ARVN Division; 2nd ARVN Division; and Republic of Korea (ROK) Marine Brigade. I could expect to spend the approximately seven months remaining until my DEROS (date of estimated return from overseas) and separation from active duty in a communication bunker or van at a division or battalion headquarters, if I was lucky, or a small remote site if I was less fortunate.

After waiting with this uncertainty for a couple of days, I received word to report to the office of the Communications Standards Branch. It was temporarily under the charge of a sergeant major until a new signal officer arrived to be branch chief. The sergeant major informed me that I was going to be the group's quality assurance NCO in charge of a small team of three or four that was currently being assembled. Col. D. W. Ogden Jr., the group commander, had created the QA team and its "communication evaluation" mission because, I was told, he was tired of receiving complaints from the combat commanders (termed "customers") in I Corps about the quality of signal support their units were getting from 1st Signal Brigade. The army, navy, marine, and air force combat commands had their own signal assets, but they depended upon units of 12th Signal Group to link their tactical networks through 1st Signal Brigade installations to the corps tactical zone; the Integrated Communications System, Southeast Asia (ICS, SEA); and worldwide networks operated by the Strategic Communications Command headquartered at Fort Huachuca. The technology of this vast system—sometimes referred to as the AT&T of Southeast Asia—was powerful. Through state-of-the-art tropospheric scatter, line-of-sight microwave, cable, and other electronic assets, a commander could connect securely by voice, teletype, or data from a combat bunker to anywhere in the world as long as 1st Signal Brigade units in the field kept the complex system up and working. [2]

It was a daunting task for well-educated and thoroughly trained signal soldiers with access to reliable equipment. At the time I took on the quality assurance challenge, I never heard anyone consider whether the ARVN would be able to manage this critical military infrastructure on its own, especially in the short time in which Washington wanted to accomplish Vietnamization. Although I know that Col. Ogden was briefed, I was unaware at the time I served that the brigade issued a regulation on March 26, 1970, requiring its commands to create a program called Buddies Together (*Cung Than Thien*) that was to train RVNAF signalmen in highly technical communications skills. Units like ours were also expected to conduct "surveys by combined teams" in each corps tactical zone "to determine where integration can take place and a single facility or system replace dual operations," and where American operators could turn over equipment and operations to the South Vietnamese. [3]

I had been doing my job for about two months when the new officer in charge (OIC) of the Communications Standards Branch arrived. Initially, in addition to myself, there was another sergeant who was an electrical generator mechanic; three spec.4s who served as drivers, guards, or assistants in various tasks; and the sergeant major, who had been in the army longer than I had been alive. Two of the enlisted men were draftsmen, and one was a radio operator just out of training, who had actually been in my classes at Fort Huachuca. I spent much of the first few weeks in Phu Bai assembling a library of manuals and reference materials and familiarizing myself with their contents. The new OIC was Maj. John Champion, who was commissioned through ROTC and on his second Vietnam tour. By the time he came on board, the three spec.4s in the office were gone. Two had gone home, and the other was on TDY in Da Nang. Our QA team by the end of March was myself, the sergeant major, the major, and sometimes the generator sergeant, whom we borrowed from another office. In April we got two more spec.4s back in the office. In June a signal corps captain replaced Maj. Champion. He was Capt. Amos, who had graduated from the corps of cadets at Texas A&M in January 1968.

The colonel had originally wanted a sergeant first class (E-7) to be the QA NCO, but senior NCOs were in short supply in Vietnam. He had settled for me because of my education and instructor experience, and my rank was at least a hard-stripe NCO. There were less than ten E-5 and E-6 NCOs in the group headquarters. The team's sergeant major (E-9) was not the group's command sergeant major, and seemed to have few specific routine duties. He traveled with our team primarily to back me up if the issues at the site turned out to be related to command or personnel problems.

The US Army history of military communications in Vietnam describes the urgency of the task at hand, much of it created by the completion of the automated digital network (AUTODIN). This automated system could transmit an average of 1,500 words per minute, but the tactical teletype circuits to which it was connected passed traffic at 60 to 100 words per minute. The 1st Signal Brigade's personnel in the field experienced continuous maintenance problems with their overextended machines. For example, in the summer of 1970, the Da Nang tape relay received twenty flash messages (highest precedence) in a twenty-minute period from the AUTODIN. This signal company had to relay these messages to the tactical units on its circuits at 100 words per minute, which required about twenty minutes per message. This volume of traffic, in turn, overheated the recipients' equipment, requiring transmission to be slowed to 60 words per minute. As the official history records, "Besides such technical problems, tactical operators lacking special training on the operation of the new Automatic Digital Network were bewildered by its formats and procedures. The 1st Signal Brigade had to keep troubleshooting teams constantly on the road to help inexperienced operators."[4]

We worked seven days a week, and once Maj. Champion arrived, we made site visits on average about three times a week, sometimes going to multiple sites in one day. The group's Operational Report—Lessons Learned (ORLL) for the period ending July 31, 1970, and the one ending October 31 recorded that "major emphasis during the past quarter was placed on improved communications thru Quality Assurance Inspections."[5] We were responsible for maintaining the efficient and effective performance of installations operated by seventeen units in five provinces. The group's ORLLs for the second and third quarters of 1970 reported that the QA inspection team conducted thirty-three site inspections in one quarter and twenty-four in the next. The colonel established a policy of conducting a minimum of one QA inspection per quarter at each site. The mission of these inspections stressed equipment maintenance, operator efficiency, site operating procedures, and customer satisfaction. According to the ORLLs, "Partly due to the effort of the Quality Assurance team the high standards of customer service provided by units of the 12th Signal Group were maintained or bettered."[6]

I became quite a jack-of-all-trades. My training had been radio telephone and teletype operations, and on the job I added manual and automated telephone switchboard operation and maintenance to my skill set. After each site visit, it was my responsibility to write the report documenting our findings and whatever improvements we had made or had recommended for follow-up action. The major or captain signed the report, and my name never appeared in the 12th Signal Group permanent files, which are now in the Modern Military Records of the National Archives.

It was amazing how the smallest detail could become so significant when dealing with modern electronics. In I Corps the soil was red clay (red mud in the rainy season and red dust other times), which made it extremely difficult for the signalmen to establish a working electrical ground for their transmission system. Our team had a Megger Earth Tester, which was a null balance galvanometer to measure the true resistance in the station's ground. In some cases, poor signal quality or even interrupted transmission was owing to where and how deep the metal grounding rods were installed. We would test them and supervise reconstruction of the grounds as necessary. Without this basic setup at a tactical location, all of the immense technical power of connection to the corps level and global system was of no use. It was a new variation on the "for want of a nail" adage. In this case, for want of a ground, the message was lost; for want of a message, the battle was lost.

Although I had originally expected to spend my time in one communication bunker in one place, my QA job took me to signal sites scattered from the DMZ that bordered North Vietnam southward to the Batangan Peninsula (the area made infamous as the location of My Lai). Traveling usually by UH-1 Huey helicopters, our team visits included Camp Carroll (the 1st ARVN Division's forward command post overlooking the DMZ), Quang Tri, Dong Ha, Tan My, Hai Van Pass, Da Nang, Hoi An, Tam Ky, Chu Lai, Duc Pho, and Quang Ngai. Our work also included small fire bases and landing zones, such as Hawk Hill (five miles northwest of Tam Ky), LZ Sharon (between Quang Tri and Dong Ha), and FB Birmingham (southwest of Camp Eagle). We went by jeep or three-quarter-ton truck to sites in Phu Bai, Hue, and Camp Eagle (headquarters of the 101st Airborne, which was about five miles from Phu Bai). We always tried to get into and out of a site (especially remote ones) in one day without having to stay overnight. We often traveled to the more distant sites with other people from our headquarters who needed to visit there for some reason.

On one occasion, because helicopters were ferrying combat troops and some signal problem at III MAF needed urgent attention, I made the trip from Phu Bai to Da Nang in an open jeep along Route 1 over Hai Van Pass with only one other soldier to ride shotgun. That we could make that drive at all was an indication that by 1970 the level of enemy activity along this key road had declined significantly. My sense was that the enemy was not deterred by the growing size of the ARVN, but was waiting for US troop withdrawals to continue. Unknown to me was the CIA's Special National Intelligence Estimate of February 5 that "Hanoi may be waiting until more US units have departed, in the expectation that this will provide better opportunities with lesser risks, and that Communist forces will be better prepared to strike."[7]

Phu Bai itself was a large and relatively secure base. It had included the headquarters of the US Army's XXIV Corps until that command moved to Da Nang in March 1970. The corps HQ controlled all combat elements in I Corps. Phu Bai did not have all the clubs, shopping, and services of Cam Ranh Bay, but there was a sign at the front gate proclaiming "Phu Bai is Alright." It did receive periodic mortar and rocket bombardment, especially aimed at runways, helipads, and signal towers. Although US infantry and military police had primary responsibility for overall base security, the security plan assigned a portion of the perimeter to our signal group headquarters detachment to defend. Signalmen were expected to be soldier-communicators who provided specialized skills and defended their installations against enemy attack. We had to detail personnel to man about five bunkers on the perimeter each night and to have a quick reaction team on standby duty in the event of an assault on the base. Our signalmen had very little training, if any, on the use of M60 machine guns, M79 grenade launchers, hand grenades, or Claymore mines, but we were provided these weapons when on guard or reaction duty. Each of us also had our personal M16 rifles, flak vests, steel helmets, gas masks, and utility belts. Since there was a shortage of junior NCOs in the detachment, I drew the duty of being sergeant of the guard, reserve force NCO, or staff duty NCO at least one night a week.

On most nights, the duty was routine, but some nights stand out in my mind. As sergeant of the guard, after ensuring that each bunker was properly staffed and equipped, the primary responsibility was to move from post to post during the night to be sure everyone was alert and to be available to call for support from the reserve forces if any breach occurred. One night, the OIC had briefed the NCOs that VC sappers recently had been probing the defenses at nearby Camp Eagle, and that one of these probes had caught men off guard in a bunker and killed them. The details may have been embellished, but we were told that the Americans were stoned on marijuana and their throats were cut. Although marijuana was readily available and widely smoked, simple concern with survival usually prevented its use by perimeter guards or troops engaging the enemy.

As I made my rounds one night after that briefing, I approached a bunker from the back (or dark) side—the front facing the enemy had floodlights illuminating the concertina wire—and detected the unmistakable smell of marijuana smoke. Without even going into the bunker, I yelled to the men inside that I did not want to smell that stuff when I returned. As I neared the post about a half-hour later in the dark, but carrying a flashlight, I did not know what to expect. I was genuinely frightened that my own men might shoot from being high or confused or even angry at being caught. I identified myself and entered the sandbagged enclosure. All was cleaned up and in order, and I never reported them. Years later, I learned that the 43rd Signal Battalion at An Khe—the original destination on my travel orders to Vietnam—had a soldier in early 1971 dealing heroin. This local "drug lord and assassination expert" fragged two officers who tried to break up his business before he was finally arrested, tried, and sent to the military prison at Fort Leavenworth, Kansas. [8]

There were several issues at work among the troops in 1970. There was a lull in enemy activity in our area, and soldiers were aware that troop withdrawals were under way. Phu Bai seldom experienced ground attack, although there were frequent mortar and rocket hits to try to keep us uncomfortable. There was a false sense of security among many of the soldiers whose duties never carried them outside the wire. During one rocket attack, I was unable to wake a sleeping soldier in my hooch and get him to the bunker outside because he was so drunk. Also, soldiers were known to openly defy command authority, as the American mission in Vietnam had become unpopular with all Americans, including draftees and enlistees. The young lieutenant in command of our detachment was an extremely unpopular martinet and in other times and places would probably have never qualified to be an officer. Although we were not a combat unit, I believe that he actually feared his troops. The word was that he slept with a pistol under his pillow. I had a very close relationship with my QA team and with all the men in the detachment and experienced no personal hostility, but I had felt real apprehension when I had to be the disciplinarian of the pot-smoking guards, even if they probably knew my order was for their own good.

I did experience one enemy ground operation against the Phu Bai combat base. It was in my last month in Vietnam before my DEROS—that is, I was "short"—and I had the duty as NCO of the detachment's reserve force. Perhaps Charlie knew I was short, because enemy bombardments and ground probes of Camp Eagle, Camp Evans, and Phu Bai increased markedly in July and August. Actually, the PAVN and VC were testing the progress of Vietnamization at that time. Around 0200 one night, the police whistles blew and sirens sounded alerting a possible assault on the perimeter and activating the reaction forces. Sleeping in my sandbagged hooch in my underwear, as was typical, I hastily threw on my fatigues and boots and grabbed my gear (rifle, helmet, flak jacket, and gas mask). With nine men in my charge, we proceeded in a deuce-and-a-half truck to a point on the perimeter as directed by the military police. There, an infantry lieutenant had me post my men in a dispersed rank behind the perimeter bunkers. He said it was not a drill, and that there was perhaps a company-size enemy force outside the wire.

I could see and hear ordnance going off in the dark beyond the floodlit area, and illumination flares were in the air. I got a whiff of tear gas, and word quickly passed along our defense line to put on our masks. I suspect the gas was ours, not the enemy's. It was definitely tense to be in the dark and the tropical heat with the limited visibility provided by a gas mask, holding a loaded M16 at the ready in a kneeling firing position, and not having any clear idea of what to expect next. After about an hour, which seemed a lot longer, the lieutenant came by and told me it was all clear and I could take my men back to our detachment area. I never saw any enemy soldiers and did not know if there was an actual assault, or if the alert had been a precaution against possible attack. Either way, I was back at my desk shortly after sunrise doing my regular job and thinking that I was way too short for nights like that one.

There were ARVN troops at many of the bases that I saw in 1970, but most of them were providing perimeter security, manning artillery pieces, or handling supplies—not operating signal equipment. Similar to what I had witnessed at the 361st Signal Battalion in Cam Ranh Bay, there were a few ARVN officers and NCOs shadowing American counterparts, but I observed little interaction or hands-on communication activity by Vietnamese. I was aware of Vietnamization and wrote home on May 29: "The Vietnamization program is really going on in earnest over here, and [the Cambodian Incursion] should give that program a little more time to achieve some real results. Even 12th Sig. Gp. is getting in on the ARVN training program. We have about 20 ARVN at various sites in the Group receiving on-the-job training on a buddy system basis." In retrospect, my estimate of twenty ARVN signalmen over a five-province area suggests that the number being trained was woefully small. With the exception of Camp Carroll, which was an ARVN command post, I seldom heard Vietnamese spoken at signal facilities.

Even at our headquarters detachment in Phu Bai, there was no visible Vietnamese presence except for laundry women of unknown age (mama sans) and elderly men (papa sans) using diesel fuel to burn latrine waste in cutoff fifty-five-gallon drums. I tried to communicate with the woman who worked in our hooch, washing and drying uniforms and underwear, but the language barrier reduced the conversation to mostly sign language. I did discover that she had lost four sons in the ARVN and lived near the Our Lady of Perpetual Help Roman Catholic Church in Hue. I could never tell what she thought of her personal sacrifice. Aware of it, however, I have always had an ambivalence about whether our presence or that of the communists was the source of her personal tragedy. It probably was both. When I left, I gave her my inexpensive AM/FM radio, which she had always listened to while she worked. I carried the radio with me in the cab of the truck in which we transported the workers home to Hue. The MPs would never have let her off the base with it. She took it home and may have kept it, sold it, or given it to the VC to use for spare electrical parts. I will never know.

One revealing incident at a signal site stands out clearly in my memory. My team was doing its work testing equipment and observing operational procedures at a line-of-sight microwave installation near Chu Lai when a group of visiting American military and civilian officials appeared. There were ARVN signal soldiers at the site. A high-ranking US officer in the group asked the American signal officer escorting them how long it would be before the Vietnamese would be ready to assume operation of this station on their own. There was a long pause as the escort seriously considered the question. Finally, he said in an even voice, with no editorial tone, that he estimated about eight years. That response was a reasonable assessment because it took the US Army two years to train specially selected American soldiers with good civilian educational backgrounds just to become entry-level operators and maintainers of this complex equipment. One Army Security Agency sergeant who had gone through a year of training at Fort Devens, Massachusetts, and served a year in Vietnam as a communication monitor, went back for a second tour during Vietnamization and provided instruction in signal security. When asked later about Vietnamization, his recollection was vague but hardly positive: "We'd have a unit be taken over by them basically as far as the duties . . . [and] send the American troops home. It didn't seem like it was working that well."[9]

Unknown to me at the time, the education requirement in the ARVN for promotion to major was a ninth-grade diploma, and the average enlisted ARVN signalman had a sixth-grade education.[10] Beyond basic education, it required two years or more of hands-on field experience for signal operators to develop the technical knowledge, leadership attributes, and problem-solving skills for this military occupation. The Nixon administration's timetable for Vietnamization and turning over the defense of the RVN to its own military was, however, measured in months, not years.

As I observed this interchange at Chu Lai, I was unaware that Lt. Gen. Walter Kerwin in III Corps had estimated in 1969 that it would take five years for the ARVN to be self-sufficient, and that Washington's goal was to have Vietnamization completed by January 1973. I also did not know that my former unit, the 361st Signal Battalion, had been designated in 1969 before I arrived as a test of 1st Signal Brigade's buddy effort to turn over the fixed communication system to the South Vietnamese Signal Directorate. That initiative explains the presence of the ARVN captain in the battalion S-3 while I was there. ORLLs from that unit in 1969 estimated, "If the current rate continues, it will take sixteen years to staff the system (ICS, SEA) with Vietnamese" because the RVNAF lacked "the broad scientific and technical education base to provide sufficient input of students to allow takeover of the ICS in [a] short time frame."[11] This study concluded that it would take a minimum of four years for the South Vietnamese to take control of ICS facilities, and a more realistic estimate was eight to ten years.

A parallel to my observations of how this technology gap impacted Vietnamization was a *New York Times* correspondent's report on a Mekong Delta river patrol in February 1970. As part of Vietnamization, the boats were operated by Vietnamese crews with US Navy advisers and instructors. Although the Americans were critical but not despairing of the Vietnamese sailors, one of the Vietnamese interviewed complained that the Americans sometimes criticized them for being lazy, when in fact their English was too poor to understand what the Americans wanted them to do. "I do not want Americans to come here and say 'you are lazy, you're not working,'" he protested, "just because they don't understand us." The journalist summarized what his reporting had found:

> While such frictions and misunderstandings can be overcome—and often are—by tactful men on both sides, two problems are proving more pervasive: the difficulty of training enough Vietnamese quickly in the complicated fields of logistics and electronics, and the lack of middle-level officers. Without qualified men, such things as communications with air force and artillery units for support, the repair of electronics equipment, and troop supplies will have to depend on American advisers for years to come.[12]

Determination of the size of the US Signal Corps presence in South Vietnam was under continual review and change. There were constant rumors while I was at Phu Bai that the group headquarters was definitely moving to Da Nang, but the move never occurred while I was there. Apparently, the delay was the time required for another US unit to depart in order to free space designated for us near the Da Nang Air Force Base. With US Army and Marine combat units leaving the county, the 1st Signal Brigade's primary mission of support for US forces (not RVNAF forces) was narrowing. Abrams had wanted to keep a residual US combat support element to bolster Vietnamization, but the Pentagon mandated across-the-board reductions. By late March 1970 the brigade was over-strength by Washington's calculations. Men who had a DEROS in April and May were being released early. I had already been reassigned once in the personnel shuffle and was not authorized another permanent change of station. One of my AIT friends had arrived in the RVN considerably after the rest of our cohort and got the bad side of the brigade's downsizing. Rather than sending him to a fixed signal installation, headquarters in Long Binh transferred him to the 17th Armored Cavalry at Pleiku, just in time for the fighting in Cambodia.

All the action in Cambodia was actually good for us in I Corps because the war got really quiet in our area during May and June. I recorded my own thoughts about Cambodia in a letter home on May 29: "I think the president made the right decision. All those supplies and ammunition that have been captured will never be used to kill American GIs." Through *Stars and Stripes* and Armed Forces Radio and Television, we were aware, at least in part, of the protests following the US and ARVN operations into Cambodia. In a letter on May 10, I remarked, "There has been a lot of violence in the news lately—as much at home as over here. So far, I have managed to not see any combat, and I sure don't want to come home and see any."

The army granted my request for early separation from active duty on an "early release" so that I could start graduate school classes at the University of Virginia. I left Vietnam on September 8 and arrived in Charlottesville on September 17. It was a strange experience to transition so quickly from the war zone to a university campus, especially one that had endured the same intense emotions of many other schools the previous May after Ohio National-al Guardsmen had killed four students at Kent State.

I had served on active duty for one year, ten months, and twenty-six days, and was in Vietnam for eight months and five days. My work in the 12th Signal Group constantly had been under arduous and sometimes dangerous conditions, and to my surprise I was twice decorated, receiving an Army Commendation Medal and a Bronze Star (one of the few awarded in our headquarters detachment). I believed then, as I do now, that the United States made a terrible public policy mistake with its massive and sustained military intervention in Vietnam, but for me personally, as I shared with my parents, "Although I wouldn't want to see everyone come over here, I think Vietnam is a good experience." A few weeks after my departure from Phu Bai, the 12th Signal Group relocated to Da Nang as US forces in Vietnam further downsized and consolidated their remaining strength. US signal assets in I Corps were turned over in a matter of months to the ARVN. American aid paid private contractors to operate the network as a stopgap to meet the South's military communication requirements, but the days were almost gone when the US Congress and public would supply such funding.

While I was at the 12th Signal Group in Phu Bai, Maj. Michael Eggleston was the deputy commander of the 43rd Signal Battalion at Pleiku. A West Point graduate and career officer, he had a better seat than I did to watch the action, but his recollections of the Vietnamization of communications-elec-tronics are similar to my own. In 1970, his unit was transferring signal equipment and responsibility to the ARVN 620th Signal Battalion. He has written about some of the challenges:

> Transferring signal equipment was more complicated than transferring other items such as rifles and artillery that the RVNAF already had in large quan-

tities. Some of the 43rd equipment was new and had not been used by the
RVNAF. I had spent a few years training US troops in the operation and
maintenance of US signal equipment, such as radios and satellites. This takes
months of training time, with English-speaking people using manuals written
in English. We had none of these luxuries during the period of Vietnamization.[13]

There were no operator or maintenance manuals in Vietnamese. Although
most of the RVNAF officers Eggleston dealt with spoke some English, the
equipment they had to deal with was simply too complicated to be mastered
quickly. "For such sites, such as the tropo communications complex at Pleiku," he explained, "the army turned to the US private sector to run them, and
Federal Electric took over the Pleiku complex." It tried to train Vietnamese
for the work, he noted, but the company "was still in place long after we
departed. . . . Years after the war, these tropo dishes had disappeared and the
sites were overgrown with weeds."[14]

My two assignments in Vietnam—as an impromptu interpreter and as a
quality assurance NCO—give insight to some of the problems with Vietnamization that were apparent in close observation of the program on the ground.
Operational studies of combat support at the time and soon after the war
make frequent references to what I witnessed—limitations on the effectiveness of Vietnamization based upon language differences between the
RVNAF and its American trainers, and on the level of expertise required to
be learned to support modern combat operations. In an otherwise upbeat
report on Vietnamization at the end of 1969, Laird had singled out as a
"serious concern" the challenge specialist training posed. "More English
language instructors and more trained technicians to man military and civil
communications systems are required," the secretary of defense admitted. He
added—and I can confirm—that there was a "need for a nationwide system
of manpower priorities since there were simply not enough qualified persons
in the Vietnamese manpower pool to fill all the demands for technical
skills."[15] The bravery of the ARVN soldiers and their ability to shoot straight
were necessary but not sufficient for battlefield success, as Gen. Abrams had
perceived when first receiving his marching orders from Washington. As a
nation-state, the RVN had major structural weaknesses to overcome before it
could field a modern military establishment.

Chapter Six

Vietnamization Tested

Lam Son 719 and the Easter Offensive

During and after the cross-border operations in Cambodia in May and June 1970, President Nixon publicly trumpeted the success of Vietnamization. His focus remained fixed on how the Vietnam War would affect his campaign for reelection in 1972, and he was determined to present the case that his plan for an orderly withdrawal of US forces was working. In a June 3 update to the American people, he boasted that the "splendid performance of the South Vietnamese Army . . . had far exceeded our expectations" and "demonstrated that our Vietnamization program is succeeding."[1] In response to his critics, he reasserted earlier arguments that the move into Cambodia was to protect the security of the 400,000 US troops still in Vietnam, while at the same time he promised that another 50,000 would be home by the end of October.[2] Behind this political rhetoric, however, Nixon's inner circle in the White House and his commanders in the field had serious concerns about the prospects of the RVN.

THE MOUNTING STRESS OF WAR

In private briefings, Nixon had asked Abrams outright if the Cambodian operation had resulted in greater confidence in our Vietnamization program, and the general had responded with one word: "Yes."[3] He did not use any adjectives like "splendid," and also, at Nixon's prompting, promised not to keep any American soldiers in Cambodia "one extra day longer" than needed.[4] It was clear from the public outcry that the administration would never again use American ground forces outside the borders of South Vietnam in Cambodia or Laos. Congress eventually codified this restriction in the Cooper-Church Amendment passed in December 1970.[5] In addition, Kissinger worried about RVNAF units being away from needed security functions within their own country. He advised Nixon that "if the ARVN becomes obsessed with Cambodia, Vietnamization and pacification could suffer."[6] Despite these forebodings, Saigon's military forces made a thrust into Laos some months later, with predictable and disastrous results.

Washington's redeployment schedule remained undeterred. In addition to the 50,000 US troops withdrawn by October 1970, another 40,000 were out by December. The total for the first four months of 1971 was 60,000, bringing US forces down to 284,000 by April 30. American strength was about half of what it had been at its peak in April 1969. The RVNAF total of regular, regional, and popular forces was 968,000 by the end of 1970, an increase of about 100,000 since 1969. PAVN and VC soldiers estimated to be in combat battalions in the South numbered about 200,000. With the total of US Army advisers reduced, Abrams made a telling adjustment. He decided that Saigon's regular forces were performing well enough to have fewer advisers, but expert assistance now needed to be channeled to combat support, such as logistics, communications-electronics, and intelligence, as well as to the persistent civilian performance problems in government services and economic development.[7]

After years of bearing the burden of ground combat, the ARVN soldiers were a battered and dispirited army. Over the course of the war, they suffered four to five times as many killed in action as did American units. "The ARVN, having fought so long and suffered so much," US Marine Corps veteran Andrew Wiest has written, "was not a historical parody, peopled by cardboard cutout officers and men."[8] In the eyes of Saigon's soldiers, Vietnamization and pacification relied upon them to "do much of the dirty work." Nguyen Van Hieu, an ARVN corporal, recalled that Vietnamization "did not change the fact that we were poorly trained, poorly led, and suffered from low morale."[9] Abrams and his military advisory mission understood that effective ARVN leadership was critical to the goal of achieving Vietnamization, but cultivating quality officers and NCOs took not only time but social reform. The high cost of living in South Vietnam, family breakups, urban slums with poverty and prostitution, inflation, and low pay for soldiers gave the Saigon government little legitimacy. War weariness in the RVN was tangible, and to many the sacrifices of war seemed no longer worth the costs. The war had also produced massive social dislocation. "In the end, Saigon's inability to cope with the massive influx of refugees tells us much about the counterrevolution's failure," Robert Brigham has observed. He concluded that "the lack of imaginative or sophisticated social programs to deal with the new urban refugees was a strong indicator that Saigon was going to lose the war."[10]

The term *corruption* often appears in descriptions of the Saigon regime under President Thieu, but the word hardly begins to capture the magnitude of this particular social pathology. A US Army sergeant at a remote outpost in the Central Highlands observed the province chief, a position appointed by Saigon:

> There was giant corruption with the gasoline, . . . [but] the worst part was the food because . . . all the rice supplies were centralized in a warehouse run by the province chief. . . . He was the colonel and the mayor and the governor of the state of Phu Bon. . . . There were about eighteen-hundred ways you could tap into this to make tremendous money, and they did. . . . Sixty to 80 percent of the [American] supplies disappeared. We are in effect supplying both sides, the medicines, the cloth, the da da da. . . . In Vietnam illegitimately 60 percent vanishes. . . . Of the legitimate 40, that's going to get illegitimately used as well. It's going to go to the province chief who sells it or denies it. And you didn't even have to buy the police force to do it. [11]

One extreme case was that of Lt. Col. Hoang Duc Ninh, a first cousin of Nguyen Van Thieu, whom the president made province chief in Bac Lieu in the Mekong Delta. As described by journalist Neil Sheehan: "Ninh was boundless in his rapacity. He levied tribute on almost every commodity sold in the province from gasoline to cigarettes; he sold government supplies, too, and had his troops steal back some of the government gasoline he sold so that he could sell it a second time; . . . no one retained a safe assignment in Bac Lieu town or in one of the district centers without a fee to Ninh." [12] Sheehan's litany of the colonel's blackmail and extortion continues at length, and notes that Ninh brushed aside efforts by American advisers to restrain him with the declaration that his cousin was the president. Ninh eventually obtained a higher command in which his opportunity to enrich himself was even greater. He would, for example, demand a bribe from a garrison under PAVN or VC attack before authorizing an artillery barrage. [13]

The war's stress on life in the United States and South Vietnam was evident by late 1970 and was wearing on the DRV as well. Under the stubborn leadership of Le Duan, however, the Politburo in Hanoi forged ahead. The US-RVN cross-border campaign in Cambodia had mixed outcomes for North Vietnam. Although the operation found no PAVN Pentagon of bamboo huts inside Cambodia as Nixon had suggested existed, it had severely disrupted, at least for the moment, PAVN command and logistics networks there. Conversely, the extreme antiwar outburst in the United States presented an opportunity for Hanoi. The Vietnamization program concerned Le Duan—not because he thought Saigon's leadership competent, but because the exit of American forces made Hanoi's propaganda and political program against foreign devils more difficult to sell to people in the South. With little confidence in the protracted diplomatic talks in Paris, Communist leaders in the North invigorated efforts to disrupt Vietnamization and pacification.[14]

Although there is little evidence that Nixon even knew who Le Duan was, the two leaders were stubbornly committed to their own individual beliefs that force and willpower would prevail. In the wake of the Cambodian campaign in the spring, Nixon continued to pound the Ho Chi Minh Trail with American airpower and to accept ARVN ground raids in Cambodia to stop DRV troops and supplies from reaching the South. Despite these interdiction efforts, Hanoi kept steady traffic moving down the trail. Abrams knew that the RVNAF was not ready for a major showdown with the PAVN and VC, but his intelligence reports indicated that a Northern offensive might be in preparation for 1971. Intelligence is seldom definitive, however. Hanoi could have been stockpiling supplies in caches in Cambodia and South Vietnam while waiting for complete withdrawal of all US forces likely to occur in 1972, at which time the DRV would then launch a major offensive, if negotiations had produced no political resolution.

In South Vietnam itself, the enemy was relatively quiet. The VC harassed pacification efforts with sporadic rocket and mortar attacks on villages and targeted Vietnamization with harassment of ARVN units to disrupt US training efforts. Although some American observers at the time—and historians later—pointed to improved rice harvests, physical elimination of some VC cadre, and less armed violence in the countryside as evidence that pacification and Vietnamization were working, the RVN's systemic deficiencies and the known flaws in its military and political structure remained unaddressed. There was good reason to doubt that disrupting or even cutting the Ho Chi Minh Trail would solve Saigon's real problems of legitimacy and lack of effectiveness. Although the supply route out of the DRV through Laos and Cambodia was an important logistics element for the PAVN in the South, the trail was not the life support system of the Southern insurgency. Since its birth in 1955, however, the regime in Saigon had never demonstrated that it could survive on its own without itself receiving outside military and economic nourishment. As one South Vietnamese general poignantly summarized, "After nearly 30 years of war, . . . whether the Republic of Vietnam, which had been supported by a long US commitment, survived or perished almost entirely depended on American will."[15]

With little movement occurring in either diplomatic conference rooms or the villages of South Vietnam, the importance of the trail increased for both sides. In December 1970, the JCS tasked Abrams to develop contingency plans for South Vietnamese cross-border operations in Cambodia and Laos. In April and September 1971, the RVNAF engaged the North Vietnamese in battles around Snuol in Cambodia. The Southern forces suffered heavy losses in the first battle but bloodied the PAVN in the second. The results were a strategic stalemate, but US observers worried that Saigon was endangering its security inside the RVN while flailing around in Cambodia.[16]

SOUTH VIETNAM'S OPERATION LAM SON 719
(FEBRUARY 8 TO MARCH 24, 1971)

In coordination with Thieu and Gen. Cao Van Vien, head of the ARVN Joint General Staff (JGS), Abrams designed what would become a major offensive in Laos targeting the once-thriving market town of Tchepone, a major transfer point along the trail. It had already been bombed to rubble, but forty to sixty trucks a night passed through it with soldiers and supplies headed south. Such an attack was a high-stakes gamble. Washington and MACV wanted to forestall any possible Northern invasion to continue to buy time for Vietnamization. If the RVNAF pulled off the attack, the success could showcase the progress of Vietnamization and give Nixon the kind of "big bang" he desired, both politically and diplomatically. Conversely, failure could be a major setback for Washington and Saigon. Abrams accepted the challenge largely because he believed it would have a better chance of success while there still were enough US combat support elements in the RVN to backstop the offensive.[17]

The South Vietnamese code-named the operation Lam Son 719, recalling a famous Vietnamese defeat of the Chinese in 1427. The mission included some of the ARVN's best units—the 1st Infantry Division, the Airborne Division, ranger and armor units, and the Marine Division—under the operational control of the I Corps commander, Gen. Hoang Xuan Lam, who had never led an operation of this size. The United States established a staging area with American air and artillery assets on the Vietnamese side of the border, but no US infantry or armor was to cross into Laos in accord with the Cooper-Church restrictions. The US Army's 1st Signal Brigade constructed a microwave relay network from Quang Tri along the hilltops to the Laotian border and built a tropo-scatter multichannel system from Quang Tri to Khe Sanh. When enemy rockets knocked out the cable head at Qui Nhon that provided service to the ARVN's I Corps headquarters at Da Nang, American signal units rushed contingency equipment and operators from outside South Vietnam to restore communications.[18]

The RVNAF offensive launched on February 8, 1971. The plan called for a conventional road movement along the forty-kilometer distance of Route 9 from the border to Tchepone. Fire support bases were built along the way to protect the route, and once at the destination the RVNAF units were supposed to establish a base from which they could make continued attacks on the Ho Chi Minh Trail. The task force proceeded about halfway to the target in two weeks before coming under heavy enemy attack. During the planning, intelligence estimates had assessed that the PAVN in the area were mostly logistics personnel with relatively light security forces. Having gotten its own intelligence weeks earlier from its super spy in Saigon—Pham Xuan An, who worked as a correspondent for *Time* magazine—and other sources within the RVNAF, and having leaked information published in international media, Hanoi had moved five divisions into the area with armor and field and antiaircraft artillery.[19] Low clouds, antiaircraft fire, and lack of separation between the opposing ground troops limited use of American B-52 and fighter bomber attacks on the enemy.[20]

Thieu ordered Lam to make an air assault on Tchepone, and US Huey helicopters escorted by Cobra gunships lifted two ARVN battalions into the town on March 6. Finding no PAVN in Tchepone, Thieu declared the mission completed and ordered Lam to withdraw all of his forces back to the RVN. With Northern troops outnumbering the Southern force by about two to one, and PAVN units equipped with tanks and artillery, the extraction came under intense attack. Using tanks, mortars, and field artillery, the PAVN overran several of the fire bases, and the retreat became a rout in the narrow Laotian valleys. Most of the RVNAF forces were out of Laos by March 25. Lam's command suffered about 5,000 killed and wounded and 2,500 missing. The United States lost about 700 helicopters and 253 lives, ferrying South Vietnamese into and out of the battle zone.[21]

Hanoi had responded in strength to Lam Son 719, leading to a huge setback for Vietnamization and providing a big morale boost for the North. This violent engagement revealed much about Vietnamization. Fighting for their lives, many of the South Vietnamese soldiers performed bravely and inflicted heavy losses on the PAVN. When weather permitted, US airmen killed large numbers of the enemy. The Northern forces suffered an estimated 13,000 killed, many lost in human wave attacks pummeled by bombing— a sacrifice that likely surpassed Viet Minh deaths at Dien Bien Phu in 1954. It was the planning and especially the leadership of the RVNAF, however, that was seriously flawed. On the planning side, the American style of war the Southern commanders had been taught did not work. Reliance on air cover and fixed fire bases had proved deadly for the ARVN. In the foggy Laotian mountains, air support of ground troops and helicopter airlifts had been difficult to execute. The dug-in fire bases proved to be rich targets for the PAVN's artillery and heavily armed ground attacks. There was little maneuvering and attacking in the RVN assault plan.[22]

A career US Army medical evacuation officer, who logged thousands of hours as a dustoff pilot, later recounted that "the intensity of fire in Lam Son 719 far exceeded anything that I'd ever seen in my lifetime as far as fire on rescue ships."[23] Their helicopters attempting to land in the besieged ARVN bases received fire from radar-guided surface-to-air missiles, antiaircraft artillery, quad .50 caliber machine guns, and small arms. As this pilot described the action, "[I]f we got into the LZ, . . . we could not stay on the ground but about three seconds. We'd count to three and pull pitch if we got into the compound. If we stayed longer than that, we would be barraged with mortars and be nailed while we were on the ground."[24] Under attack from huge numbers of PAVN armed with tanks, every soldier—wounded or not— who could walk rushed the aircraft trying to escape. "We had to use force on many occasions to push . . . the people that were on the ground away from the aircraft to pull off," he added, explaining that "we had to do that or we would be overloaded and unable to pull out of the LZ. They were overcrowding the ships . . . in the three seconds that we were on the ground."[25] News photographs of ARVN soldiers hanging onto helicopter skids correctly conveyed that Saigon's troops were overwhelmed, but the Southerners were not cowards in the eyes of this witness. He thought the Vietnamese he knew "were doing as much as they could" with the amount of training and resources they had.[26]

An American combat assault (CA) pilot expressed a similar judgment of the soldiers grasping for the skids: "But I still can't help but feel sorry for those people, 'cause they really didn't want this thing to happen. . . . The people we CAed in Laos didn't even know they were going there until we put 'em down on the damn ground. That's pretty bad in my book."[27] He faulted MACV because "it throws them out there on the damn mountaintop and expects them to do damn wonders. . . . It's the United States' advisers and the Vietnamese higher-ups who don't know what in the hell they are doing."[28] Gen. Lam received most of the criticism, but JCS chairman Adm. Thomas Moorer recorded in his diary that the responsibility went all the way to senior US leaders in Vietnam. He listed by name Abrams, Ambassador Bunker, and the top two three-star American generals in I Corps—Michael Davison and James Sutherland. "I am appalled," he wrote, "that they did not take into consideration at that time Gen. Lam's incompetence. As a matter of fact, none of my Army advisers . . . gave me any reason to believe that Lam could not hack it. . . . They failed to appreciate that the President had so much riding on this golden and last opportunity to punish the enemy."[29]

When the heaviest of the fighting began during the retreat, there was a major breakdown in RVNAF command and control. Many company and field-grade officers simply did not have the ability to adjust to the counterattack. Without US advisers on the ground, the South Vietnamese officers were unable to coordinate air and artillery support. In their haste to withdraw, they abandoned large amounts of supplies even when there was time to regroup.

Worse was the bickering and confusion among the senior officers. Abrams and his staff wanted the Vietnamese to stay in Laos and reinforce the ground already taken. The RVN airborne and marine commanders complained about redeployment and replacements, leading US observers to charge that Lam lost control of his subordinates. Thieu declined to support Lam, reportedly because some of his challengers were among the officers most personally loyal to the president. Thieu himself intervened at critical points and made the key decision to withdraw. Gen. Cao Van Vien of the JGS claimed later that Thieu was ignoring the recommendations of the general staff and the field commanders. Thieu apparently "had decided at the outset," according to ARVN Maj. Gen. Nguyen Duy Hinh, "that once Tchepone had been entered by the RVNAF, the withdrawal should begin without delay."[30] When Abrams pressed him to reinforce the 2nd ARVN Division, the RVN president expressed "concern that ARVN divisions were unprepared for a strategic task," and argued that he would only reinforce if a US division entered the battle, which all knew was impossible.[31]

The White House was dismayed with Thieu's sudden termination of Lam Son 719. Kissinger cabled Ambassador Bunker in Saigon: "It would be hard to exaggerate the mystification and confusion caused here by the ARVN's latest scheme of maneuver which envisages a rapid pull-out from Laos."[32] He wanted Bunker to make Thieu understand the danger of losing Nixon's confidence, and "that this may be his last crack at massive US support."[33] Kissinger's deputy, Gen. Alexander Haig, reported from Lam's headquarters in Da Nang that "it is now obvious that [the] ARVN has lost its stomach for further operations in Laos and that [the] main problem now faced by Gen. Abrams is not getting ARVN to stay but rather to influence them to pull out in an orderly fashion."[34]

In a joint assessment of the RVNAF operations in Laos and Cambodia, Abrams was guarded. He reported that there were "disappointments and failures as well as successes" in those operations. He thought that it spoke well of Vietnamization that Saigon was able to mount offensives in two areas at once, that the RVN had taken the initiative from the enemy, and that it had bought time to strengthen its internal security.[35] In reviewing the implications of the Laos operation, Kissinger mused: "We cannot yet tell whether the pace of Vietnamization would have to be slowed, but right now I doubt it." He acknowledged that "Thieu may be hurt politically for having launched a venture [Lam Son 719] which was not a full success."[36] As Maj. Gen. Hinh later wrote, the goal "to strangle the enemy's supply route could not be accomplished."[37]

On April 7, 1971, betraying no loss of self-confidence, Nixon boldly announced on national television, "Tonight I can report that Vietnamization has succeeded."[38] Lt. Gen. Phillip Davidson later labeled this statement "an Orwellian untruth of boggling proportions."[39] Vietnamization had failed the test in Lam Son 719. There was plenty of blame to go around, including faulty US intelligence and an overreliance on airmobile warfare training. For example, the RVN's forces were woefully underequipped and untrained for the tank assaults they encountered. The deep-seated flaws in RVN military and political leadership were so daunting that Davidson, for one, believed that the final success of Vietnamization was "years, probably decades, away."[40]

By the spring of 1971, the Vietnamization clock was ticking loudly. Lt. Gen. James W. Sutherland, the commander of all US forces in I Corps (redesignated in July 1970 as Military Region 1, or MR1) and Gen. Lam's American counterpart, gave an optimistic assessment of the ARVN's performance but, in the process, revealed the daunting challenges still facing the transition from US to RVN responsibility for the war against the PAVN. Although the performance of ARVN units in Lam Son 719 had been uneven, Sutherland declared it progress that the Southern army had for the first time initiated and coordinated a multidivisional offensive without US advisers on the ground, damaging the enemy in Laos. He even went so far as to conclude that, on balance, "the results of Lam Son 719 indicate that Vietnamization is progressing well in MR1." He felt compelled, however, to advise the Pentagon, as he transferred his command in June, that there were still shortcomings: "a lack of effective long-range planning by higher-level staffs, a serious disregard for communication security, a general lack of supply discipline, and a failure to delegate authority to subordinates."[41] These were deeply rooted deficiencies because they revealed, according to a USMC history, "the technological dependence—tactically and logistically—that the United States had bred into the RVNAF."[42] The most glaring failure of all was the total dependence of the South's forces on US helicopter and fixed-wing support both for the initial attack and the rescue of its troops from its own mistakes. Saigon's military had yet to demonstrate that it could defeat Hanoi's army in a major conventional battle. USMC historians summarized concisely that timing was at the heart of the problem: "Vietnamization, whatever progress could be reported, remained an unequal contest between the slow pace of RVNAF improvement and the inexorably quickening pace of American withdrawal."[43]

In his April 7 address, Nixon announced the withdrawal of an additional 100,000 American troops by the end of the year. It was clear that Lam Son 719 had not derailed the redeployment schedule, but journalists were openly doubting Nixon's confident claims of Saigon's success. The president dismissed as isolated incidents the disturbing press photos of ARVN soldiers clamoring to board US helicopters escaping the battle zone. Kissinger told his staff that the pictures of men hanging from helicopter skids were proof of ARVN "order and discipline—particularly when one sees that the troops are bringing with them their rifles and other gear, hardly a characteristic of panic-stricken soldiers."[44] The images gave the American public a very different and powerfully negative impression of their South Vietnamese allies. From the perspective of an antiwar journalist reporting for the *Village Voice*, the operation was a debacle: "The ARVN abandoned something like a hundred armored personnel carriers and were clinging to the skids of helicopters to get out of there. It was pretty clear that Vietnamization wasn't working any better than Americanization."[45] A Harris poll in May 1971 indicated that 45 percent of the public considered Lam Son 719 a failure, and only 24 percent agreed with the president that it was a success. Many Americans were convinced that South Vietnam would never stand on its own, and that further US attempts to shore up the RVNAF were not worth the cost.[46]

Secret US intelligence reports supported what the public was sensing. The CIA's National Intelligence Estimate (NIE) dated April 29, 1971, began with a rather pro forma comment that "the past three years have produced . . . considerable progress in Vietnamization." The report quickly shifted to analysis of the future prospects, however, and began a litany of warnings. The paragraph on the RVNAF zeroed in on deficiencies that MACV had long known:

> In attempting to cope with the communist military threat, South Vietnamese forces will probably require substantial US support for many years. ARVN lacks the logistical system and technological and managerial skills required to maintain and support a modern fighting force. There are also serious personnel problems, including a shortage of qualified leaders and a propensity for enlisted ranks to desert. Problems of leadership and morale are even more severe in the territorial forces and village militia, key elements in the campaign to control the countryside.[47]

The NIE painted a bleak picture on almost every subject. It noted the current and likely continuing "durability of the communist party apparatus." Looking at the South's economy, it found that Saigon was unable to meet rural and urban needs and expectations and, in the face of protests that were often anti-American, "the regime might . . . rely on its coercive powers, thereby leading to instability and risking political disintegration."[48] At the end, the report focused specifically on Vietnamization and the burning question of the ability of the South Vietnamese "to cope with the communists and face the country's problems on their own." The analysts declined to offer a "clear-cut estimate" but concluded with this sobering picture:

> In our view, the problems facing the GVN, the uncertainties in South Vietnam about the magnitude, nature, and duration of future US support, doubts concerning the South Vietnamese will to persist, the resiliency of the communist apparatus in South Vietnam, and North Vietnam's demonstrated ability and willingness to pay the price of perseverance are such that the longer-term survival of the GVN is by no means assured.[49]

Inside the White House, Nixon and Kissinger were also grappling with reality. As they had attempted with the sending of American forces into Cambodia, the duo had sought to gain time for Vietnamization and negotiations, but lack of success only increased public pressure to get the United States entirely out of Vietnam. Kissinger knew that time was running out to get a negotiated settlement with Hanoi. The administration turned with greater urgency to diplomatic efforts with China and the Soviet Union to construct a global strategy that looked beyond Vietnam to improving big power relations. In preparation for secret meetings with Chinese prime minister Zhou Enlai that would lead to Nixon's blockbuster trip to Beijing in 1972, Kissinger made a note in July 1971 to assure Zhou: "We are ready to withdraw all of our forces by a fixed date and let objective realities shape the political future. . . . We want a decent interval."[50] A year later in Beijing, while meeting with Zhou after Nixon had traveled there and to Moscow, Kissinger could not have been more specific about a decent interval when talking about his cease-fire negotiations in Paris: "It is important that there is a *reasonable interval* between the agreement on the cease-fire, and a reasonable opportunity for a political negotiation. . . . The outcome of my logic is that *we are putting a time interval between the military outcome and the political outcome.*"[51]

SOUTH VIETNAM'S "ONE-MAN ELECTION"

"Objective realities" in the RVN meant specifically the degree of stability and survivability of Thieu's presidency. He had been elected president in 1967 with 37 percent of the vote in a negotiated deal with other military leaders, including Nguyen Cao Ky, who had become vice president. Under the RVN constitution, written with American advice, the presidential term was four years. Elections were looming for October 1971, and US officials knew that Thieu's political performance would be a crucial test of Vietnamization. Abrams warned Secretary of Defense Laird that Thieu was not taking Vietnamization seriously. The RVN president was behaving as if he had a guarantee of American support whatever he did, and that Washington would not really reach a point where it would let his authority collapse.[52]

In the months before the scheduled election, it became evident that Thieu was not going to allow any real challenge at the polls. Both Laird and Kissinger believed that a one-man contest would have damaging consequences for Vietnamization. The American officials calculated that a Thieu loss would be a major blow to the war effort, but they preferred that his win appear to be evidence that he had a genuine popular base in the RVN. A demonstration that South Vietnam was becoming a democracy could counter antiwar activists who criticized Washington's support of what they claimed was dictatorship in Saigon. Kissinger also believed that evidence that Vietnamization was enhancing Thieu's standing could provide bargaining leverage with Hanoi. Nixon's negotiator had rejected DRV demands that the removal of Thieu was necessary for a peace settlement, and Kissinger was holding out for the Communists to concede to America's refusal to abandon the RVN leader.[53]

Thieu marched to his own drummer and knew he had US backing—at least for the time being. The RVN national assembly under Thieu's control created legislation that made ineligible for the ballot the two leading opposition candidates—Ky and Gen. Duong Van "Big" Minh. Both of these men had participated in the coup that had toppled Ngo Dinh Diem in 1963, and each had his own backers in South Vietnam. Over the previous four years, the CIA had provided millions of dollars to Thieu to shore him up, and he now dispensed part of this political war chest to bribe legislators and provincial officials to facilitate disqualification of Ky and Minh and ensure his reelection.

On the eve of the election, Kissinger penned an analysis for Nixon on "where we are on Vietnam" that revealed a great deal about the progress of Vietnamization. He was thinking ahead about how "the manner in which we end the war" would affect the United States globally and domestically. With clear suggestion of a decent interval, he wrote that "a swift collapse in South Vietnam traced to precipitate American withdrawal would seriously endanger your effort to shape a new foreign policy" and would likely "swing us from post–World War II predominance to post-Vietnam abdication, instead of striking the balanced posture of the Nixon Doctrine."[54] Referring specifically to himself and the president, Kissinger noted that "we have consistently followed the two strands of Vietnamization and negotiation since the outset of your administration."[55] They had always been uncertain about the outcome of Vietnamization and preferred a negotiated settlement with an orderly US exit from the RVN. For a time, Vietnamization had put pressure on Hanoi to negotiate and had bought time for Saigon, but now, he complained, domestic pressure and "the indiscipline of the bureaucracy" had hastened the American troop withdrawals, which withered away the bargaining asset.[56] The comment about the "bureaucracy" was a swipe at Laird, who had always pushed Abrams for a faster redeployment schedule than the MACV commander or Kissinger liked.

Kissinger described the DRV diplomats as "insolent" in their attitude. He put primary blame, however, on domestic antiwar critics who were zeroing in on Thieu. He believed that it would be a mistake to push forward right away with the goal of completing Vietnamization in 1972. "Should a total withdrawal be announced," he reasoned, "we will then be in a passive posture while Hanoi and our domestic opposition slowly slice the salami."[57] Instead, he recommended to Nixon that, after Thieu's one-sided victory, the United States offer to Hanoi through Chinese or Soviet intermediaries the holding of a new presidential election in the RVN five months after the signing of an agreement for a US total withdrawal.[58]

On September 20, 1971, the National Security Council met, and Laird, Rogers, and other officials had the opportunity to weigh in on Vietnam. Having given his views privately to Nixon two days earlier, Kissinger kept largely silent during the discussion. The president asked Laird for his analysis of Vietnamization, and the secretary of defense declared that the military and diplomatic situation was "quite favorable." The logistics buildup was ahead of schedule, and tactical air support had been turned over to the RVNAF. He projected that, by December 1, 75 percent of US combat forces would be gone from the RVN. He hastily added, however, that US air support for the South Vietnamese remained, and that B-52 missions could be mounted anytime the Southern forces needed them. He cautioned that a major war was still going on, and that tens of thousands of Vietnamese were dying on both sides. He recalled that when he first went to Vietnam in 1969, Abrams had "asked him how much time do we have—12 or 18 months. We've done pretty well; that was three years ago."[59]

Nixon concluded the meeting by musing on how difficult it was to conduct an election in Vietnam under wartime conditions:

> Our choice may be difficult, but the only one there who can run the country is Thieu. Whether there will be a referendum or elections, and the people vote for or not for, Thieu is the only one there. Ky can't do it, and Minh is unbelievable. There's a real war on, finding a new leader is very difficult, and we're going to back Thieu. . . . Whoever thought that we would be in this position, with Vietnamization working, and the Vietnamese capable of defending themselves?[60]

His final thoughts turned to his outreach to China and the Soviet Union. It was important that those major powers and the "little countries" know that the United States can be depended upon. For that reason, he affirmed, "we have to see it through, and the way is to stand by Thieu and support him. We will make another announcement on Vietnamization in November, and face up to it. We must stick through this way."[61]

On October 3, Thieu won what RVN ambassador to the United States Bui Diem labeled a "one-man election," with an endorsement of 78.7 percent of the voters, who represented a turnout of 87.7 percent. A "fatigued and dispirited" Diem later recorded: "Outside South Vietnam, as well as inside, the image of the Thieu regime as a corrupt and repressive dictatorship got a rousing confirmation."[62] In an overt public information production, Nixon sent California governor Ronald Reagan to Saigon as a personal envoy to show US support of Thieu. In a press conference, Reagan complimented the RVN president for the successful "referendum" and actually compared Thieu to George Washington, who also ran unopposed.[63]

Nixon sent a letter of congratulation to Thieu, but he also had Ambassador Bunker meet with the RVN president to recommend a number of reforms. The administration wanted Thieu to reach out to his political opponents, implement economic and political changes, appoint more competent ARVN division commanders, and crack down on corruption.[64] In a news conference on November 12, Nixon announced that the United States was withdrawing an additional 45,000 troops over the next two months, with another announcement to be made by February 1. The rate and duration of withdrawals in that later announcement would depend upon three things: the level of enemy activity, the progress of the Vietnamization training program, and the progress on negotiations for release of American POWs and for a cease-fire in all of Southeast Asia.[65]

After Thieu's so-called reelection, US envoys in Paris tried to restart peace talks, but Hanoi rebuffed the move. The steps that Nixon was taking toward entente with the PRC and USSR gave the Vietnamese Communists a sense of urgency in breaking the continuing stalemate on the ground in Vietnam before further negotiations. Although Moscow and Beijing did not exert the diplomatic pressure on Hanoi that Nixon and Kissinger desired, Le Duan and the DRV leaders believed that their forces should make a preemptory move to topple Thieu. The South Vietnamese debacle in Laos gave them confidence in launching their own offensive. Hanoi may have been overconfident, however, because Nixon continued to have faith in American airpower and was willing to use it.[66]

NORTH VIETNAM'S EASTER OFFENSIVE (MARCH 30 TO SEPTEMBER 16, 1972)

The PAVN's official history of the war reveals that Vietnamization had captured the attention of the DRV's Central Military Commission but had not dimmed its confidence. Hanoi's historians maintain that "the American imperialist 'Vietnamization' policy had suffered a severe defeat" in the spring of 1971, and the withdrawal of 300,000 US troops had left Saigon's forces spread thin. Consequently, the Politburo decided to go on the offensive "to defeat the American 'Vietnamization' policy, gain a decisive victory in 1972, and force the US imperialists to negotiate an end to the war from a position of defeat."[67] The official history does not acknowledge that Le Duan and advocates of the offensive also worried that the Vietnamization-inspired logistical buildup was strengthening the RVNAF, and that the operation had to begin as soon as it could be readied.[68]

On January 20, Kissinger met with Nixon to consider how to react to urgent reports from Abrams that Hanoi was preparing for a major military campaign against the RVN concentrated in I Corp and II Corps (now labeled MR1 and MR2). Intelligence indicating that the PAVN was stripping all of its reserve divisions from the North to launch a massive offensive led Kissinger to remark wistfully to the president that "if we could land one division up North, we could drive to Hanoi."[69] He knew Congress and the public would never tolerate sending US troops, but Kissinger's recommendation was that "we have to hit them early in February" with bombing of the staging areas.[70]

Nixon had announced on January 13 that US troops in South Vietnam would be down to 69,000 by May 1. Despite the secret discussions of renewed fighting, he decided to go ahead with a national address on January 25, unveiling "a plan for peace that can end the war in Vietnam." With his trip to Beijing on the horizon for February, another journey to Moscow to follow, and US elections coming in the fall, the president chose to present himself as a reasonable leader who had done all he could to make peace and to make no preemptive air strikes. He boasted to his listeners about the drawdown of US forces and dramatic reduction in American casualties, but he termed Vietnamization the "long haul." The "shortcut," he said, was negotiations, and he revealed for the first time that Kissinger had been meeting secretly in Paris with the North Vietnamese since August 1969. He then listed numerous peace proposals from the United States that had been met in return by "a step-up in the war" by the other side. He made public the points of the current US position: "Within six months of an agreement,

- We shall withdraw all US and allied forces from South Vietnam.
- We shall exchange all prisoners of war.
- There shall be a cease-fire throughout Indochina.
- There shall be a new presidential election in South Vietnam."[71]

He added that President Thieu had indicated he would resign one month before the proposed election to ensure an independent voting process.[72]

Nixon reaffirmed that the United States was ready to negotiate immediately, but would never "join our enemy to overthrow our ally." He did not expect the speech itself to move Hanoi in the negotiations because the DRV had rejected these terms many times. For his American audience, he closed with a combination of Vietnamization and threat: "If the enemy rejects our offer to negotiate, we shall continue our program of ending American involvement in the war by withdrawing our remaining forces as the South Vietnamese develop the capability to defend themselves. If the enemy's answer to our peace offer is to step up their military attacks, I shall fully meet my responsibility as Commander in Chief of our Armed Forces to protect our remaining troops."[73]

Preparations had taken a year, but on March 30, 1972, the PAVN began the first phase of a planned three-pronged conventional invasion that Americans quickly labeled the Easter Offensive. As one cabinet member in the Provisional Revolutionary Government (PRG) put it, without the departed American combat troops, "an untried South Vietnamese army . . . was about to face a savage baptism."[74] Equipped with Soviet- and Chinese-supplied armor and heavy weapons, the Northern forces struck first in I Corps, with three divisions crossing the DMZ aimed for Quang Tri City. Three days later, three additional divisions came out of Cambodia and headed toward An Loc in III Corps. After two weeks, two more divisions crossed from Laos into South Vietnam's Central Highlands, targeting the provincial capital at Kontum in II Corps. The objectives were all population centers of political importance. Their captures would not only expose Hue in the north and Saigon in the south to direct attack, but also would enhance the PRG's claims for recognition in the peace negotiations as a legitimate authority in South Vietnam.[75]

The invaders severely battered the defending ARVN divisions, captured Quang Tri, and laid siege to Kontum and An Loc during the initial fighting. After three weeks, the Southern forces regrouped and reinforced the defenders, with the JGS even transferring one unit from the unthreatened Delta to III Corps. Briefly, Abrams was optimistic about the RVNAF performance. Its troops had fought bravely, and their commanders had utilized their reserves and managed to provide logistics support. An ABC News cameraman remembered the ARVN fighting hard to defend Kontum and "making the enemy pay for every foot of ground. . . . They went with a lot of courage and determination from house to house, street to street, corner to corner, driving back the enemy troops. It reminded me of the old newsreels of the German and American armies as Patton and Montgomery drove the Nazis out of Europe."[76] The combat support deficiencies that Abrams had worried about, however, plagued the ARVN. One of its logistics officers at An Loc reported that it had to transport tons of materials to the battle by human labor. Over the summer, the siege warfare around the key cities became a bloody stalemate, only relieved finally in September by US aerial bombardment.[77]

The move of some troops from IV Corps—the Delta—to the III Corps tactical zone was something the ARVN corps commanders and President Thieu had resisted in the past, and revealed how desperate the situation was. One of the flaws of the RVNAF was its immobility. Its divisions stayed in their home districts, where they were close to their families and provided security for their own villages. Their officers were deeply involved in local politics. Even after two years of Vietnamization and the departure of US maneuver battalions, South Vietnam's almost one million soldiers with their enhanced armor and artillery remained immobile.[78]

The Easter Offensive was Hanoi's effort to force Nixon's hand in the negotiations in an election year. The Politburo's military commission assessed that Nixon would not stop troop withdrawals, which were popular with American voters. In addition, the offensive would divert attention from the RVN elections and Nixon's trips to the PRC and USSR and would highlight the weaknesses of Vietnamization. Their reasoning seemed correct at first, as the White House reacted cautiously to the offensive, not wanting a big battle in an election year. When Abrams reported that the threat was "very serious," however, Nixon and Kissinger decided to act. The heavy Soviet-made arms the PAVN was using would mark a success for Moscow as well as Hanoi if the offensive succeeded. [79]

"We are not going to let this country be defeated by this little shit-ass country," Nixon can be heard screaming at Kissinger on the secret White House tape-recording system. [80] The president ordered the bombing of the North in an operation code named Linebacker. Laird objected on political grounds, and Adm. Moorer had operational concerns because of the US drawdown. The Pentagon delayed the bombing, blaming weather. Nixon and Kissinger were outraged with Laird, the JCS, and Abrams for dragging their feet. Caution was merited, however, because the bombing would cause civilian casualties in the DRV that would set back any domestic political advantages from the January 25 speech and would produce a sharp international reaction. [81]

Operation Linebacker sorties began on April 10. It was the first bombing north of the 19th parallel since October and November 1968, and the first B-52 strikes on DRV surface-to-air missiles and similar strategic sites since November 1967. American aviators provided air support to the ARVN at An Loc and elsewhere, and B-52s and fighter bombers attacked military supply depots at Haiphong. For US public consumption, Kissinger contended that the goal of the bombing was to get North Vietnam to stop its attacks so that Washington could continue its troop withdrawals and then leave political settlements to the Vietnamese. To rally American conservatives, he asserted that Washington was defending America's honor. [82]

MACV's analysis of the fighting indicated that South Vietnamese units had sustained heavy casualties but still had mustered fierce defenses and counterattacks that ultimately forced their enemy back. Abrams concluded, however, that it was American air support, not RVNAF ground fighting, that saved the situation. Moorer complained privately to US Air Force general John W. Vogt Jr. that whenever the ARVN "spot a sniper up a tree . . . they immediately dig a hole and call for F-4s." [83] Vogt responded that Westmoreland taught them to fight that way, but the JCS chair contended that Abrams and his successor at MACV, Gen. Frederick C. Weyand, did the same thing. Moorer maintained that the RVNAF was "too dependent on airpower and must begin to operate along the same austere lines as the North Vietnamese." [84] By 1972 and after, however, the North Vietnamese forces were not just guerrillas and light infantry, but were well equipped with armor and artillery. "From the start of Vietnamization planning in 1968," the JCS official history later summarized, "MACV, with the support of the JCS and OSD [Office of the Secretary of Defense], had rejected South Vietnamese requests for additional heavy ground force equipment."[85] MACV's planning assumption had been that American airpower would be available as it had been in response to the Easter Offensive, but that was not always going to be true.

Nixon and Kissinger knew that Vietnamization had failed. They did not explicitly say so, but increasingly they turned to airpower alone as their only remaining leverage. Operation Linebacker had targeted roads, bridges, enemy bases, and supply depots in one of the largest aerial bombardments in history. It also included some of the first-ever uses of laser-guided missiles. Unlike the Johnson administration, the Nixon White House placed no restrictions on targets in North Vietnam, with the exception of a thirty-nautical-mile buffer along the Chinese border and a requirement for approval of individual targets within ten nautical miles of Hanoi. US aircraft also dropped mines into Haiphong Harbor. On the ground in the South, the PAVN's tanks were heavier than ARVN armor and required US air and rocket ordnance to defeat. Once the attacking forces dug in around their objectives, they provided fixed targets for massive US bombing, including B-52 "arc light" strikes. US airpower killed approximately 50,000 PAVN and destroyed an estimated 225 tanks and heavy artillery pieces. After-action assessments found that key locations, including the town of An Loc, would have been lost if the handful of American advisers still remaining had not been available to direct air strikes and bolster local commanders. [86]

Hanoi's Easter Offensive failed to topple Thieu from power. Many RVNAF troops fought well, despite being overwhelmed in many cases. The loss and almost total destruction of the city of Quang Tri—although eventually retaken many weeks later on September 16—cast a particular cloud over Vietnamization. One American colonel complained that some ARVN units needed "to get over the mental attitude that the great American silver bird is going to do it all."[87] Thieu arrested and imprisoned Brig. Gen. Vu Van Giai, the commander of the 3rd ARVN Division, as a scapegoat for the failure to hold Quang Tri. The division had only been activated in October 1971 at one-third strength. Lt. Gen. William J. McCaffrey, one of the highest-ranking US generals in South Vietnam, expressed the following judgment: "I honestly think that the 3rd ARVN Division conducted itself creditably during the 28-day battle at Quang Tri." He added that "under the circumstances, I doubt if *any* general, US or Vietnamese, could have done much better." He put more blame "on the higher command levels than on the 'poor little bastards fighting on the ground.'"[88]

The fate of Brig. Gen. Giai is emblematic of the obstacles that Vietnamization faced. Col. (later Maj. Gen.) Victor J. Hugo Jr. commanded one of the last operational US artillery battalions in Vietnam and had mentored Giai "on our own," as he described it, because he knew Abrams was "pushing" Vietnamization. After the events at Quang Tri, Hugo reflected:

Everybody was talking about, [O]h, the Vietnamese can't fight, and the rest of it. Now, that's pure baloney. . . . The Vietnamese airborne was outstanding. Vietnamese marines were super good. [Giai] had a regiment and then it became a division, and you know the way commanders do this all the time. They take the riffraff and give them to the new unit, and they *did it*. And I will never forget that Gen. Lam who had I Corps. He should have been shot. He didn't give them anything in the way of help. . . . Thieu threw Vu Van Giai in jail. And then when the war ended, the NVA came in and threw him in jail again.[89]

In a reprise of Lam Son 719, the Easter Offensive exposed the most serious problem in the RVN—Saigon's failed leadership. Coordinated defense proved impossible, as commanders of units called in as reinforcements often refused to take orders from local commanders. When this happened at Quang Tri, Gen. Lam (who had been in charge during Lam Son 719) refused to leave his I Corps headquarters in Da Nang to sort out the problems at the front. Thieu himself added to the confusion by personally sending directives from Saigon to field officers. Thieu finally removed Lam—whom Abrams and the senior US adviser in I Corps declared incompetent—and made some other leadership changes, but, because Saigon had a shortage of qualified general officers, those relieved, including Lam, often ended up in other positions. In the midst of this turmoil, Thieu was also forced to remove the minister of defense and a number of officers for a scandal involving deductions from soldiers' pay.[90]

The long-term prospects did not bode well for Vietnamization. Laird himself acknowledged to Nixon that the problems in the recent fighting had not been from equipment shortages or even organizational defects in the RVNAF, but "deficiencies in leadership and will."[91] Multiple studies continued to reference pervasive and gross examples of corruption. Social inequities, political malfeasance, and economic dependence on the United States gave many in the South little reason to continue to resist the unrelenting regime in the North. Especially problematic for Saigon was long-range planning at a time when the US Congress was weighing the future of assistance to the RVN. Kissinger was talking with DRV representatives in Paris about final withdrawal scenarios. Thieu was well aware of his government's vulnerability and was becoming extremely wary of what a negotiated settlement would mean for him and South Vietnam.[92]

Chapter Seven

Vietnamization's Final, Failed Test, 1973–1975

The political will to continue American intervention in Vietnam was gone once Richard Nixon had begun Vietnamization and the unilateral withdrawal of US troops. A narrow plurality of voters elected him president in 1968 with the expectation that he would end the expenditure of American lives and treasure in a fight that no longer seemed worth the sacrifice. Having discovered during his first six months in office that his initial instinct to threaten or to use massive airpower against North Vietnam was unacceptable to most Americans, and ineffective with Hanoi, Nixon and his chief aide Henry Kissinger turned to Vietnamization to buy time with the public and hopefully to signal to both Saigon and Hanoi the need to come to a negotiated resolution of their bloody conflict. The drop in the number of Americans in harm's way in the RVN gave the White House some political space, as Secretary of Defense Melvin Laird had argued in support of Vietnamization, but the staged withdrawal of US troops also raised the expectation that the complete end of direct American participation in the war was fast approaching. Fixated on winning reelection in 1972, Nixon believed he had to fulfill that expectation by Election Day. Ruining his plans, however, was the inability of the RVN to realize the three selfs—self-defense, self-government, and self-development—while the DRV remained resilient in its determination to rule the entire country. For Nixon and Kissinger, negotiations had always been on a parallel track with Vietnamization, and they turned to negotiation in earnest during the 1972 presidential campaign season.

WASHINGTON NEGOTIATES ITS FINAL EXIT FROM VIETNAM

With the peace talks in mind, both Washington and Hanoi made big moves in 1972. Nixon went on highly publicized trips to Beijing and Moscow for a variety of reasons, but in large part to convey to the DRV the possibility that its communist allies might lessen their support in order to gain something from Washington. Never one to be passive, Le Duan launched the Easter Offensive to try to affect negotiations with a battlefield victory. Both sides were disappointed. The United States gained no diplomatic intervention with the DRV from the PRC or USSR, and had to resort to aiding the beleaguered RVN with massive air attacks on the PAVN and with the mining of Haiphong Harbor in the North. In June Nixon transferred an exhausted Gen. Creighton Abrams to the Pentagon as US Army Chief of Staff—marking the end of the "better war" the general's admirers would later extol. The president made Abrams's deputy, Gen. Frederick Weyand, head of the American forces in Vietnam, which now numbered only 47,000. The DRV knew that, although all US combat troops were gone from the South by August, Nixon's willingness—and even eagerness—to employ damaging airpower remained. Le Duan had underestimated Nixon's ruthlessness in the past, and the DRV had paid a price.[1] Consequently, Washington and Hanoi, each for their own reasons, entered into direct talks during the summer of 1972.

In face-to-face conversations with North Vietnam's Le Duc Tho, Kissinger refused to abandon Thieu, but he did not inform Thieu of the substance of the talks or take Thieu's concerns seriously. The national security adviser was more sensitive to how public revelation of the peace terms would affect the global credibility and diplomatic influence of Washington than he was about the fate of the Saigon regime. When Kissinger and Tho met in Paris on September 17, both wanted an agreement. The Republicans in the White House believed that Nixon had enough support from conservative and working-class voters to defeat the strongly antiwar Democratic candidate George McGovern. With guarded political optimism, Nixon and Kissinger wanted to move beyond Vietnam to pursue an agenda of improved relations with China and the USSR.[2]

For the DRV, the Linebacker operation had been severely damaging, and North Vietnam needed time to heal. Kissinger was ready to concede virtually every point to Hanoi. He was willing even to allow the cease-fire to come at signing and not earlier, which would allow the PAVN a final grab of territory. Kissinger thought this arrangement would allow the United States to keep bombing until the last minute. Tho made one major concession in allowing Thieu to remain in office for discussions with the PRG, rather than persisting in Hanoi's earlier insistence on Thieu's resignation and a coalition government in Saigon at the time of the cease-fire. There were no specific penalty provisions in the draft if either side violated the cease-fire. All Thieu would have were assurances of US support made outside of any written conventions among the parties. [3]

On October 2, Kissinger's deputy Alexander Haig met with Thieu in Saigon and revealed to him the good news that the draft agreement on a cease-fire in place provided for temporary continuation of Thieu in office. He also gave Thieu the bad news that the agreement allowed PAVN units to remain in the RVN after all US forces had departed. These terms would leave only the RVNAF to defend South Vietnam against an enemy within its borders after having repeatedly demonstrated its ineffectiveness to perform on its own. Thieu rejected the plan and publicized its contents. He condemned it as a sellout of the RVN that would fulfill Hanoi's goal to destroy the Saigon government. Kissinger instructed Haig to inform the RVN president that he was being "insolent"—one of Kissinger's favorite labels for both Thieu and Le Duc Tho—and to threaten Saigon with "unilateral disengagement" of the United States. In private conversations with Nixon, Kissinger acknowledged that "our terms will eventually destroy him [Thieu]."[4] Kissinger was clearly frustrated with Thieu and was feeling the pressure of a deadline that he himself had imposed to have an agreement with Hanoi by Election Day in the United States. Still, his harsh assessment of Saigon's prospects gives credence to the argument that Kissinger had determined that Vietnamization and negotiations were only meant to provide a decent interval between US withdrawal and the end of an independent South Vietnam. [5]

Kissinger's negotiations had failed. Hanoi accepted separation of the military and political settlements, agreeing to a cease-fire and a postponement of the definition of the government in the South. It believed the balance of forces in South Vietnam was in its favor, and that it would eventually "win bigger victories."[6] Thieu had always envisioned a Korean-style cease-fire, with a heavily guarded DMZ and US forces remaining in the South. Instead, what he saw coming was a complete American withdrawal, PAVN forces in the South, and a weak commission (including the PRG) to oversee the cease-fire. Kissinger assured Thieu of continued US support, but Thieu saw abandonment of him and of South Vietnam. [7]

Nixon had supported Kissinger's arrival at the terms negotiated with Tho, and Kissinger even announced publicly on October 26 that "peace is at hand."[8] The president now chose to delay, however. He did not want to go to the polls appearing to have abandoned the Saigon government. In the campaign, he had managed to portray his Democratic opponent as an antiwar radical, who had once cosponsored an unsuccessful Senate resolution for immediate US withdrawal from South Vietnam, and who would recklessly run out on America's international commitments. Nixon also had been able to dodge allegations in the press that White House staff members had participated in a break-in at the Democratic Party headquarters in the Watergate office building.

Nixon secured a one-sided reelection victory—60.7 percent of the popular vote, and all but seventeen electoral votes—but the Democrats kept control of both houses of Congress, and were intent upon terminating funds for the war. Nixon sent Kissinger back to Paris to resume talks with Le Duc Tho. As Le Duan's closest Politburo ally, Tho's position somewhat paralleled Kissinger's partnership with Nixon.[9] In addition, the White House ordered Operation Enhance Plus that would send thousands of items, including tanks, aircraft, and artillery, to the RVNAF, and he addressed confidential letters to Thieu assuring future technical assistance to his military forces and B-52 air support if the DRV ever threatened to overwhelm Southern territory. Both Saigon and Hanoi decided to hold out for more favorable terms for their respective sides. Although the Kissinger and Tho meetings in December eventually narrowed the differences down to a couple of very small points, Nixon and his aide lost patience and reverted back to their frustrated penchant for force, which they believed had been successfully employed in Operation Linebacker in response to Hanoi's Easter Offensive.

On December 14, Kissinger met with Nixon to review the status of his talks in Paris. He summarized that "Saigon wanted total victory," but that Nixon had always said only that "he would give them a reasonable chance to survive." Kissinger estimated that Hanoi "will not give them a reasonable chance to survive. So, Saigon's objections never had a chance." He then recommended that "we start bombing the bejeezus out of them within 48 hours of having put the negotiating record out."[10] After about two weeks, the US side would offer to withdraw completely for the return of American POWs. About the time Congress returns in January, Kissinger proposed, the administration would announce that "It [has] now been proved that the negotiations are too complex involving all Vietnamese parties. Let them settle their problems among each other. The South is strong enough to defend itself."[11] It was clear from numerous comments throughout the meeting that the last assertion was disingenuous. At various points Kissinger refers to Thieu as a "bastard" and "incompetent," and complains that "we lost the gamble [of recent negotiations] 80 percent because of Thieu."[12]

The Nixon administration put this plan into effect on December 18 with Operation Linebacker II, which journalists quickly labeled the Christmas Bombing. It continued until December 29. US B-52s and fighter bombers dropped 20,000 tons of high explosives on targets in the North, some near Hanoi itself. Nixon remarked to a group in the White House that Hanoi, Beijing, and Moscow "might think they are dealing with a madman" and settle in order to avoid a wider war.[13] In a phone call to JCS chairman Adm. Moorer, the president bellowed, "This is your chance to use military power to win the war, and if you don't, I'll consider you responsible."[14]

Once the bombing stopped, what happened next was not a US-RVN victory. After a month of final conversations in Paris, the four parties—the

United States, DRV, RVN, and PRG—signed an "Agreement Ending the War and Restoring Peace in Vietnam." The key terms were virtually identical to those reached in October. The bombing had not forced any meaningful concession from Hanoi, and had come at a heavy price for the United States, with twelve tactical bombers and fifteen B-52s lost, and their surviving air crews taken prisoner. The White House understood from the beginning that public outrage would make it impossible to keep up the operation very long, but Hanoi was the one who requested resumption of talks on December 26. Despite unprovable assertions by strategic bombing advocates that the huge air attack had brought a successful conclusion to the conflict, which could have been achieved long before, at less cost to America and Vietnam, the survival of the RVN—the principal objective of US policy throughout the war—remained precarious. Although he stalled briefly, Thieu accepted the terms as a fait accompli. Hanoi signed the agreement on January 27, because it still needed to regroup from the Easter Offensive and now from the Christmas Bombing, but it was not defeated. [15]

Within days of the signing, both sides made thousands of violations of the cease-fire. There was heavy fighting in the Delta and Central Highlands, with over 6,000 ARVN killed and 200,000 refugees fleeing the fighting. While this violence was occurring, Nixon was proclaiming "lasting peace in Indochina and Southeast Asia" in his second inaugural address. [16] In March 1973, and in keeping with the agreement, the remaining 23,000 American service personnel departed South Vietnam, leaving in Saigon only an embassy guard detachment of 159 Marines and a Defense Attaché Office (DAO) with 50 US military personnel. Hanoi released 591 American POWs from its prisons, but of greater strategic importance, 170,000 PAVN combat troops remained in the RVN, with another 100,000 in support across the border in Cambodia and Laos. US financing and advice had ballooned the RVNAF to a million troops listed on its rosters in an array of components and commands. [17]

SOUTH VIETNAM FACES NORTH VIETNAM ALONE

The final test of Vietnamization now began. Thieu had a vaguely worded document in his files in which Nixon had pledged to respond with "full force" if Hanoi strengthened its units in the South. [18] Some sharp critics of Nixon have argued that the cease-fire agreement was a sham; that the stubborn president, abetted by Kissinger, intended "to bomb the North Vietnamese again in early April or May" after the US POWs were released; and that only the expanding Watergate investigation stopped them. [19] Nixon had always been driven by the requirements of his own political survival, however, and he exhibited no sense of obligation to leaders in Saigon, whom he despised. He had managed the Vietnam issue through his reelection and had given repeated indications long before Watergate began that he would sacrifice the RVN as long as his hands were clearly away from its final demise. For better or worse, Vietnamization had run its course. Saigon's military and civil structure was now on its own to defend itself. In March 1973, Adm. Moorer recorded in his diary that Nixon only needed South Vietnam "to remain viable for perhaps a year, [and] then he could say we gave them everything and they could not handle it."[20]

In the first months after the cease-fire agreement, it appeared that the RVN might still have a chance to survive. Ambassador Bunker cabled Nixon privately that "Vietnamization has succeeded," citing several successful ARVN operations, but he also acknowledged three qualifications to that assessment. Saigon still needed to address 1) problems of leadership and motivation in the military; 2) corruption that "corroded" the effectiveness and integrity of civil and military officials; and 3) lack of domestic and international confidence in Thieu's government. Despite the ambassador's upbeat tone, these cautions were major issues.[21]

Although he was extremely unhappy that Northern forces remained south of the 17th parallel, Thieu's mood was buoyed by the size of the RVNAF and the expectation that Washington would provide at least some of the continued backing it had promised. Meanwhile, Le Duan's forces were exhausted, and morale in the North needed shoring up. He and the Politburo were also uncertain of what Washington might do if major fighting were to erupt. They were cautious, concerned that Hanoi's allies in Beijing and Moscow might now be less helpful with the Americans gone. The gambler in chief in Hanoi, Le Duan, decided to move carefully for a while. Relatively speaking, Saigon initially violated the cease-fire-in-place provision of the Paris Agreement more than did Hanoi. Determined not to yield any RVN territory—a choice that in time would prove very dangerous—Thieu deployed forces in all provinces and engaged them in both small and large clashes with the enemy. The PAVN launched some operations of its own, and—also with great future significance—upgraded the Ho Chi Minh Trail and added new logistics networks with paved roads, sturdy bridges, and pipelines that enabled it to bring southward supplies and fighters in amounts previously unseen.[22]

Nixon had set out upon Vietnamization and had repeatedly heralded its success—despite his knowledge that it was a weak option always dependent upon Thieu's survivability—to keep at bay political critics of the war and to lay a basis for his reelection. Ironically, it was politics that continued to limit his Vietnam options, even after his victory at the polls, and with American troops now withdrawn. After the Cambodian operation in the spring of 1970, Congress had become increasingly emboldened to challenge the White House on the use of American forces, and in June 1973 the House and Senate overrode a presidential veto and passed the War Powers Resolution to limit executive powers. That summer congressional hearings and a special prosecutor exposed Nixon's role in the Watergate burglary, and the president became fully engrossed in efforts to avoid impeachment. A serious war in the Middle East and an embargo on the sale of oil to the United States further demanded attention. Thieu and his problems were rapidly becoming old and neglected business for Washington.

In the early months of 1974, the RVN president ordered attacks to punish PAVN forces in the South. These operations killed thousands of Hanoi's troops and destroyed large quantities of equipment. In April, a major ARVN thrust into the Parrot's Beak along the Cambodian border killed 1,200 enemy soldiers and disrupted PAVN operations in this critical area. It proved to be the last move of this size by Saigon. These successful sweeps had been fought American-style as Vietnamization had taught the RVNAF, which meant air mobility, tactical air support, and lavish use of ammunition and supplies, especially fuel. By the summer of 1974, the materiel needed for this type of warfare was drying up. Saigon held on to the hope that Washington would fill the gap. The Joint General Staff gave no evidence of devising new tactics, but of necessity began retrenchment. For example, it provided ARVN soldiers only eighty-five bullets each per month. It reduced fuel allotments for tanks, trucks, river boats, helicopters, and aircraft by almost 50 percent. Meanwhile, DRV forces in the South continued to grow stronger in both men and materiel.[23]

The RVN's dire financial straits had a devastating impact on the size and morale of the ARVN units. Short of funds, Saigon cut soldiers' pay, provided units with fewer replacements, and reduced ammunition and medical supplies. RVNAF units, especially combat elements, became seriously understrength. The soldiers in the ranks saw increasingly less for which to fight. Some deserted, and those who stayed might absent themselves from their duty stations to work a part-time job, sell their weapons and equipment on the black market, or steal from peasants to get money for their own families. PAVN and VC forces in the South were able to obtain many essential items—food, fuel, medicine, radios—from the black market in areas supposedly under government control. These commodities may have been provided by VC sympathizers, but often the seller of the goods was either a petty entrepreneur seeking a profit or a desperate citizen needing cash.[24]

Rather than crack down on this behavior, senior officers indulged in their own illegal activities. They embezzled funds through schemes like collecting pay for "ghost" or nonexistent soldiers, selling supplies, and profiteering in other ways. The corruption spread also to the civilian workforce, and the cost of living jumped more than 25 percent in the first half of 1974. Inflation and unemployment produced recession. The departure of US forces meant the loss of thousands of jobs that had been created by the large American presence. Rising world prices added to inflationary pressures, and by the end of 1974 the inflation rate was 90 percent. Peasants at the lower rung of the economy were hardest hit, and it was from their families that most of the ARVN soldiers came. [25]

The economic lifeline of the RVN from its inception in the 1950s had been US aid. Where was it now? From the beginning of Vietnamization, the Nixon administration had declared that US support for the RVN was not open-ended. In what sounded like tough love, the president himself had asserted in 1969 in the Nixon Doctrine that the United States "had the right to expect that this problem [of military defense] will be increasingly handled by, and the responsibility for it taken by, the Asian nations themselves. . . . If the United States just continues down the road of responding to requests for assistance, of assuming the primary responsibility for defending these countries when they have internal problems or external problems, they are never going to take care of themselves." [26] In that vein, Laird had characterized Vietnamization as the critical test of the Nixon Doctrine, because its goal was to make the RVNAF completely self-sufficient with no residual US force. [27]

Facing impeachment and likely removal from office for his role in the criminal cover-up of the Watergate break-in during the 1972 election campaign, Nixon resigned his office on August 9, 1974. Vice President Gerald Ford immediately succeeded him as president. This dramatic turn shook Thieu, who was relying on Nixon's personal messages of support, but it mattered little who actually occupied the White House. Funding America's high-technology war had required about $3 billion a year with US forces, and that funding level had dropped immediately to $2.27 billion when the last American troops withdrew. For the fiscal year ending July 1, 1974, Congress had lowered the military spending for the RVN to $1.01 billion. Ford had supported Vietnamization, and upon taking office immediately assured Thieu of continued US support. President Ford was not aware at the time that Nixon had promised the "full force" of US power if needed. The RVN president tightened his belt and continued to expect a last-minute bailout of US dollars, and perhaps even bombing. Ford knew the American public would not tolerate the reinsertion of US ground or air forces into the war, but he pressed Congress to maintain the $1 billion funding level. Mirroring the mood of American voters—that the United States had already done enough—Congress authorized only $700 million in economic aid to Saigon in the coming year. [28]

When he learned of this congressional action, an unbelieving Thieu recalled that "first the Americans told me at Midway to agree to the withdrawal of a few thousand troops and I would still have a half a million Americans left to fight with me." As the pace of American withdrawal quickened, he continued, Washington told him, "Don't worry . . . we will give you a substantial increase in military aid to make up for all that. . . . Now you are telling me American aid is cut by sixty percent. Where does that leave us?" [29]

After the war in which the DRV ultimately triumphed, Kissinger and some others, including President Ronald Reagan, made Congress a scapegoat for Saigon's failure. The argument was that Nixon and Kissinger had combined Vietnamization and negotiation into a plan that would have led to a viable RVN, if Congress, which represented the American people, had not lost the political will to bankroll the Saigon regime.[30] Former RVN ambassador Bui Diem complained bitterly that the callous Americans, not willing to spill American blood, were reluctant even to spend a few million dollars.[31] This criticism begs the question, however, of whether a plentiful supply of US aid would have enabled the RVNAF to withstand the PAVN onslaught when it came. Although impossible to answer with certainty, the most reasonable conclusion is that the organic pathology of South Vietnam's government and armed forces caused their defeat—not the termination of their life-support system. The head of Saigon's JGS, Gen. Cao Van Vien, sharply criticized the lack of US support of the RVN at the end, but he recognized that "after many years of continuous war, South Vietnam was approaching political and economic bankruptcy. . . . Riddled by corruption and sometimes ineptitude and dereliction, the government hardly responded to the needs of a public which had gradually lost confidence in it. . . . The whole nation appeared to some to resemble a rotten fruit ready to fall at the first passing breeze."[32]

Vietnamization never found an answer to the societal weaknesses and corruption that handicapped the exercise of leadership in the South, and these deficiencies also nullified the benefits of American materiel aid or expertise. During the period of Americanization of the war under Johnson and the various stages of Vietnamization under Nixon, the United States supplied the RVN with a great deal of sophisticated technical equipment that required skilled operators and managers to utilize and maintain. Aviation, armored vehicles, communications-electronics, logistics systems, civil engineering, and other tools of modern warfare required a level of skills and education that were in short supply in the RVN. Abrams had worried about the challenges of the RVNAF providing its own combat support in his first drafts of the Vietnamization plans. Perpetuating the problem was weak, corruption-ridden South Vietnamese leadership that had failed to provide adequate training and drill for combat and support troops. By late 1974, the vehicles, equipment, and supplies already provided to South Vietnam were sitting rusting or in crates, or otherwise undistributed and unused. There is little reason to believe that more assistance would have been better assistance, or produced positive results.[33]

From September 30 to October 8, 1974, the Politburo met in Hanoi and assessed the North's improving prospects and what to do next. They no longer had to guess what the mercurial Nixon might do, and were confident that Ford and the American Congress would never countenance reintroduction of US military units in defense of Saigon. The balance of forces on the ground inside South Vietnam was in the PAVN's favor, as the degrading of RVNAF personnel strength and materiel was evident. Street protests by Buddhist priests and even usually loyal Catholic clergy against the Saigon regime's misrule were causing Thieu to use force against the demonstrators, which further weakened him politically. Seeking to preempt China's influence with Hanoi, the USSR had just made a renewed military commitment that was providing hundreds of advisers and more surface-to-air missiles to the PAVN. In addition, Beijing had just moved to occupy the Paracel Islands and to improve relations with the Khmer Rouge in Cambodia, actions that pushed Hanoi's Politburo closer to Moscow and made it feel pressure to conclude the long war. Despite reasons for confidence, DRV leaders, including Le Duan, remembered that they had prematurely launched "war-ending" offensives in 1968 and 1972 that had failed.

The Politburo's decision was to make a military probe of the Western Highlands, which it knew was only lightly defended. Its top spy in Saigon, Pham Xuan An, provided this intelligence gained from his knowledge of Thieu's strategy sessions inside Independence Palace. The Communist high command continued to project final victory in 1976 after a sequence of conventional mechanized attacks, using roads when possible, rather than one multifront assault on ARVN bases, like the Tet and Easter Offensives.[34]

On December 13, Hanoi's military began its test assault on the capital of Phuoc Long province north of Saigon, along the Cambodian border. The probe was on the line that divided the ARVN's II Corps and III Corps regional commands and was lightly guarded by RF and PF units. Although military headquarters in Saigon helicoptered in an ARVN battalion and two ranger companies as reinforcements, the attacking force of two infantry divisions with armor and artillery battalions in support scored an overwhelming victory. Of the 5,400 ARVN defenders, only 850 survived. The province chief died trying to retreat, and the provincial officials who were unable to escape capture were executed.[35]

The province was in DRV hands by January 6, 1975, and Thieu's repeated appeals to Washington for assistance went unanswered. The US Air Force's B-52s that had protected RVNAF units in the past had been removed from their hangars in Guam and redeployed elsewhere in the world, which Hanoi knew from Soviet intelligence sources. Congress remained unresponsive to Ford's request for supplemental financial aid to Saigon. Certain now that Washington was leaving the RVN completely on its own, Le Duan recommended to the Politburo that the target date for liberation be advanced from 1976 to occur before the onset of the rainy season in April. He declared that the "opportune time" for "a complete total victory" had arrived.[36]

The complete and final collapse of the RVNAF and the final demise of the government in Saigon came quickly, and with it the exposure of the total military failure of Washington's Vietnamization policy. The PAVN attacked Ban Me Thuot in the Central Highlands on March 10, and by April 30 the Northern army had swept through all of South Vietnam and was in possession of Saigon itself. The RVN's military organization had been one of the largest and best equipped in the world in January 1973, when the cease-fire had been declared, and in the spring of 1975 it simply evaporated. As the enemy's offensive proceeded quickly from the Central Highlands to the population centers of Hue and Da Nang, and then southward along the central coast and finally to Saigon itself, many of the ARVN officers and men surrendered or simply discarded their weapons, removed their uniforms, and went home. Large numbers of US-supplied artillery pieces and vast quantities of ammunition were abandoned, providing the advancing PAVN with instant resupply.

Thieu belatedly changed his mind about trying to contest every inch of his country, and called units back from outlying areas to defend the cities, but this shift in the face of the offensive created panic in the civilian population. The roads became choked with civilians and soldiers alike, fleeing in fear of falling victim to a communist bloodbath. They were justifiably terrified, remembering that VC cadre had gone door to door in Hue after capturing the city during the 1968 Tet Offensive, immediately executing anyone with any connection to the Saigon regime. When well led, ARVN soldiers could fight, and some units did try to stand their ground.

One of the most notable examples was the ARVN 18th Division, a unit not considered an elite force, which held off superior enemy strength at Xuan Loc, forty miles east of Saigon, for two weeks. It killed more than 5,000 PAVN and destroyed thirty-seven tanks before being overwhelmed by the DRV juggernaut.[37] After the war, an ARVN lieutenant, who only entered his army in 1972, reflected, "I am very proud I was in the army, but very disappointed with the corruption with all the big shots. They talk big, but they just run away quickly—very cowardly."[38]

The tragic but predictable fate of the heroic division at Xuan Loc had been sealed years before. Just as there are many American anecdotal accounts of dispirited and unwilling ARVN troops, there are numerous cases of courageous and accomplished soldiers. ARVN colonel Le Cau rose through the ranks with battlefield promotions and citations—including the US Silver Star and the RVN's highest commendation, the National Order of Vietnam—for repeated acts of bravery and leadership in decisive battles. He was captured in 1975 and spent thirteen years in a reeducation camp. A US Army study of the war after 1973 lamented that there were men like Col. Cau who deserved unflagging US support, but it was not to be. "Convincing reforms were needed in South Vietnam long before the cease-fire of January 1973," the report concluded, "in order to have reversed the momentum of decreasing American support."[39] The specific reform identified was one with which

Washington had wrestled beginning with Ngo Dinh Diem's First Republic and continuing with Nguyen Van Thieu's Second Republic: "What was missing was a national leader of great stature and strength who was committed to personal sacrifice, willing to get tough with inept or corrupt subordinates, and able to rally the support he would need to stay in office. Such a man did not emerge."[40]

On April 21, the day before the surrender of Xuan Loc, President Thieu resigned and flew out of the country. Largely by chance, the US Congress voted down an emergency funding request from the White House for the RVN as the Ban Me Thuot attack was beginning. The long-suffering RVN diplomat Bui Diem described the vote, coming when it did, "like a kick in the groin, deep and painful."[41] US Ambassador Graham Martin kept up a bold, and perhaps even self-delusional, avoidance of the inevitable almost to the day the PAVN armor rolled up to the gates of the presidential palace in Saigon.

President Ford inserted a carefully worded line into a speech to college students on April 23 that the war in Vietnam "is finished as far as America is concerned."[42] The RVN also was finished, and the end was not pretty for America and its ally. Largely because of Martin's resistance, the final exit of American officials in the capital and a few Vietnamese closest to them came in the form of a chaotic and humiliating helicopter lift from a rooftop near the US embassy on April 29. When Thieu's successor, the old ARVN general Duong Van Minh, sought to negotiate his government's surrender the next day, the arriving DRV forces informed him that there was nothing left to negotiate. They simply assumed control.[43] Nixon's policy of Vietnamization and negotiation had failed him, the United States, and the Republic of Vietnam.

Chapter Eight

Vietnamization and the End of the Republic of Vietnam

An Assessment

Was there ever a chance for Vietnamization to achieve its strategic goal? As the policy took shape after 1969, the Nixon administration's aim was to enable the Republic of Vietnam to defend itself alone against the Democratic Republic of Vietnam's ruthless determination to unite all of Vietnam under its own political and ideological control. What obstacles needed to be overcome? Maj. Gen. Nguyen Duy Hinh, the ARVN officer who wrote the historical monograph on Vietnamization for the US Army, concluded that "by far the widest loophole of the Vietnamization program was its failure to provide the RVN with enough time for an overall improvement. The program was initiated out of American domestic political consideration, and it was implemented with too much haste." He was frank, however, about the historical limitations his country faced. Troop strength was achieved fairly rapidly, he acknowledged, but "it was impossible to improve the quality and technical capabilities of a one-million-strong military force within the space of a few years," while also battling armed subversion and overt aggression. His assessment was that the RVN "needed more time . . . to become truly self-reliant."[1]

Was more time the panacea, and if so, how much time? The question of whether the policy could have worked if it had continued longer or started earlier is a counterfactual query, but one of enormous significance. Unaccustomed to and frustrated with failure, American strategists searched for lessons learned in failure, and some seized upon the speculation that Vietnamization—the building of a self-reliant RVN—could have worked, especially if begun sooner, perhaps from the beginning of US assistance to Saigon. The classic counterinsurgency formula calls for a sequential process to clear away the armed rebels, hold the cleared territory from further threat, and build the state institutions to eradicate the economic and social grievances upon which the rebellion had grown. For US assistance to South Vietnam in the 1960s and 1970s, the major challenge was the last step of building a self-sustaining state to effectively govern the RVN.

This chapter assesses Vietnamization as a counterinsurgency strategy by first reviewing the different historical analyses of the program's results. This debate generally engages the issue identified by Maj. Gen. Hinh—that Saigon needed more time. A discussion of timing raises questions of when to have undertaken Vietnamization, and for how long, leading to consideration of the history of Vietnam beginning in 1945, in the second part of this chapter. This historical analysis suggests that by 1969, when Nixon announced Vietnamization, Saigon had never possessed and had not, over basically two decades, developed a foundation upon which to build an effective Vietnamese leadership alternative to the regime already ensconced in Hanoi. Although all of Vietnam—and all of Indochina itself—had long been a colony, southern Vietnam continued to exhibit evidence of an inadequate native social, economic, and educational base left from years of colonial damage. The narrative of Vietnamization from 1969 to 1975 repeatedly notes the problem of poor leadership as the South's weakest feature. The final section of this chapter then describes fatal flaws in the RVNAF leaders and soldiers that continued to make the South's military incapable of reform and of meeting the survival needs of the South Vietnamese state.

THE DEBATE AMONG HISTORIANS

Military historian Lewis Sorley contends "that there came a time when the war was won," and that "this achievement can probably best be dated in late 1970."[2] By then, he argues, pacification had been completed, and "South Vietnam's armed forces, greatly expanded and impressively equipped, were substantially more capable than [they were] even a couple of years earlier."[3] For him, the decisive period of the war was the period of Vietnamization under Gen. Creighton Abrams's leadership, from the spring of 1968 through 1970. James Willbanks, Gregory Daddis, Kevin Boylan, and other military historians dispute Sorley's evidence of victory, but if Sorley is correct, even in part, what went wrong after 1970? Sorley faults Nixon for losing faith in Abrams and giving up on the winning strategy of Vietnamization. He quotes James Schlesinger, Melvin Laird's successor as secretary of defense, that "the military in Vietnam were pushed into the invasion of Laos by civilian officials who thought it would be a good idea. And when it failed, Gen.

Abrams was beaten up and there were calls for his removal. It was quite unjust, but not untypical."[4] If Nixon undermined his own Vietnamization policy, was it ever a serious military strategy, or was it primarily political rhetoric? Sorley believes Nixon was serious about Vietnamization as a strategy, and cites Ambassador Ellsworth Bunker's assessment of blame. After himself placing in Thieu's hands Nixon's written assurances of support if Hanoi violated the cease-fire, Bunker later claimed, when the other side ignored the terms, "we never came to [Saigon's] assistance, because Congress refused to appropriate the money."[5]

Nixon and Kissinger repeated this same accusation several times in their memoirs, asserting that Vietnamization and negotiation worked until Congress lost the will to continue the war.[6] Congress expressed the will of the public, however, not just constitutionally but also in accord with popular sentiment as measured by public polling and congressional election results. Blaming Congress is to argue that the American people lost the Vietnam War. This line of thinking reflects an overinflated faith in American power and rectitude that the nation is so strong and correct that only Americans can defeat themselves. It arrogantly refuses to acknowledge that there are limits to American power, or that others—in this case, Vietnamese—may have their own strengths and weaknesses that shape historical outcomes.

Among Sorley's critics, Daddis examines the period of the war after the Tet Offensive—that is, from when Abrams took command of MACV in 1968. His study specifically critiques Sorley's claim that Abrams's "one war" was the decisive strategic innovation, and finds that there was no significant change from Westmoreland to Abrams in how the US military conducted its operations. He challenges Sorley's statistical evidence of progress in pacification, and sees no victory in 1970 because this continuation of US tactics had no better chance of success under Abrams than under his predecessor. Daddis further discounts the credit Sorley gives Abrams by making a strong case that Nixon—thinking always of politics and the 1972 election—controlled the goals and implementation of policy from Washington. Consequently, Abrams was in no formative way the architect of the final four years of the American war in Vietnam.[7]

Willbanks's analysis generally parallels that of Daddis, but considers whether Vietnamization could have been more effective if started sooner—that is, at least by 1963, and the coup against Ngo Dinh Diem. It is historically doubtful that a Vietnamization program of the type attempted by Nixon would have been at all possible in politically chaotic Saigon in the early 1960s. Regardless of the political context, US training of the ARVN from the beginning was more concerned with conventional attack from the North than with counterinsurgency, Willbanks notes, and had created an army in the South geared to static defense, high technology, and heavy use of munitions. In his view, "technology became a source of dependency and distraction for the ARVN."[8] Furthermore, the arrival of American combat troops in 1965 to fight the "big war" pushed the locals aside and devastated their confidence and morale. As one South Vietnamese colonel put it, the "ARVN completely lost the notion of being an independent army."[9]

Examination of the earliest American experiences in Vietnam is essential to understanding the defects in Vietnamization, and especially in RVN and RVNAF leadership. Journalist David Halberstam, a critic of the American war in Vietnam, wrote that he and other Americans failed to appreciate fully "what the French Indochina war had done to Vietnam, how it had created in the North a modern dynamic society and how it had given us as allies a dying post-feudal order. . . . We did not from the start make clear the impossibility of the struggle."[10] Halberstam's postwar comment following Hanoi's victory may be overstated, but his point is valid that Hanoi had an enormous advantage from early on, not only in its ruthless discipline and particular patriotic appeal, but also in the serious and dangerous—potentially fatal—flaws in the Saigon government. It would be ahistorical to claim that the defects in the South's leadership were so obvious at the beginning as to be undeniable. The United States had other allies in Asia in the 1950s, such as Syngman Rhee in South Korea and Chiang Kai-shek in Taiwan, with similar serious liabilities. The United States continued to recognize Chiang's Republic of China, rather than the People's Republic of China (PRC), as the representative of the Chinese people, although Chiang had already lost the civil war in China as much through his own errors as the astute tactics of his communist enemy. Ngo Dinh Diem was a familiar model to US officials. In a meeting with the French foreign minister in May 1955 to discuss Diem, Secretary of State John Foster Dulles blandly asserted that "in that part of the world, there was no such thing as a 'coalition' government, but one-man governments."[11]

VIETNAMIZATION IN THE SHADOW OF HISTORY

A review of Vietnamese history after World War II reveals why Vietnamization as an American initiative in the South did not begin earlier. In the patriotic struggle against France's efforts to restore its former Indochinese colony, Ho Chi Minh had seized the leadership initiative by boldly declaring independence in September 1945, almost immediately after Japan's surrender. Ho was a Communist, and his Viet Minh front was only one political faction, but they had organized Vietnamese resistance to Japanese occupation during the Pacific War and then stepped into a similar role against the colonial power. The Viet Minh defiance of French military reoccupation of Indochina escalated to full-scale war, and Paris soon knew that the popularity of the Viet Minh among the Vietnamese was a major element of its strength.

To counter Ho and the Viet Minh, the French government recognized a new State of Vietnam headed by Bao Dai, the heir of the country's last royal line, the Nguyen. The French role in the birth of the new regime in July 1949 made Bao Dai's State of Vietnam appear to be a colonial puppet, and Bao Dai's declaration of his new government in its capital in Saigon was a non-event. There were no banners or parades or speeches as had heralded Ho's declaration of independence in Hanoi. Although the United States and Britain soon joined France in recognizing the new state, it was not the equal of Ho's DRV in power or popularity. Some Vietnamese chose to align with Bao Dai because they feared or disagreed with the communist ideology of the Viet Minh leaders. Some also had social, family, or economic ties to the French, and they believed they would be better served by a traditional state with Western connections than a revolutionary socialist one. This constituency gave the State of Vietnam a collaborationist identity that clung to the government in Saigon until its end in 1975.

When historians begin looking back in time for a road not taken in US policy, dating the start of the American war in Vietnam is problematic. In the most basic terms, the United States inserted itself directly in Vietnam's internal political struggle at the end of the Geneva Conference. Washington stood aside during the conference itself while France negotiated withdrawal from its Indochina war. The model of a negotiated withdrawal was thus available from 1954. In the weeks after the conference, the Eisenhower administration decided that it was unwilling to trust the final outcome in Vietnam to diplomatic and political processes alone. It would facilitate the survival of a regime in South Vietnam to contest the communist government in Hanoi that had outlasted the French Expeditionary Corps and finally forced Paris to end its attempt to repossess its former colony.

Several considerations influenced US thinking. There is little question that the Cold War in Europe and Asia was foremost in Washington's calculations. The United States had provided financial assistance to France in Indochina in large measure to keep faith with an important NATO ally against presumed Soviet threats to Europe. Paris was pulling back in Southeast Asia and turning its attention to another colonial war in Algeria against insurgents there seeking independence from France. In the midst of the Cold War, and concerned that insurgencies might be susceptible to communist infiltration, Washington made no objection to this particular French redeployment. Containment of communist expansion was America's prevailing national strategy, and it had just fought a war in Korea against two communist armies, those of the PRC and the Democratic People's Republic of Korea.

Other factors were less direct but still obvious. Eisenhower and his advisers harbored a prejudice from their World War II experience that devalued for them the quality of French political and strategic management. There was a tendency to attribute the French failure in Indochina to problems in Paris, rather than strengths in Hanoi or to particular geostrategic hurdles in Southeast Asia. In addition, American strategists operated in a cultural environment that might be characterized as neocolonialist—that is, one that looked down upon Asian society and Asians as weaker or less able than Western society and Westerners. The bloody war in Korea should have disabused that notion of weakness, but old biases die hard. Americans would do for the Vietnamese what they presumed the Vietnamese could not do for themselves.

After the Geneva Conference temporarily divided Vietnam into two parts, Washington created the Southeast Asia Treaty Organization (SEATO) as one link in a chain of defensive arrangements aimed at the PRC—including bilateral defense pacts with Taiwan, Japan, and South Korea, and the ANZUS pact with Australia and New Zealand. SEATO did not require US military defense of South Vietnam, but it provided a kind of diplomatic cover for continued US involvement in Vietnam in the 1950s and on into the 1960s. As long as Eisenhower was president, Washington cautiously avoided sending more than a few hundred uniformed American military personnel to the country, but on numerous occasions it demonstrated determination to keep South Vietnam separate and independent from North Vietnam as an American Cold War outpost in Asia. The Geneva Agreements had included a proposal for nationwide elections in Vietnam in 1956 as a mechanism for political unification of the country. In retrospect, this election that never happened was possibly a missed opportunity to avoid the massive bloodletting that began in the 1960s.

Preoccupied with the Cold War in Europe after 1945, American officials had paid little attention to Vietnam's internal politics until the Cold War spread to Asia in the form of the Chinese Communist Party's victory in 1949 in China's Civil War and communist North Korea's offensive against South Korea in 1950. When the Geneva Conference appeared to be headed toward a communist success in securing international recognition of the DRV in North Vietnam, the Eisenhower administration found a possible leader in South Vietnam around whom to build a pro-American state, similar to Rhee in Korea and Chiang in China. Some Vietnamese had remained fence-sitters during the Franco–Viet Minh War, and had tried to remain politically aloof from both sides. The most prominent of these anticommunist, anti-French independents was Ngo Dinh Diem and his large family. Within a year after the Geneva Conference, Washington had decided to give "wholehearted" support to Diem as its ally in Southeast Asia, although many American officials harbored doubts about his leadership ability to construct and govern a viable state. [12]

In November 1963, Diem was assassinated in a coup by his own military leaders, and it has become commonplace to view him as a fatally flawed leader. Relying heavily on his family and a close circle of Vietnamese Catholics—his coreligionists who were a minority in the Buddhist country—Diem was more capable according to recent scholarship than was once thought, but his inability to build a popular political base plagued his presidency.[13] American officials were well aware of the challenges to political survival that the Saigon regime faced throughout its existence. There was continuous debate within the US country team in Saigon over whether to press Diem to reform with threats of withdrawal of American assistance or to allow him to find his own way with the confidence that he had Washington's backing. This argument was essentially about counterinsurgency, although not usually posed in those terms. By the end of the 1950s, Saigon faced an armed and increasingly dangerous insurgency from the National Liberation Front (NLF), and requirements for protecting the security of the South often prevailed over seemingly abstract notions of political and social betterment. When senior officers in the RVNAF overthrew Diem's government, both they and their American advisers—whose extent of involvement in the coup remains unclear—believed that the demise of an independent South Vietnam was eminent.

For two years after the coup, South Vietnam's government was essentially leaderless. Diem had spoken boldly about the need for a social revolution in the South but had never delivered one, and the generals who executed the coup had no apparent understanding of this need. They offered no constructive ideas of how to restructure the country or even how to respond militarily to the enemy. Concepts like land reform, for example, were not part of their vocabulary. Gen. Duong Van Minh, who led the junta that took control, was popular but remote from the people. He also failed to deal with the evils of corruption in Saigon and left many venal and incompetent Diem-era officials in their jobs.

Although not a revolution, the new leadership group in Saigon marked a change from the past. Originally from the old imperial capital of Hue, Diem and his Ngo family represented a traditional, so-called mandarin style of government. The generals now in charge came mainly from the middle class of Cochinchina, the rich provinces around Saigon. After almost a decade of Diem's repressive rule, they had a distrust of government and partisan politics and had no specific political constituency. The Saigon area had profited from international market connections under the French, and it continued that pattern with external US aid. It mattered more to the generals that their army kept the NLF insurgents out of Saigon than out of the countryside.[14]

In recognizing the junta, Washington crossed a significant threshold. The United States was now more deeply committed to sustaining Saigon in the hopes of better results against the Communists than with the previous regime. There was so much rivalry within the junta, however, that American attempts to influence it were largely futile. In January 1964, Gen. Nguyen Khan executed his own seizure of control in a plot that did not surprise the

Americans. Khan's move was simply a power grab indicating that the paramount political force in South Vietnam was the army. Gen. Paul Harkins, US MAAG chief, liked Khan and the "Young Turks" who supported him. These young officers had combat experience—some had trained at Fort Bragg—and they represented a generational change from the Minh junta, who had served in the Vietnamese National Army, a *jaunissement* (or French "yellowing") of its forces in the First Indochina War somewhat similar to American Vietnamization in the Second Indochina War.

The United States had invited itself into the internal conflict between the RVN and DRV to pursue its own geopolitical interests, believing that American wealth, power, and good intentions could prevail over any challenge as it had against fascism and militarism in World War II. Once, in a letter to a woman seeking advice, Mark Twain counseled that "all you need in life is ignorance and confidence, and then success is sure."[15] In Vietnam, the United States had confidence in its own ability and ignorance of the place it was entering. In what became America's Vietnam War, ignorance led to failure, not success. Vietnamization was one of the American-made approaches that failed. Americans often expressed dismay that the Saigon regime could not be more like Washington, but such solipsistic desires were ahistorical and failed to understand Vietnam and the Vietnamese. The Politburo's political control over DRV society and the PAVN remained firm throughout the conflict because of the Leninist discipline of the Lao Dong—or Workers Party, as the Communist Party of Vietnam labeled itself—and the ruthlessness of Le Duan and others in Hanoi's leadership. The political and historical origins of the DRV government, especially the heroic mantle of having defeated the French colonizers, was an advantage from the 1950s to 1970s in the struggle with the ad hoc, chaotic, and thin structure of all the Southern governments.

The Young Turks had very little education, especially in economics, diplomacy, management, political theory, and other knowledge required to govern. Reminiscent of Mark Twain, some Americans, like CIA analyst George Carver, actually welcomed their combination of confidence and ignorance, and termed it "a fundamental shift in the locus of urban political power and a basic realignment of political forces—in short, a revolution."[16] There was no revolution. Carver's opinions notwithstanding, the idea of relying upon these leaders in a manner similar to the Vietnamization initiative begun later was not apparent or considered. The Young Turks were no more able to go to the people than Diem had been. Without education and nationalist credentials, their short careers had been as self-promoters. They had maneuvered politically to the rank of general in what journalist Frances Fitzgerald described as "the corrupt, inefficient, demoralized Diem army."[17]

On June 12, 1965, Radio Saigon transmitted an announcement that ARVN general Nguyen Van Thieu of the Armed Forces Council was replacing civilian premier Phan Huy Quat, whom the council had installed the previous August to give an appearance of political openness. Sharing top authority with Thieu was Air Vice Marshal Nguyen Cao Ky, the flamboyant and mercurial head of the RVN Air Force. This transfer of power marked the fifth government in Saigon since Diem's assassination. A few days earlier, Senator Mike Mansfield of Montana, a longtime congressional advocate for US support of South Vietnam, had shared his thoughts with President Johnson on the new MACV commander Gen. William Westmoreland's desire for more American troops: "As I understand it, Westmoreland will respond to requests from the Vietnamese *military*, not the Vietnamese *government*. This underscores the fact that there is no government to speak of in Saigon."[18]

US officials were pessimistic about the RVN's political future under these particular Young Turks. Thieu was forty-two years old, and Ky was thirty-five. William Bundy, the assistant secretary of state for Far Eastern affairs, recounted later that the Thieu-Ky duo "seemed to all of us the bottom of the barrel, absolutely the bottom of the barrel."[19] Unforeseen at the time was that Thieu would remain head of the RVN government until its end in 1975, when another top US official—Henry Kissinger—would regularly be referring to him with words like "incompetent," "bastard," and even more demeaning terms.

In an effort to appear legitimate, the Saigon government held elections in September 1967, making Thieu president and Ky premier. The *New York Times* labeled the voting a "farce," but the British *Guardian* thought the exercise was "less of a charade than expected."[20] Unlike the firm Communist Party discipline over Hanoi's domestic politics, Thieu faced a lively legislative assembly, but over time he moved to control it as he did the military. In 1971 he went back to the voters for affirmation of his singular authority. This second election was, in part, to provide a democratic gloss on his administration to ward off growing criticism of him in the US Congress. Senator Mansfield and others warned him that continued funding of the RVN was at risk. Thieu's heavy-handed suppression of his political opponents, which resulted in no viable challenger on the ballot, produced the opposite of the desired effect. A few days after the vote, the Senate rejected a $565 million aid package for the RVN. Longtime friend of Saigon Anna Chennault warned Thieu that the Republicans in Washington were "losing patience." "I think they are looking for an excuse to get out," she worried, "and time is getting short."[21]

In formulating his ahistorical what-if scenario, Sorley begins with the appointment of Westmoreland in 1964, during the time of chaos in South Vietnam's political leadership. He assumes that South Vietnam was salvageable in 1964, despite the weaknesses of the Southern state and a decade of failure to build a political foundation. Rather than candidly assessing the client state, he concentrates on Washington's failure not to call up reserves in

1965, not to cut the Ho Chi Minh Trail in Laos and Cambodia, not to meet the persistent danger of the Viet Cong Infrastructure (VCI), not "to develop South Vietnamese armed forces during the period of American domination," and not to replace Westmoreland with Abrams earlier than it occurred. He faults "the squandering of years" when the public, Congress, and media supported the effort in Vietnam, and then itemizes the ways in which Nixon's conduct of the war was better than Johnson's.[22]

In this scenario, Sorley is oversimplifying and essentially ignoring the history of the early Cold War and the legacy of Western colonial and neocolonial attitudes toward the people of Vietnam. For years, Americans in Washington and in Saigon assumed they would make South Vietnam successful, and ignored both the limitations and desires of the South Vietnamese. The political state that led the RVN was weak, and the regime controlling the DRV was strong. The ideology of the North was seriously flawed, as the economic and social failings of the Socialist Republic of Vietnam (SRV) demonstrated from 1975 well into the 1980s. The population of South Vietnam possessed tremendous social and economic energy. Southerners helped the development of all of Vietnam once they were allowed to flourish under a chastened and modified SRV leadership that proved adaptable after 1985, just as the DRV authorities made military adjustments against the French and Americans earlier. In other words, the story of Vietnam since World War II is largely a Vietnamese story, as it should be.

Gen. Douglas Kinnard's postwar survey of American general officers who served in Vietnam found that the majority thought Vietnamization should have started sooner, and that the United States should not have Americanized the war at all. The combining of these two notions suggests that Vietnamization in the form of aid and advising should have begun in 1955, when the French Expeditionary Corps departed South Vietnam, or at least sometime before the summer of 1965, when Johnson ordered the escalation of the American role. Despite the presence of American military advisers, Vietnamization like that attempted by Abrams under orders from Washington was impossible in the 1950s and 1960s. Even with "an entire US combat brigade in direct support of pacification for eighteen months" in 1968, Boylan concludes in his study of Binh Dinh, pacification and Vietnamization could not be accomplished in that one province.[23] The RVNAF could not provide internal and external security against the communist military threat and undergo training simultaneously. The United States military assumed the lead role countering that threat when it did because Johnson declared to aides that he was not going to lose Vietnam to the Communists, as Harry Truman had been accused of losing China in the 1940s.

The Saigon government and its military officers represented a segment of Vietnamese society that was too removed from the rural masses, especially by comparison with the NLF. The regime's base was urban, tainted by association with the French and Americans, either corrupt or inept in public administration, and aligned more with landlords and moneylenders than with working farmers and fishermen. Four US presidential administrations attempted to work with what it found in Saigon to fashion a reliable containment ally. The Eisenhower team, for all of its anticommunist concern, was cautious about spending, especially in the form of foreign aid and long-term commitment to development projects by grants, or even loans. It had exercised a prudent discipline on the extent of America's commitment to Saigon.

Kennedy and his advisers abandoned that restraint and set out through its counterinsurgency plan to better arm the RVNAF and pursue nation building in the South. Johnson inherited this work in progress and came to a crossroads that would have confronted Kennedy if he had lived. The decade of American investment in the survival of an independent South Vietnam would have to be written off as the South's military and political apparatus faced imminent disappearance, or Washington had to Americanize fully the defense of the South to stave off failure. Johnson chose the latter. When Nixon replaced Johnson, Washington's bet that it could protect the South until it was viable on its own proved much more burdensome than the American public would tolerate for long. After his narrow election victory in 1968, Nixon entered the White House well aware of the political reality that he had to de-Americanize the fighting. It took him little time to give his plan the more positive sounding name—Vietnamization.

Nixon ordered Vietnamization for political reasons. He wanted to end the war quickly, but came to realize that the public would oppose an escalation of US military force to achieve that outcome. Kissinger believed that a combination of force and diplomacy could provide an American exit from Vietnam, but it was Laird's Vietnamization idea, with the attractive political benefit of starting actual withdrawal of US ground forces, that got the president's nod as a place to begin. Nixon's "peace with honor" thus became a phased unilateral withdrawal, negotiations that ultimately ended in American concessions, and the return of US prisoners of war.

The military part of Nixon's exit strategy fell to Abrams to accomplish. Laird pushed the general to design a withdrawal timetable that was much faster than Abrams believed operationally prudent. Redeployment of US troops while the South was still under fire required force protection for the remaining American units and combat support of the RVNAF in tactical and technical specialties that were woefully underdeveloped in South Vietnam. Abrams's war was still violent. Americans continued to die in Vietnam: 20 percent of all US combat deaths in the war occurred between 1969 and 1972.[24] It was not necessarily a "better war" than that fought by Westmoreland, but Abrams managed the drawdown of US forces without an immediate collapse of the RVNAF. If Vietnamization's intent was a decent interval between the departure of American troops and the end of an independent

South Vietnam, then it was a success. If its goal was, as Nixon claimed, to leave a regime in the South that could defend itself, then Vietnamization failed.

Once the steady rhythm of American unit departures was evident, the end of the process was no secret. As Kissinger understood early on, but would not publicly acknowledge, he had lost negotiating leverage. The final and predictable US diplomatic concessions came in October 1972 when there were no more US ground troops in the RVN. More than anyone else, Thieu knew, with the American forces gone and with PAVN units in the South and on its borders, the RVN would not survive. Despite some personal promises of emergency support from Nixon, who was no longer president, Thieu was alone; he had never been able to demonstrate that he could manage on his own, or that his senior military commanders had the leadership required to defeat the PAVN and VC.

SOUTH VIETNAM'S MILITARY LEADERSHIP DEFICIT

The South's chronically poor political and military leadership compounded each other's faults that were at the heart of the failure of America's Vietnamization strategy. Since the RVNAF was always under separate command from MACV, US commanders had to let Saigon's generals do their job whether Abrams and others thought they were competent or not, especially since many of these officers had close ties to Thieu. Journalist Arnold Isaacs reported from South Vietnam: "Neither in leadership nor in the population at large—except for the Communists—was there any conviction that the future could be grasped in their own hands. But the Americans, imprisoned in their own faulty doctrines and their ignorance of Vietnamese realities, never found a way to influence the ruling system. . . . Power in South Vietnam was used only for the personal ends of those who held it."[25] The Nixon administration did not want Saigon to fall as long as US troops were in the country—that is, it wanted to keep a decent interval. It intervened with air support and other assistance in 1970–1972 because it would not yet leave Saigon totally on its own and risk premature failure during the American withdrawal period.

Since both sides in the struggle were Vietnamese, frustrated Americans in the racialized vernacular of the time asked "Why can't *our* gooks fight like *their* gooks?" The answer was in the social and political culture of each side. The life experiences of the top command of the PAVN and ARVN were poles apart. The senior PAVN officers, such as Gen. Vo Nguyen Giap—who created the PAVN and had studied military theoreticians that included Napoleon, the Chinese writer Sun Tzu, and T. E. Lawrence, the World War I British officer who advised Arab insurgents against the Ottoman Turks—had been fashioning successful tactics against Western technology and style of war since the late 1940s. It was a painful trial-and-error process. The communist forces had some great successes, such as the RC4 campaign on the Tonkin–Chinese border in 1950, and the famous siege at Dien Bien Phu in 1954, but they also had made costly mistakes in which they sometimes lost 5,000 men in one battle because of premature assaults, human wave attacks, or other miscalculations. They learned strategy, tactics, and logistics and how to take advantage of their common border with Communist China, difficult terrain along that border, and often dense cloud cover over the mountains. The geostrategic proximity of China cannot be overstated, especially after the Chinese Communist Party came to power in 1949. These factors made the flow of military materiel into the DRV from Chinese and Soviet sources easier, and base areas inside China were readily accessible as training centers, supply depots, and safe havens for parking MiG aircraft.[26]

PAVN officers received leadership training in China in critically important staff functions. Staff work is not glamorous, but it makes tactics work. The commander orders the movement of forces from one valley to another; the staff organizes all the details of the route, equipment, feeding, and shelter to ensure that troops arrive at the right place, on time, and prepared to fight. These management skills turn orders into reality and are essential to the effectiveness of any military enterprise. Giap could not have carried out his successful operations at Dien Bien Phu without Chinese or other foreign advisers because he did not yet have officers with the education and experience for large operations. By the Second Indochina War, the PAVN had operational ability, although it still had foreign technical assistance. The RVNAF did not have staff competence among its senior officers, and relied heavily on US advisers to conduct its operations. Saigon had done too much staffing based on politics, rather than merit, and had a shortage of senior officers because of lack of education and trust within the officer corps.[27]

US Marine Corps analysis of Lam Son 719, for example, zeroed in on the staff and combat support deficiencies evident in that and other large-unit RVNAF operations: "the inadequacies in high-level staff work, the questionable ability to maneuver effectively units of greater than battalion size, the reluctance of commanders to delegate authority to staffs, the absence of long-range logistical planning, the disregard for the rudiments of supply discipline, and the inability to exercise communications security."[28] This critique recalled the concern Abrams had expressed to Laird two years earlier about the technological dependence—tactical, logistical, and electronic—that Americanization of the fighting had bred into the RVNAF. Experience revealed especially that Saigon's military forces simply did not possess the level of combat-support expertise to fight a war on their own with the modern tools the United States provided. Knowing that South Vietnam's security depended upon it, MACV had argued without success for residual combat-support elements along with the continuation of materiel supply. Under pressure from the White House to meet a political timetable to get Americans home, the US Army's history of this period notes that "the question of how the South Vietnamese were to continue the war alone was completely side-stepped."[29] Technology and language problems, for example, might have been overcome with several years of social and educational development within the RVN, but the time required was not available because of the American public's war fatigue and Saigon's inept leaders, who were running the RVN into the ground.

Relegating ARVN units to pacification duties after US forces entered South Vietnam in combat formations in 1965 had dampened the fighting spirit of the Southern troops that was not rekindled until they took on more combat burden defending their bases during the Tet Offensive. Americaniza-tion also meant that the bulk of materiel and modern technology went to the American forces. Even the morale of American officers assigned to be ARVN advisers suffered. They thought the duty undesirable and harmful to their careers since they were not line officers in combat units. With the decision to Vietnamize the war in 1969 and better equip the ARVN, its unit leadership improved somewhat, including better rapport of its field-grade officers with US advisers. These tenuous connections caused US officers to hesitate to recommend relief of unsatisfactory Vietnamese unit commanders, however, for concern about negative reflection on themselves or the under-cutting of what influence they had established with the South Vietnamese military.[30]

US advisers often complained about the senior RVNAF military leader-ship. Unlike the PAVN high command, the older officers in the South had begun their careers under the French and did not have the benefit of going through their own discovery/learning process for tactics particularly suited to Vietnamese geography, history, and society. Since both the Diem and Thieu governments had little political legitimacy due to corruption, favoritism, nep-otism, and other flaws, the RVNAF was constructed to defend against the North but also to protect the president from domestic political opponents. Top commanders were often chosen for personal loyalty to the regime, rather than military expertise. The DRV had its own internal military debates and made mistakes—the Tet and Easter Offensives were premature and costly—but it had a leadership capable of learning and adapting.

A US Army major general, who served as deputy senior adviser in II Corps in 1966–1967, described ARVN officers as being from the middle and upper classes, the old aristocracy, the families of officers who had served the French in the First Indochina War, and the urban business and commercial sector. Although some were outstanding, he judged that many lacked "ag-gressiveness, leadership ability, and a full professional commitment." They seemed to prefer rear-area assignments and political jobs "so that they could avoid the rigors, boredom, and dangers of training and combat, and a few (I suspect but cannot prove) [sought] to use their positions for personal or even financial gain."[31] From his long years of experience in Vietnam, journalist Stanley Karnow corroborated this image. ARVN officers had to be high school graduates, he observed, "which meant that if you were a high school graduate, the chances are you came from a middle-class family, and the chances are you didn't know anything about the countryside, you didn't know anything about the peasantry. And your aim when you become an officer is not to go out in the countryside. . . . So the South Vietnamese Army was really quite incompetent."[32]

The historical background of the leadership of the Northern and Southern armies shaped each in fundamental ways during the American war. In addition to their hard-learned lessons in tactics from their war against the French, the PAVN as an institution also had an ideological model in Maoism and Leninism that provided discipline and a political curriculum that could be used to motivate and control its followers. This element of control or discipline was a genuine part of the North's ideology and practical knowledge drawn from successful methods developed by Vladimir Lenin in the Bolshevik Revolution and Mao Zedong in the Chinese Revolution. The political regimentation of the Lao Dong had been honed during years of survival under a harsh French colonial regime that had not allowed peaceful or democratic change, and left only violent revolution and covert or stealth tactics for these Vietnamese nationalists.

On the other hand, the RVNAF leadership had not had the opportunity for hands-on strategic and tactical learning as young officers or subalterns in the French-led Vietnamese National Army, which was better remembered as *L'Armeé Nationale Vietnamienne* (AVN), a French creation. After the French Expeditionary Corps' departure in 1955, Americans directed the training and education of the ARVN, successor of the AVN. American methods showed scant evidence of learning from the French experience against the Viet Minh. For example, Vo Nguyen Giap and PAVN planners had developed ways to defend against and attack land-air bases, a model widely employed by American forces, and later under Vietnamization used by the ARVN. The French called them *bases aéro-terrestres*, known to Americans as Fire Support Bases (FSBs), and they provided artillery emplacements, secure aircraft landing zones, supply dumps, and communication facilities to support infantry operations. In the First Indochina War, the battles at Na San (1952) and Dien Bien Phu (1954) stood as examples of this type of installation. The French withstood the Viet Minh attack at Na San, but experienced a costly defeat at Dien Bien Phu. In the Second Indochina War, Ia Drang (1965) had parallels with Na San with regard to lessons believed to have been learned about effective use of air-mobility, and Lam Son 719 paralleled Dien Bien Phu in terms of overreliance on FSBs and air-mobility. Lt. Gen. Sutherland, who commanded the US Army combat helicopter support for the

Laos operation, considered it to be what James William Gibson terms "another *'test'* in the laboratory" of technocratic warfare—one that the ARVN and its advisers failed.[33]

The initial equipping and training of the ARVN were largely to fashion it as a conventional force to defend against a Korean War–style invasion. The modern American way of war, practiced with relative success in World War II, emphasized firepower—aircraft, artillery, armor, and heavy infantry weapons—to best utilize science, engineering, and a deep well of resources to minimize friendly casualties. As military technology developed, the US military itself made increasing use of the latest thing, especially electronic technology—such as the 1st Signal Brigade's long-distance communications—and modern aircraft ranging from US Army and Marine Corps helicopters to US Air Force heavy bombers. When Washington Americanized the war, the development of the RVNAF was further compromised. Assigned to pacification and local security, ARVN officers got limited combat command experience, particularly in large-unit movement and combat support, and lost whatever opportunity they might have had to develop an aggressive fighting spirit in the style of US traditions, such as the marines' Semper Fi or the army's Hooah battle cries. Nguyen Cao Ky told journalist Stanley Karnow, "when the American forces came in, the South Vietnamese Army didn't want to fight—let the Americans do it."[34] The instinctive quasi-colonial mentality of American leaders imposed a model that was not necessarily wrong but was not indigenous to its trainees; in addition, it did not recognize the social and educational deficiencies of their charges or the inherent strengths the Vietnamese themselves had.

The American general assessing the leadership he witnessed in II Corps chose his words carefully, but a military historian who has studied the French war in Indochina and drawn parallels between the ARVN and Paris's local allies, the ANV, provided a blunt answer to the question of why the communist soldiers outperformed the State of Vietnam forces: "Bao Dai's army failed to command the loyalty of Vietnamese peasants because disinterested service and civic honesty were almost unknown in the Vietnamese governing classes who should have led them, and because the Viet Minh promised them a better future."[35] Washington did not know its enemy and often undervalued the communists' nationalism. Moreover, it did not have much detailed knowledge of the PAVN as a military structure. There were few wartime handbooks or guides to opposing forces like the ones the US military had developed in previous wars. Many Americans had a conception that the PAVN and VC were organizations held together by fear. While true that the DRV was a police state, the Lao Dong had highly focused political education beginning in the 1940s that motivated soldiers, even those deployed far from the North and in small units. The twenty-four-page pamphlet *Know Your Enemy: The Viet Cong,* provided to American soldiers, warned that the emphasis of the VC was "placed on terror and murder," but also acknowledged that "appeals to the mind and the heart are the principal way in which the Viet Cong seeks to control its members."[36]

American soldiers often commented on lack of motivation among many ARVN enlisted men. The recollections of American Vietnam veterans from the 1969–1972 period often begin with a caveat that some individual ARVN units fought well, especially elite troops like the airborne, marines, and elements of the 1st Infantry Division in I Corps. Overall, however, a common GI assessment is that the ARVN soldiers and their company-grade officers did not seem to have their hearts in the fight. They seemed dispirited, and "did not have the will" to persist, a medevac pilot observed, because "they had been fighting so long."[37] They would hunker down in defensive positions or conduct "pantomime operations" intended to create the illusion of patrolling. A warrant officer in an American assault helicopter company remembered transporting ARVN on operations: "It didn't seem like they had the fire to take a fight to somebody." To ensure that the South Vietnamese unit would sweep an area, the American pilots would land them at one location and pick them up somewhere else. "That way," he explained, "you've guaranteed that they went somewhere as opposed to just being put in and [setting] up a perimeter and stay[ing] put until it's time to go back to where it's safe."[38]

These GI accounts often express sympathy with the common South Vietnamese soldier. In the spirit of the "brotherhood of arms," they ascribed the malaise of the ARVN to evidence of corruption and petty politics in their officers. In Boylan's words, "the rot came from the top," and poor motivation of the rank and file came from their poor leadership.[39] Most of the ARVN troops were conscripts with little understanding of internal or external politics. An American Friends Service Committee volunteer who taught English to high school students in My Tho in the early sixties remembered the teenagers in his classes standing in the morning and dutifully singing the RVN national anthem. It was the only country they knew, he reflected. They were not aware of Ngo Dinh Diem's toleration of corruption or America's Cold War strategy or any of that, and because of where they lived, many of the boys would someday be drafted into the ARVN. It did not seem to occur to him that some of them may also have become VC.[40]

As an operational term, *Vietnamization* meant the complete transfer of the defense and security of South Vietnam from a force of more than a half-million US ground forces with American air and naval support to the Republic of Vietnam Armed Forces. As publicly declared many times by President Nixon, the process provided an honorable American exit from a long and costly conflict. Combined with negotiations and a last-minute bombardment of North Vietnam, Vietnamization was a political success for Nixon and Kissinger. For Kissinger it was part of "a formula that holds the thing together a year or two, after which . . . Vietnam will be a backwater . . . [and] by January '74 no one will give a damn."[41] Privately to his national security adviser, Nixon termed the final cease-fire "cosmetics," and reasoned that South Vietnam "doesn't have to survive forever. It's got to survive a reasonable time. Then everybody can say 'goddamn we did our part.' . . . I don't know that Saigon can survive forever."[42]

Despite the political spin, Vietnamization was a strategic failure, and the symbol of that failure to create a self-sustainable RVN government was the raising of the flag of the triumphant VC and PAVN forces over the presidential palace in Saigon in April 1975. The military and political roots of this outcome rested firmly in the country's history before 1969. The debate over timing and whether an earlier turn to Vietnamization would have produced a different result is beside the point. "Over a span of two decades," a US Army historian wrote after the war, "a series of regimes had failed to mobilize fully and effectively their nation's political, social, and economic resources to foster a popular base of support."[43]

Gen. Cao Van Vien, the chairman of the RVNAF JGS during the final years of the war, provided his own postmortem on his military's leadership. His narrative begins with French colonial rule that left the RVN without its own military leaders. Under Ngo Dinh Diem, military authority centered in the president's office, not the JGS, and largely because of the influence of Diem's brother Ngo Dinh Nhu, "cronyism" undermined military promotion at the cost of professionalism. The 1963 coup that overthrew the Ngos had long-term consequences because it ingrained political preoccupation in the RVNAF officers. Ironically, since he had supported the coup, Nguyen Van Thieu was always looking over his shoulder. "Political-mindedness" and corruption remained persistent problems. RVNAF at times prosecuted corrupt officers, Vien maintains, but there was such a shortage of experienced combat leaders that Saigon had to tolerate corruption in order to field an army at all. There were some good generals and leaders, but just not enough. It was this shortage, the general concludes, that contributed more to the demise of the RVN than did corruption.[44]

The fight for government control in Vietnam and for the future of the country was always in the hands of the Vietnamese—not the Americans—to decide. Coming from differing historical approaches, two American scholars have affirmed this truth with strikingly similar conclusions. Informed by his study of the operations of the US Army's 1st Cavalry Division and 173rd Airborne Brigade, military historian Kevin Boylan concluded: "While Americans can fairly argue that South Vietnam would have survived if it had not been for massive North Vietnamese military intervention, the GVN almost certainly would have fallen in 1965 had it not been for massive US military intervention."[45] Writing from the perspective of a Vietnamese-speaking international relations scholar in touch with Vietnamese culture, who spent much time in Vietnam, David Elliot offered his "wild history"—that is, his informed personal reflection—that "the Vietnamese noncommunists could not have won without the United States, but could not have won by dependence on the United States either."[46]

In the context of counterinsurgency warfare, the case of Vietnamization should be humbling and cautionary for American strategists. For politicians, it was self-deceptive, self-serving, and disingenuous. For American military commanders, it proved to be an impossible task imposed upon them against their better judgment because it did not square with reality. The COIN model is clear, hold, and build. The Americans could use their weapons and tactics to take and hold territory and to supply and tutor the RVNAF, but to build a secure Republic of Vietnam on a foundation of social and historical quicksand was not within their capability. Vietnamization was a case of means without ends.

Chapter Nine

Vietnamization's Postwar Counterinsurgency Legacy

Almost three decades after the end of the Vietnam War, media accounts of a new American military deployment in Iraq began to draw some disturbing parallels between the conflicts. In March 2003, President George W. Bush ordered an invasion to remove from power Saddam Hussein, the Iraqi dictator alleged to possess weapons of mass destruction and have links to international terrorists—both of which possibilities the White House defined as threats to US national interests. The rapid advance of US forces into Baghdad forced Saddam out of his capital, but that beleaguered nation quickly devolved into internal chaos and violence that trapped American troops in a lengthening and bloody war. In November, an editor at the *New York Times*, who had been a reporter during the Vietnam War, wrote: "'QUAGMIRE,' 'attrition,' 'credibility gap,' 'Iraqification,'—a listener to the debate over the situation in Iraq might think that it truly is Vietnam all over again."[1] This writer and others quickly noted the many ways in which Iraq in 2003 was not Vietnam in 1973, but the connection had been made and would not go away. Over the next few years, American military thinking would evolve from conventional operations to counterinsurgency, to "indigenization," to decent interval, and to withdrawal in a pattern eerily reminiscent of the past. As planners grabbed onto these models at various stages, there seemed little recognition that they might have been good politics but not good strategy—just like Vietnamization.

The American war in Vietnam was a painful experience for everyone. Although the DRV had prevailed over the RVN-US alliance and declared a new, united Socialist Republic of Vietnam (SRV), the victory had cost Vietnam millions of lives, a bitter internal legacy of suspicion and forced "reeducation," and widespread economic devastation. Compounding the wartime losses—attributable both to lavish application of US military power and to the stubborn willingness of Communist Party leaders in Hanoi to accept this level of destruction on their own people—the SRV government dogmatically attempted to impose a Stalinist political-economic model on their underdeveloped county. Under Le Duan's chairmanship, the Politburo drove the country into further poverty and despair over the ensuing decade. During those same years, and to some extent enabled by Richard Nixon's decent interval maneuver, Americans largely tried to forget what they considered a humiliating national failure in Vietnam, and were reluctant to explore the complex dimensions of what seemed an unprecedented experience.

"NO MORE VIETNAMS"

Publicly, a national amnesia prevailed in the United States, as many people refused to think about what had happened in Vietnam and what it might mean about the power and goodness of the nation, attributes that had been largely taken for granted over the years, especially after the victories of World War II. Many American Vietnam veterans—numbering in the hundreds of thousands—felt isolated and alienated. Young Americans who had taken to the streets in protest were happy the war had ended, but many were not celebratory. A generation was uncertain what the national trauma had meant for their country and for their own personal choices. Finally, in the 1980s, with the dedication of the Vietnam Veterans Memorial funded by veterans themselves, the release of some sympathetic movies like *Platoon* directed by Vietnam veteran Oliver Stone, and the appearance of a few college courses on the war, a public discourse slowly and tentatively developed.

In professional military and foreign policy circles, the lost war challenged a host of assumptions and required reexamination of policy doctrines. The United States had failed to achieve its goals in Southeast Asia but was not a defeated nation. The national defense establishment was bruised but remained strong, and the Cold War continued. During the Vietnam War years and immediately afterward, the international security environment for the major powers moved from a nuclear arms race and big power confrontation to experimentation with conventional and small war strategies, as well as to increased diplomacy and negotiation. The United States established formal diplomatic relations with the People's Republic of China in 1979, and President George H. W. Bush joined Soviet president Mikhail Gorbachev in announcing the end of the Cold War in December 1989. Despite eruptions of ethnic violence in Eastern Europe and Africa, civil wars in Latin America, dangerous political-religious radicalism in parts of the Muslim world, and the aggression of Iraq against Kuwait in 1990, the magnitude of the threat to

American security that would come crashing into US streets on September 11, 2001, was not yet imagined.

Inside the Pentagon and various military educational and training centers, policy analysts and planners studied the US military's role in Vietnam and the unacceptable outcome. Gen. Creighton Abrams served briefly as US Army chief of staff from 1972 until 1974, when he died in office from cancer. The army named the M1 Abrams tank in his memory, and ironically, in view of his identification with "one war," combining political and military tactics, the tank along with airpower served as the principal weapons in the US offensive—Operation Desert Storm—that liberated Kuwait from Iraqi occupation in 1991. By the 1990s, the US military had been configured for maximum use of air-land-sea power, and had a very different organization and mission than in the last years of the Vietnam War.

The uniformed US armed services are proud organizations with distinguished histories, and the Vietnam War had tarnished those traditions in their own eyes. The US Army in particular felt a need to rehabilitate its reputation. As it had always done, it employed historical analysis as a serious tool for developing doctrine and improving training, and the US Army Center of Military History produced dozens of histories, monographs, and special studies to capture the Vietnam experience detailed in thousands of pages of operational records and lessons learned.

Despite this institutional analysis, however, the military ultimately is answerable to civil society through political leadership. The initial public desire was to leave Vietnam behind. Nixon, Kissinger, and Laird continued to defend their historical reputations by blaming Congress and others for their errors, but the nation sensed that the war had been an American defeat. In 1973, over Nixon's veto, Congress enacted the War Powers Resolution in a move to limit any president's commander-in-chief authority. A neo-isolationist "Vietnam Syndrome"—so named and criticized by Nixon—emerged that described the commonly held opinion that there should be "no more Vietnams."[2] Although many citizens understood this concept to mean that the United States would refrain from intervening with US troops in violent regional conflicts, for military planners it meant going into future hostilities only when objectives are sharply defined and when an overwhelmingly favorable balance of forces exists.

"If Kennedy's 1961 pledge to 'bear any burden' had announced the birth of the counterinsurgency age," historian Andrew Birtle has remarked, "then the popular refrain of the early 1970s—'no more Vietnams'—was its eulogy."[3] American officials quickly turned their backs on counterinsurgency (COIN) doctrine. By 1972, counterguerrilla warfare segments had been completely removed from the US Army's basic combat and advanced individual training curricula, to be replaced by mechanized warfare drills. Even at the John F. Kennedy Institute for Military Assistance at Fort Bragg, the entire course on "stability operations"—the term then in use for COIN—was down to a single hour of instruction by 1975. Fort Bragg's Civil Affairs and Security Assistance School no longer had a civic action course. Programs for foreign area officers or classes on civil-military relations addressed COIN topics only with great care to avoid civilian criticism. The army did not totally abandon all mention of counterinsurgency, but the focus of strategic doctrine had definitely shifted.[4]

During the mid-1980s, the White House had one serious moment of attraction to counterinsurgency in El Salvador. Students of the Vietnam War experienced an uneasy sense of *déjà vu*. The civil war in El Salvador had a very different history from the revolution in Vietnam, but the Reagan administration declared the Central American conflict a Cold War battleground. At a symposium convened by the Center of Military History in 1984, Allan Goodman warned, "We are following a dual-track strategy of El Salvadorizing the military struggle—a policy directly descended from Vietnamization and the Nixon doctrine—and simultaneously searching for a negotiated settlement."[5] He worried that the United States had identified as a vital interest the survival of a regime that was fundamentally flawed, but one that Cuba and the USSR would be delighted to see American forces get tied to in a protracted and unproductive war. He did not believe the United States could isolate itself from Third World conflicts, but had to choose its fights carefully. "We should not adopt strategies like Vietnamization only to make the best of a bad situation," Goodman advised, "but we should assess *at the outset* of our involvement the potential for our ally to perform up to our expectations and requirements."[6] If American interests are not allied from the start with the client state, the ally can argue against demands for reforms like "depoliticizing the army" on the grounds they would risk its demise. Goodman's critique could come right out of the pages of today's orthodox histories of the Vietnam War, arguing that attention needs to be paid to the origins of the war, the flaws of the Saigon regime, and leaders who placed their own political survival ahead of that of their nation. Scholarly studies of counterinsurgency in the 1980s were accurately pointing out the myths of COIN— warnings that would be discounted in its rediscovery in Iraq and Afghanistan.[7]

During the Ronald Reagan years, two paradigm shifts occurred—one in political policy, and one in military doctrine. At the highest political level— the president's Cabinet—Secretary of Defense Caspar Weinberger and Secretary of State George Shultz clashed over guidelines for deployment of US forces into foreign hostilities. This policy discussion came to a head on a bloody Sunday in October 1983 when a truck loaded with 12,000 tons of TNT destroyed a building in Beirut, killing 241 sleeping US Marines sent to Lebanon as peacekeepers in a civil war. Weinberger and his senior military aide, US Army Maj. Gen. Colin Powell, a Vietnam combat veteran, soon produced mobilization guidelines. Although not formally adopted, the Wein-berger-Powell Doctrine, as it became known and practiced, specified that US troops would only be sent into situations in which US national interests were clearly defined, goals were attainable, public support was assured, and ade-quate means had been committed to ensure success.[8]

Weinberger later acknowledged that the guidelines were intended to avoid repeating the "terrible mistake" made in Vietnam of putting Americans in harm's way without popular support and the means to win. Shultz com-plained that these criteria were the "Vietnam Syndrome in spades" and would handicap America as a world power.[9] The new deployment standards were an unspoken acknowledgment that limits to US power exist and that memo-ries of Vietnam kept that reality alive. In 1991 when Gen. Powell was chair-man of the JCS and US forces made a successful conventional assault in Desert Storm, President George H. W. Bush proclaimed "[W]e've kicked the Vietnam syndrome once and for all," although the deserts and oil fields of Southwest Asia bore little resemblance to the forests and rice paddies of Southeast Asia.[10] Further evidence that US policy was running as far as possible away from Vietnam War precedents was the White House's deci-sion not to continue the operation on to Baghdad to remove the dictatorial regime of Saddam Hussein, clearly revealing concerns over another Viet-nam-like quagmire. Powell, for one, stressed caution: "I had witnessed the contortions the government had gone through during Vietnam to avoid say-ing war is war."[11]

Regardless of the politicians' worries, on a military planning level the US Army had not conceded the effectiveness of military force and revised stand-ing military doctrine for the future battlefield. In the words of one colonel, "the Army just walked away from unconventional war" after Vietnam and began to equip and train itself for large unit warfare.[12] Col. Harry Summers's book, *On Strategy: A Critical Analysis of the Vietnam War*, became required reading for all officers.[13] One of the endorsements on the cover of the paper-back edition was by Charlton Heston, Hollywood action-adventure actor and prominent supporter of Ronald Reagan. Summers was on the faculty of the Army War College and argued that the emphasis on counterinsurgency war-fare had been a mistake. Taking his inspiration from Carl von Clausewitz's classic *On War*, his counterfactual scenario was a strategy that would have cordoned off North Vietnam from South Vietnam, treating the 17th parallel as an international boundary. Close reading of Summers's book reveals that it pays no attention to the historical origins of the war or of how that boun-dary came to be.

THE IRAQ WAR: FROM A THUNDER RUN TO A QUAGMIRE

On September 11, 2001, the debates since the Vietnam War over military doctrine took on an unexpected urgency when the United States experienced the first major foreign attack on its own soil since Pearl Harbor. Terrorists hijacked four commercial airliners and slammed three of them into the World Trade Center and Pentagon, and the White House almost immediately declared a "war on terror." The nation faced a real but shadowy danger, and the vague identification of "terror" as the enemy was of little help to military strategists. President George W. Bush and his political aides thought immediately of Saddam Hussein, but the intelligence community's assessment was clear that the perpetrators had no link to Iraq. They were a terrorist group called al-Qaeda led by Osama bin Laden that had exploded a bomb at the World Trade Center in 1993. They were Islamic fundamentalists who viewed as enemies anyone, including other Muslims, who did not share their particular theology.

The Taliban was a similar extremist movement that controlled nine-tenths of Afghanistan and provided protection and training facilities for al-Qaeda in that country. With international support generated by an outpouring of sympathy for the United States following the September 11 attacks, a small US operation dubbed Enduring Freedom—comprised of a total force of about 350 US military special forces, 110 CIA officers, and 4,000 marines—searched unsuccessfully in Afghanistan for bin Laden. At the same time, a loosely connected Northern Alliance of Afghani tribes led by Hamid Karzai—recognized by the United Nations and supported by US bombing of Taliban bases in cooperation with the North Atlantic Treaty Organization (NATO)—established a new government in Kabul in December. Identified as the "Coalition," it "appeared to have all the underpinnings of success," according to political scientist Abdulkader Sinno. US assistance provided it with a budget, Sinno estimates, that was "a thousand times larger than that of the Mujahideen, as its opponents called themselves, and its members benefited from technologies and military training that were generations ahead of those available to their ragtag opponents."[14]

During 2002, however, world and domestic American opinion began to eye the Bush administration warily as it turned its focus from Afghanistan to Iraq. The president labeled Iraq part of an Axis of Evil with Iran and North Korea, and alleged that Saddam Hussein possessed weapons of mass destruction. During an address at West Point in June, in what the press labeled the "Bush Doctrine," he announced that the United States was "ready for preemptive action when necessary to defend our liberty and defend our lives."[15] George W. Bush ordered a military offensive against Iraq to begin on March 19, 2003, but many public officials, journalists, and scholars in the United States and allied nations questioned the timing and motives of this unprovoked attack. Origins of wars are complex, but some have viewed the American action as a "performative war" for the "edification of potential opponents"—that is, to demonstrate American power, especially in the Middle East, as part of the response to the September 2001 attacks.[16]

US military commanders were sure that American ground and air forces equipped with the latest in precise and lethal technology would quickly prevail. Following only two days of aerial bombardment, the first American ground forces crossed the border into Iraq on the morning of March 21 (local time), and by April 9 they were in the streets of Baghdad. The high-speed, mechanized "Thunder Run" to the capital was intended to overwhelm Saddam Hussein's forces and to avoid creating any slow-moving formations that could be targeted by chemical or biological weapons. No weapons of mass destruction were encountered, Saddam and his guards fled, and US troops remained thinly spread along the roads to the capital. On May 1, Bush ordered an end to combat operations. In military terminology, the conventional offensive under Gen. Tommy Franks had used "dominant force" to achieve "full-spectrum superiority," and the next phase was supposed to be the establishment of security and restoration of services to the population, in anticipation of a final phase of transferring civil authority to Iraqis and withdrawing US troops. These two last phases were projected to require about six months, but inadequate planning and staffing and some frankly terrible initial decisions left the country without security and services and exposed to armed violence.[17]

Unlike South Vietnam, where the United States had gradually escalated the size of its forces in response to what it perceived—rightly or wrongly—to be external aggression, the United States invaded Iraq with an initial mass of forces that wrecked the existing social, economic, political, and military structure. This "shock and awe" beginning was supposed to be an improvement over the incrementalism of Vietnam. Although 140,000 US combat forces with 50,000 allied troops (mostly British) may have seemed a large deployment, it was far less than what military planners had wanted in Iraq, and it was woefully inadequate to manage the post-attack phase. On May 12, a Coalition Provisional Authority (CPA) under Ambassador Paul Bremer replaced the initial military assistance effort, and Bremer immediately issued orders to "de-Baathify" and demilitarize Iraq. These orders dissolved the Iraqi army and removed from their positions everyone at all levels of civil administration who had been members of Saddam's Baathist Party, the dictator's requirement for virtually all government employment. Overnight, US actions had denied Iraq it own native expertise in daily government and had left an internal security vacuum. Simple services like fresh water, electric power, and food supply were limited. Contrary to the expectations of the so-called neoconservatives, who advised Bush that Iraqis would welcome the

Americans as liberators, no political leadership emerged to direct a post–Saddam Hussein Iraq.[18]

Saddam Hussein's harsh rule through his army and a civil service loyal to his party had created a strong centralized state that kept control over a volatile mix of religious, regional, and ethnic divisions among Sunni Muslims (Saddam's faith), Shiites (the majority of Muslims in Southern Iraq), and Kurds (a distinctly different community in Northern Iraq). Even more localized were family and tribal conflicts throughout the country. Political unity and democracy were slogans, not reality, in this toxic mix. US forces captured Saddam himself in December, but his followers continued to war against the provisional government. There were tentative steps toward elected government in 2004 that brought a close to the CPA. Lt. Gen. David Petraeus transferred from command of the 101st Airborne Division to head the Multinational Security Transition Command in Iraq. Its purpose was Iraqification. As described by Thomas Ricks, "the US plan was to keep a lid on Iraq until such time as newly created Iraqi forces could take over the fight."[19] In 2006, an internationally supervised election created a supposedly permanent administration in Baghdad under Prime Minister Nouri al-Maliki. The new head of the government was a Shiite politician who had lived for twenty-four years in exile from the Saddam regime and had close ties with Iranian and Syrian leaders. The fledgling government and entire population of Iraq lived in constant threat of sectarian violence that, although not unified as had been the case in Vietnam, was armed insurrection all the same. During the summer of 2006, an average of one hundred civilians a day were dying from scores of suicide and other bombings, and even more outright sectarian murders.[20]

In Vietnam, the Kennedy and Johnson administrations had initially enjoyed fairly solid domestic support for their policies because of the Cold War consensus around the idea of containment of international communism. Political backing for Bush's invasion of Iraq had always been thin, despite the American people's acceptance since September 2001 of fighting international terrorism. The connections between the evils of Saddam Hussein and terrorist movements like al-Qaeda were debatable, and claims of weapons of mass destruction in Iraq had proved unfounded. With the bungling of the occupation of Iraq beginning in 2003, and the ongoing exposure of American fighters to dangerous combat—women as well as men in the increased gender equity of recruiting for an all-volunteer force—public outcries began to be heard that "Iraq is Arabic for Vietnam." In May 2004, the public was shocked by photographs of American soldiers mistreating Iraqi prisoners at Abu Ghraib, news of marines in brutal combat in the narrow streets of the city of Fallujah, and reports of Shiite militia attacks on US forces. Public opinion polls indicated for the first time that a majority thought fighting in Iraq was not worth American lives. Marine general Anthony Zinni, the former chief of the US Central Command, remarked, "I have seen this movie. It was called Vietnam."[21]

Within the US military, the specter of Vietnam was most troubling to the US Army. The Bush administration had resisted using the term *insurgency* in Iraq to avoid parallels to the Vietnam War—preferring the label *sectarian violence*—but there was a growing contingent within the army that was looking back to that earlier war and the idea of counterinsurgency warfare. Even before the 9/11 trauma in 2001 or the invasion of Iraq, policy pundits had been drawing attention to small-war tactics for dealing with insurgencies. In a 1999 book, Michael Lind had argued that the US military had not adapted to the requirements of a guerrilla war in Vietnam, and Max Boot complained in a 2002 work popular in military circles that the "big-war mind-set embodied in the Powell Doctrine" had been "a poor fit with the actual missions the Pentagon was forced to undertake in the post–Cold War era."[22]

In 1999, Lewis Sorley's *A Better War* appeared with its flawed argument that COIN had been successful in Vietnam. In a manner similar to Summers's earlier conventional critique of Vietnam strategy, Sorley's claims for the effectiveness of unconventional approaches became required reading for officers. In addition, Capt. John Nagl on the faculty at West Point published an article in 1999 that was expanded in 2002 into an influential book with the same title, "Learning to Eat Soup with a Knife: British and American Counterinsurgency Learning during the Malayan Emergency and the Vietnam War." Nagl charged that the "organizational culture of the US Army blocked organizational learning" about unconventional warfare after the Vietnam War.[23] A decade earlier, in 1986, David Petraeus—who would become the commander of all US forces in Iraq in 2007, and head of Central Command in 2008—published an article on lessons from Vietnam in *Parameters*, the army's infantry magazine, based upon his dissertation research at Princeton. In 2006, the ideas in the dissertation and article became the starting point for revision of the army's manual on counterinsurgency warfare.[24] In evident disagreement with what had happened to army training doctrine after Vietnam, Petraeus wrote that "Vietnam planted in the minds of many in the military doubts about the ability of US forces to conduct successful large-scale counterinsurgencies."[25]

IRAQIFICATION AND THE RESURRECTION OF COUNTERINSURGENCY WARFARE

With consideration of COIN tactics back on the table, Nagl explicitly connected them to development of local forces. A lengthy *New York Times* analysis of Nagl's arguments paraphrased his contentions: "The formation of 'indigenous' forces, as they are called, is considered a paramount element of successful counterinsurgency. In his book, Nagl emphasizes that one of the many shortcomings of American policy in Vietnam was America's inability to build a capable South Vietnamese fighting force."[26]

Since the United States under the CPA had dismantled the Iraqi army and civil service, the challenge of rebuilding an indigenous force was going to be more difficult than expanding and modernizing the RVN Armed Forces (RVNAF). Saigon's officer corps was handicapped by its colonial origins, but most of the experienced officers in Iraq had been Saddam Hussein's loyal guards. What, then, was the appeal of Iraqification to American tacticians? As had been the case in Vietnam, once the war began slipping away from a US military victory attainable at costs acceptable to Americans, shifting the fighting to Iraqis became a face-saving exit strategy. Vietnamization was a domestic political ploy, not a military strategy. Although Vietnamization had failed to create an effective and survivable RVNAF, the new defenders of indigenization insisted that it could have worked.

As if on cue, the architect of Vietnamization, Melvin Laird, published an article in *Foreign Affairs* in 2005 insisting that "I believed then and still believe today that given enough outside resources, South Vietnam was capable of defending itself, just as I believe Iraq can do the same now."[27] Laird maintained that the failure in 1975 had been in Congress, and the Bush administration had followed Nixon's example and fashioned its own blame game. Both administrations moved the goalposts closer. Laird himself acknowledged, "Unwilling to abandon South Vietnam, the United States changed its mission to self-determination for Vietnam."[28]

The Bush White House crafted its own "decent interval," putting the burden on the interim and fragile political structure in Baghdad and looking for a way to redirect blame from itself. In strikingly similar language of rationalization, the Nixon and Bush administrations created the same metric for US withdrawal. Bush frequently repeated the phrase "[A]s the Iraqis stand up, we can stand down."[29] President Nixon announced in 1969 in his Silent Majority speech, "As South Vietnamese forces become stronger, the rate of American withdrawal can become greater."[30] Like Nixon, Bush struck a resolute public posture, insisting that "failure is not an option."[31] In November 2005, his administration issued a slick brochure, "National Strategy for Victory in Iraq," featuring the shift in tactics to the classic COIN formula:

> The Security Track involves carrying out a campaign to defeat the terrorists and neutralize the insurgency, developing Iraqi security forces, and helping the Iraqi government:
>
> • Clear areas of enemy control by remaining on the offensive, killing and capturing enemy fighters and denying them safe-haven;

- Hold areas freed from enemy influence by ensuring that they remain under the control of the Iraqi government with an adequate Iraqi security force presence; and
- Build Iraqi Security Forces and the capacity of local institutions to deliver services, advance the rule of law, and nurture civil society.[32]

Despite his reelection in 2004, in part by campaigning as a wartime leader, Bush and his Republican Party were in trouble by 2006. The president's approval rating on his handling of the war stood at 34 percent, a low comparable to that of Lyndon Johnson after the Tet Offensive. As had occurred when public support for the Vietnam War waned in 1968, Melvin Small has noted, many Americans were calling for withdrawal, even though "immediate withdrawal was never in the cards" for the majority of the public then, or in Iraq.[33] In an unprecedented step during a time of war, the Bush White House acquiesced to the urgings of some members of Congress to create a bipartisan Iraq Study Group (ISG) to advise the president on how to end the war. Its eighty-nine-page report issued in December 2006 made seventy-nine recommendations, but the three most significant echoed Vietnam: 1) expand training of the Iraqi Army and national police to enable US troop withdrawal by 2008; 2) undertake negotiations with nations in the region to reduce tensions; and 3) slow aid to Baghdad to pressure the regime toward a stable, representative democracy.

The Democrats swept to control of both houses of Congress in the midterm elections in November 2006, and Bush recognized that he needed to make some changes. He essentially ignored the ISG report, however, and launched his own initiative.[34] He decided to stay with his strategy for victory publicized the previous year, and, similar to Nixon's moves after declaring Vietnamization, he took steps to buy more time for his policy to work. In January 2007, he ordered the deployment of five army brigades to reinforce the coalition forces in Iraq and appointed Gen. Petraeus to lead the effort, marking the beginning of the Iraqi surge campaign.[35]

While in command of the Combined Arms Center at Fort Leavenworth in 2006, Petraeus had supervised the writing of *Counterinsurgency*, US Army and Marine Corps Field Manual (FM) 3-24.[36] This publication marked the official resurrection of COIN doctrine for the twenty-first century. One chapter is devoted to "Developing Host Nation Security Forces." The field manual was based in part on models from France's losing wars in Indochina and Algeria, although Western powers have engaged in COIN since the fifteenth century, in terms of using military action to disseminate Western values and ideas as a foundation for indigenous social, political, and economic transformation in pivotal areas. "Small wars" became a military category in the nineteenth century, associated with imperial expansion. They were basically a "political project." In the words of historian Douglas Porch, FM 3-24 "replicates the righteousness of nineteenth-century imperialists when it brands the enemies of coalition occupation of Iraq and Afghanistan as 'elusive, unethical and indiscriminate foes.'"[37] This characterization echoes Paul Kattenburg's concern that the Kennedy administration made a conceptual error by labeling the enemy in Vietnam "insurgents," rather than "revolutionaries."[38]

Contemporary COIN practitioners refer to the tactic as "war among the people," which suggests it is as much about "soft power" or political persuasion as it is military force. Historically, however, it has targeted "the people" for assassination and brutality, including rape, destitution, internment, and intimidation, with the goal of depriving insurgents of their support base and ability to survive. This method is sometimes given the picturesque image of taking the sea away from the fish. Carl von Clausewitz deemed small wars ineffective and uncivilized, and its practitioners—in contrast to Summers's attachment to the Prussian theorist—have often dismissed von Clausewitz as irrelevant.[39]

The theoretical works of French military officer David Galula heavily influenced the writing of the army's new COIN manual. Originally published in 1963 and 1964, Galula's books were reprinted in 2006, one with a foreword by John Nagl.[40] Galula served his country in its unsuccessful efforts to defend its colonial hold on Algeria after it had lost Indochina. In both colonial wars, the native resistance to French minority rule and military occupation outlasted the French people's support of the imperial project. In his 1964 book on COIN theory, which was known and read by US officers at the time it was published, Galula did not use the word *pacification* in his step-by-step approach. He defined success as building a "political machine from the population upward," but he described no mechanism for this final step that is supposed to come after "destruction or expulsion of the insurgent threat."[41]

Galula wrote about the way France could have prevailed in Algeria, and his ideas meshed nicely with counterfactual histories like Sorley's *Better War* that criticized Westmoreland's purportedly conventional approach. Providing security and opportunity to the Iraqi people—population-centered counterinsurgency—was not a new idea, but Petraeus and fellow officers were now in a position to try to return the idea to army training and tactics. Eager to accept that winning had been possible in Vietnam and could be in Iraq, the authors of FM 3-24 and others came forward with a doctrine that would utilize small-war tactics backed by American power, and technology provided by the surge, that would save the US campaign, codenamed Iraqi Freedom. Their thinking repeated Vietnam-era mistakes of trying to impose a big military format on political reconstruction of a less-developed nation. The record of those errors had been amply documented in many of the army's own studies of the Vietnam War. In their enthusiasm for the theory, the new wave of COIN advocates was rushing to the rescue like a Hollywood movie plot. In this version, Abrams was their hero, and the villains were Westmoreland, Congress, the antiwar movement, and the media—the list of usual suspects provided by revisionist histories that discount the weight of the colonial history of the Vietnam War. Orthodox studies of the American war in Vietnam begin with examining the flawed origins of that war; likewise, Iraq had its own historical influences that shaped the strategic environment within its borders.[42]

Westmoreland surely made mistakes, but repeated studies reveal that US aid, tactical doctrines, assassinations of Viet Cong cadre, strategic hamlets, Marine Corps Combined Action Programs, and digging of water wells could not overcome the military, political, and societal deficiencies in the Saigon regime and its unwillingness and inability to reform.[43] US planners had rejected COIN after 1975 and turned to the Weinberger-Powell doctrine of employing big units in vital interest conflicts. US forces were completely unprepared to respond to the insurgency that engulfed Iraq. To attempt to salvage the operation, Petraeus and other commanders adapted conventional forces to COIN theory.

HISTORY'S WARNING: DON'T MAKE ME REPEAT MYSELF

The problem with this new interest in COIN was that it distorted the history of the "other war" in Vietnam. Strategic choices were not the problem in Vietnam. Eric Bergerud found in his province study that "the GVN, even with massive American support, could never create the essential foundation for a strong and resilient morale—the perception that it could win. The collapse in 1975 is very intelligible in this light."[44] His point complements the contention of orthodox historians that America's frustration in Vietnam was from lack of understanding of the country in the 1950s and the first half of the 1960s, rather than in the way the military tried to conduct the war from 1965 to 1973. The course of the Vietnam War demonstrated the limits of military power to influence the behavior of its politically unstable ally, and the American public came to understand that its leaders' overconfidence and ambitions had led to rising costs in areas of marginal interest to the United States and the West.[45]

The outcome of the surge in Iraq paralleled the Vietnam experience in some ways. The input of thousands of American troops and their modern materiel enabled the Iraqi forces of Prime Minister Maliki to begin to suppress the level of violence in the country. The maneuver secured control of three major cities—Baghdad, Basra, and Mosul—and enabled the removal of the additional US troops in July 2008. With fewer American boots on the ground, American casualties dropped. Republicans who had backed the original invasion began declaring victory in Iraq, as if the number of Americans killed was the metric for winning and losing. "Despite the unpopularity of the war," Melvin Small observes, "Senator McCain ran for the presidency on a stay-the-course policy, which the Democrats, backed by a majority of the population, opposed."[46]

As Nixon had done in Vietnam, however, Bush had already lowered American aims and changed the definition of winning. There was no more talk of a flowering democracy. Testifying before Congress, Petraeus claimed that the Iraqi government could defend itself and was "reasonably representative," but was not a "Jeffersonian democracy."[47] In another similarity to Vietnam, it was clear that—regardless of debates over the long-term potential of population-centered counterinsurgency—the American public had had enough. In accepting the Democratic presidential nomination in 2008, Barack Obama declared, "We must be as careful getting out of Iraq as we were careless getting in, but start leaving we must. It's time for Iraqis to take responsibility for their future."[48]

In March 2010, Iraq's parliamentary election was relatively open, but its results split basically into four factions. Meanwhile, suicide bombers and other forms of violence continued to kill sometimes hundreds of people at a time. Still, under President Obama, Washington removed all of its remaining forces from the country in 2011. Although the problems of law and order were unsolved, corruption was rampant, and the state was far from a democracy, America had lost interest in reforming Iraq and squandering American lives and fortune in the process. The new Iraqi government's inability to form a genuinely national state remained problematic. Without Baghdad's enemies having a backer on the border as the DRV had with China in the 1970s, Iraqification seemed to hold until 2014, when fighters for the Islamic State in Iraq and Syria (ISIS) stormed in and the Iraqi army disintegrated. US forces rushed back in to "stem the tide," to recall a term from the Vietnam War days.[49]

While US attention had been focused on Iraq, the Taliban moved back into Afghanistan from its hiding places in Pakistan. During Obama's first year in office, the insurgents were operating in thirty-three of the country's thirty-four provinces, and attacks on the American-led NATO forces—especially from improvised explosive devices (IEDs) that could flip over an armored vehicle like a toy—were constant occurrences. Meanwhile, the seemingly hopeless corruption and ineffectiveness of the Hamid Karzai government, in what one columnist called a "tribal narco-state consisting of some 40,000 mostly rural villages," was driving people toward either local warlords or the Taliban.[50] The massive flow of international aid into Kabul's immature government structure, in the assessment of Gen. H. R. McMaster, "converted a backwater failed state into a casino of corruption that further delegitimized the Karzai regime."[51]

Obama decided to repeat Bush's surge tactic and sent 30,000 additional US forces to Afghanistan in 2009. Also, he turned again to Petraeus to command what was a total NATO force of 100,000. The mission was explicitly described as counterinsurgency—clear, hold, and build—and its purpose was reminiscent of Vietnamization. The marine general in Helmand Province told his troops fighting with the Afghan National Army that "we cannot win this war, we cannot possibly win it, but we can help the Afghans win it."[52] With the modern technology of Predator and Reaper drones operated by the CIA out of secret bases, Obama's surge forced the Taliban terrorists back into hiding, and food crops began to replace opium fields in southern Afghanistan. "As in Vietnam," in historian Terry Anderson's account, "the enemy trades space for time, waiting for the allies to tire and eventually go home."[53]

Afghanistan has earned, for good reason, the reputation as "the graveyard of empires," and there was only so much the United States and NATO could do. The fate of the country was ultimately up to its own people. Obama withdrew the surge force in 2012, still leaving more than 60,000 Americans in-country. None of the objectives outlined by Petraeus and the JCS had been accomplished, and echoes of Vietnam could be heard in the litany of deficiencies. Karzai never agreed with the counterinsurgency campaign because he wanted more forces on the Pakistani border and not in the tribal areas. Pakistan did not provide meaningful pursuit of the Taliban in its territory. Afghani soldiers tended to stay back and let America do the fighting, and all the while Americans at home complained about what the war was costing. By 2015, government institutions in Kabul remained dysfunctional, and the militants, including the Taliban, had not been significantly weakened. "The civil war is likely to continue in earnest after most or all of the foreign Coalition troops withdraw," one analyst concluded, "with many of the participants [in the civil war] tracing their lineage to the pre-2001 belligerents."[54] When Donald Trump became president, American troops and civilians working for military contractors still remained in Afghanistan, making the US deployment there the longest and costliest war in dollars spent in American history. The Vietnam War had once held the distinction of longest, and still ranks only after the World Wars as America's deadliest foreign war.[55]

Insurgencies and civil wars are politics carried out by violence, and they are countered in the end on a broadly defined strategic and political level, not simply by the way military forces are deployed. The surge in Iraq did not rescue the American reform project from failure. The Shiites consolidated their power in the central government through political exclusion and sometimes outright "ethnic cleansing" of hostile regions. Whether Sunnis and Kurds could participate effectively in sustainable state-building remained an open question. The surge in the name of counterinsurgency in Afghanistan was even more dubious in its results. It used violence to stabilize a corrupt and illegitimate regime that was left with little except lofty rhetoric to defend itself against ruthless opponents.[56]

In South Vietnam, failed social and political programs would have continued to erode and finally force out President Thieu, even without the PAVN offensive in 1975. Military security is essential, but the political war is decisive. In Iraq and Afghanistan, a combination of security and social programs was required. Lack of reform had doomed the nation-building effort in South Vietnam, according to historian Robert Brigham, who has studied the RVN extensively, and his assessment of the Iraq war was the same: "that security and social progress must proceed in tandem, or nation building cannot succeed."[57]

When the threat to public safety is an armed insurgency, the strategists must determine what counterinsurgency tactics are appropriate. The strategic analysis should begin with a careful examination of the origins of the insurgency. Its roots may be strong and locally appropriate due to a history of oppression or other injustice. The insurgents may not offer the best course forward for the nation. The Marxism-Leninism of the Workers Party in Vietnam created a sense of grievance and provided a playbook for revolutionary war, but the most appropriate design for modernization and a successful and moral society may not have been in a Maoist reinterpretation of the European industrial revolution. It may well have existed in the culture of the rational peasant guided by Confucian and ancestral patterns of social order or some other indigenous anthropological model.

Vietnamization failed—not because Abrams and US military planners did not attempt to address recruiting, training, and leadership deficiencies in the RVNAF, but because there was no civil base upon which to build—step three of COIN's sequential process. The Iraq-era COIN advocates demonstrated little historical perspective on whether the ends—the final step—were appropriate to the means available. COIN as practiced by a powerful developed nation in a less-developed postcolonial state continues paternalistic attitudes originally evident in pacification of colonized peoples. "Counterinsurgency becomes," in Douglas Porch's colorful phrase, "adult intervention in a school yard of bullied children." As he explains, terms like *nation building* and *democracy* serve as soothing substitutes for *white man's burden* and *civilizing mission.*[58]

John Kennedy's military adviser and later ambassador to the RVN, Gen. Maxwell Taylor, reflected on Sun Tzu's dictum on the art of war—"Know your enemy; know yourself"—with this thought: "First, we didn't know ourselves. We thought we were going into the Korean War, but this was a different country. Secondly, we didn't know our South Vietnamese allies, . . . and we knew even less about North Vietnam. . . . So until we know the enemy and know our allies and know ourselves, we'd better keep out of this dirty kind of business."[59]

If there is no reasonable chance from the beginning of a conflict that the ally can do the job, it should be a warning that outside aid and commitment will not last long enough to make it happen. During Vietnamization, Kissinger and Nixon in Washington and US advisers in the field often expressed disdain for South Vietnam's leaders and officers. Too seldom did Americans even ask the local allies what their interests were and what they wanted. Ignorance and confidence can be complementary, as Mark Twain observed. Nixon always projected a lot of certainty, despite his personal insecurities, but George W. Bush seemed to believe, as David Elliott describes it, "that unflinching confidence has an almost mystical power," or as one Bush aide asserted, "[W]e're an empire now, and when we act, we create our own reality."[60]

Attempting to create effective military allies in Iraq and Afghanistan, the US COIN approach suffered from the same colonialist and American-centric blinders worn in Vietnam. Both the enemy and the client had their own agency, which American self-interests and arrogance obscured. Iraq and Afghanistan demonstrated that the structure and fate of those countries is their story, not America's. The events of 9/11 were a violent criminal act. Instead of isolating Osama bin Laden and his small band as the criminals they were, by both Western and Middle Eastern standards, the perpetrators were made into a pseudo-political movement to which the United States gave substance by declaring a war on terrorism—a war on an idea. Rather than an American war, the response could have been a transnational movement against criminals who threaten global peace and stability. How to respond to a perceived threat to national security requires thorough historical and cultural knowledge of the states and parties involved to know how to provide materiel and technical resources that can produce positive results. How does the outside power align its interests and the means it possesses with the interests and methods of the recipient? Today's military, with its foreign area officer programs and language training, is moving in positive directions, but the knowledge required—especially at the strategic planning level—is vast, because the cultural gaps to be bridged can be enormous.

Despite the massive application of US power in Vietnam, the United States did not get its way. The war took a heavy toll on the US military in terms of operational readiness, self-esteem, and public support, from which it took nearly two decades to recover. Eventually Laird and Sorley and others argued that the United States actually had won in Vietnam and had withdrawn prematurely. The lesson for them was to stay the course in the face of adversity. In defending his authorization for the surge in Iraq, George W. Bush informed the Veterans of Foreign Wars convention in 2007 that our problem in Vietnam was that we did not stay long enough: "Unlike in Vietnam, if we withdraw before the job is done, this enemy would follow us home."[61] "What the United States really lacked in Vietnam," according to journalist Arnold Isaacs, "was not persistence but understanding."[62] Vietnamization overlooked the historical evidence about the limits of one nation, even with overwhelming wealth and firepower, to ensure that its allies are successful if the allies are not up to the job.

Notes

PREFACE

1. David L. Anderson, "One Vietnam War Should Be Enough and Other Reflections on Diplomatic History and the Making of Foreign Policy," *Diplomatic History* 30 (January 2006): 1–21.

2. Stephen Biddle, "Seeing Baghdad, Thinking Saigon: The Perils of Refighting Vietnam in Iraq," *Foreign Affairs* 85 (March/April 2006): 2–14; Frederick Kagan, "Iraq Is Not Vietnam," *Policy Review* 134 (December 2005–January 2006): 3–14.

3. James William Gibson, *The Perfect War: The War We Couldn't Lose and How We Did* (New York: Vintage Books, 1988), 461.

4. Kevin Boylan, *Losing Binh Dinh: Failure of Pacification and Vietnamization* (Lawrence: University Press of Kansas, 2016), 6–7.

5. Eric M. Bergerud, *The Dynamics of Defeat: The Vietnam War in Hau Nghia Province* (Boulder, CO: Westview Press, 1990).

6. Kosh Sadat and Stan McChrystal, "Staying the Course in Afghanistan: How to Fight the Longest War," *Foreign Affairs* 96 (November/December 2017): 8; Emma Sky, "Mission Still Not Accomplished in Iraq: Why the United States Should Not Leave," *Foreign Affairs* 96 (November/December 2017): 15.

INTRODUCTION

1. Andrew J. Birtle, *U.S. Army Counterinsurgency and Contingent Operations Doctrine, 1942–1976* (Washington, DC: US Army Center of Military History, 2006), 4.

2. Ibid., 368–69.

3. Gregory A. Daddis, *Withdrawal: Reassessing America's Final Years in Vietnam* (New York: Oxford University Press, 2017), 83.

4. Abdulkader Sinno, "Partisan Intervention and the Transformation of Afghanistan's Civil War," *American Historical Review* 120 (December 2015): 1811.

5. Ibid.

6. Robert D. Schulzinger, *A Time for War: The United States and Vietnam, 1941–1975* (New York: Oxford University Press, 1997), 329.

7. See, for example, Michael Lind, *Vietnam: The Necessary War* (New York: The Free Press, 1999).

8. John Prados, "Introduction to Roundtable XX-13 on Gregory A. Daddis, *Withdrawal: Reassessing America's Final Years in Vietnam,*" H-Diplo, November 12, 2018, http:// www.tiny.cc/Roundtable-XX-13. For a discussion of Vietnam War historiography, see David L. Anderson, "No More Vietnams: Historians Debate the Policy Lessons of the Vietnam War," in *The War That Never Ends: New Perspectives on the Vietnam War,* ed. David L. Anderson and John Ernst (Lexington: University Press of Kentucky, 2007), 13–33.

9. Lewis A. Sorley, *A Better War: The Unexamined Victories and Final Tragedy of America's Last Years in Vietnam* (New York: Harcourt, 1999), xv.

10. Mark Moyar, Donald Kagan, and Frederick Kagan, *A Question of Command: Counterinsurgency from the Civil War to Iraq* (New Haven, CT: Yale University Press, 2009), 161–63.

11. James H. Willbanks, *Abandoning Vietnam: How America Left and South Vietnam Lost Its War* (Lawrence: University Press of Kansas, 2004), 279, 287; Daddis, *Withdrawal,* 10–13; Gregory A. Daddis, *Westmoreland's War: Reassessing American Strategy in Vietnam* (New York: Oxford University Press, 2014), 170–72; Boylan, *Losing Binh Dinh,* 2–6.

12. Buffalo Springfield, "For What It's Worth," 1966, Genius, accessed February 14, 2019, https://genius.com/Buffalo-springfield-for-what-its-worth-lyrics.

13. David L. Anderson, *Trapped by Success: The Eisenhower Administration and Vietnam, 1953–1961* (New York: Columbia University Press, 1991), 167–68.

14. Bergerud, *Dynamics of Defeat,* 234.

15. Ibid., 235.

1. VIETNAMIZATION BEFORE NIXON

1. Ronald H. Spector, *Advice and Support: The Early Years, 1941–1960* (Washington, DC: US Army Center of Military History, 1983), 223.

2. Ibid., 115, 222–23, 255–56, 261–62.

3. Ibid., 273; Anderson, *Trapped by Success,* 167; Birtle, *U.S. Army Counterinsurgency,* 309.

4. William J. Lederer and Eugene Burdick, *The Ugly American* (Greenwich, CT: Fawcett Publications, 1962), 234.

5. Lawrence Freedman, *Kennedy's Wars: Berlin, Cuba, Laos, and Vietnam* (Oxford, UK: Oxford University Press, 2000), 336.

6. Birtle, *U.S. Army Counterinsurgency,* 314. See also Harve Saal and Spencer C. Tucker, "Counterinsurgency Warfare," in *Encyclopedia of the Vietnam War: A Political, Social, and Military History,* ed. Spencer C. Tucker (Santa Barbara, CA: ABC-CLIO, 1998), 136–39.

7. Freedman, *Kennedy's Wars,* 287–90.

8. Ibid., 291.

9. Ibid., 306.

10. Ibid., 307.

11. Ibid., 308–9.

12. John Prados, *Vietnam: The History of an Unwinnable War, 1945–1975* (Lawrence: University Press of Kansas, 2009), 544.

13. *The Pentagon Papers: The Defense Department History of United States Decisionmaking on Vietnam,* Senator Gravel, ed., vol. 2 (Boston: Beacon Press, 1971), 667–69.

14. David L. Anderson, *The Columbia Guide to the Vietnam War* (New York: Columbia University Press, 2002), 109, 144–45.

15. Freedman, *Kennedy's Wars,* 356–57.

16. Quoted in Robert Dallek, "Lyndon Johnson and Vietnam," *Diplomatic History* 20 (Spring 1996): 148.

17. US Department of State, *Foreign Relations of the United States,* 1961–1963, vol. 4: *Vietnam, August–December, 1963* (Washington, DC: Government Printing Office, 1991), 637 (hereafter FRUS, followed by years, volume, and page number).

18. Freedman, *Kennedy's Wars*, 404.

19. *Congressional Record*, 88th Cong., 2d sess. (1964), vol. 110, part 14, pp. 18, 132.

20. Lyndon B. Johnson, "Remarks in Memorial Hall, Akron University," October 21, 1964, *Public Papers of the Presidents*, The American Presidency Project, https://www.presidency.ucsb.edu/node/242136 (hereafter PPP followed by URL).

21. Quoted in John M. Carland, *Combat Operations: Stemming the Tide, May 1965 to October 1966* (Washington, DC: US Army Center of Military History, 2000), 13.

22. Ibid., 14.

23. James Lawton Collins, *The Development and Training of the South Vietnamese Army, 1950–1972* (Washington, DC: US Army Center of Military History, 1991), 35, 56–63.

24. William C. Westmoreland, *A Soldier Reports* (New York: Dell, 1980), 126.

25. Collins, *Development and Training*, 48. See also George C. Herring, *America's Longest War: The United States and Vietnam, 1950–1975*, 4th ed. (Boston: McGraw-Hill, 2002), 164–67.

26. Lyndon Baines Johnson, *The Vantage Point: Perspectives on the Presidency, 1963–1969* (New York: Popular Library, 1971), 232.

27. Brian VanDeMark, *Into the Quagmire: Lyndon Johnson and the Escalation of the Vietnam War* (New York: Oxford University Press, 1991), 218.

28. Anderson, *Columbia Guide to the Vietnam War*, 286, 288.

29. Sorley, *Better War*, 18.

30. Ibid., 6–7, 18.

31. Andrew J. Birtle, "PROVN, Westmoreland, and the Historians: A Reappraisal," *Journal of Military History* 72 (October 2008): 1216–17, 1219.

32. Quoted in ibid., 1222.

33. Westmoreland, *Soldier Reports*, 149.

34. Birtle, "PROVN," 1224.

35. Ibid.

36. Ibid.; Sorley, *Better War*, 6–7; Daddis, *Withdrawal*, 83, 101.

37. Boylan, *Losing Binh Dinh*, 1–10; Max Boot, *The Road Not Taken: Edward Lansdale and the American Tragedy in Vietnam* (New York: Liveright Publishing, 2018), xxxix, xlv–xlvii; Phillip B. Davidson, *Vietnam at War: The History, 1946–1975* (New York: Oxford University Press, 1988), 410–14; Lewis A. Sorley, *Westmoreland: The General Who Lost Vietnam* (Boston: Houghton Mifflin Harcourt, 2011), 68, 103–4, 218.

38. Lewis A. Sorley, *Thunderbolt: General Creighton Abrams and the Army of His Times* (New York: Simon & Schuster, 1992), 214–19.

39. Nguyen Duy Hinh, *Vietnamization and the Cease-Fire* (Washington, DC: US Army Center of Military History, 1980), 181. See also Prados, *Vietnam*, 261.

40. Jeffrey J. Clarke, *Advice and Support: The Final Years* (Washington, DC: US Army Center of Military History, 1988), 300.

41. Daddis, *Withdrawal*, 44.

42. Walter LaFeber, *The Deadly Bet: LBJ, Vietnam, and the 1968 Election* (Lanham, MD: Rowman & Littlefield, 2005).

43. David F. Schmitz, *Richard Nixon and the Vietnam War: The End of the American Century* (Lanham, MD: Rowman & Littlefield, 2014), 35.

44. Ibid., 35; Jeffrey Kimball, *Nixon's Vietnam War* (Lawrence: University Press of Kansas, 1998), 41.

45. Schmitz, *Richard Nixon*, 36–37.

2. NIXON ANNOUNCES VIETNAMIZATION

1. FRUS, 1969–1976, vol. 6: *Vietnam, January 1969–July 1970*, 3n2; Schmitz, *Richard Nixon*, 37.

2. FRUS, 1969–1976, vol. 6: *Vietnam, January 1969–July 1970*, 5.

3. Henry Kissinger, *White House Years* (Boston: Little, Brown, 1979), 261.

4. Pierre Asselin, *Vietnam's American War* (Cambridge, UK: Cambridge University Press, 2018), 168–69.

5. H. R. Haldeman, *The Ends of Power* (New York: Times Books, 1978), 81.

6. Kissinger, *White House Years*, 262; Dale Van Atta, *With Honor: Melvin Laird in War, Peace, and Politics* (Madison: University of Wisconsin Press, 2008), 162.

7. Robert K. Brigham, *Reckless: Henry Kissinger and the Tragedy of Vietnam* (New York: Public Affairs, 2018), 25.

8. Ibid., 9–10; Daddis, *Withdrawal*, 60.

9. Van Atta, *With Honor*, 176.

10. FRUS, 1969–1976, vol. 6: *Vietnam, January 1969–July 1970*, 116.

11. Ibid., 115, 118.

12. Brigham, *Reckless*, 35–38; Ronald B. Frankum Jr., *Like Rolling Thunder: The Air War in Vietnam, 1964–1975* (Lanham, MD: Rowman & Littlefield, 2005), 135; Willard J. Webb, *The Joint Chiefs of Staff and the War in Vietnam, 1969–1970* (Washington, DC: Office of the Chairman of the Joint Chiefs of Staff, 2002), 136; FRUS, 1969–1976, vol. 6: *Vietnam, January 1969–July 1970*, 121–23.

13. Haldeman, *Ends of Power*, 82–83, emphasis in the original.

14. Schmitz, *Richard Nixon*, 62–65.

15. FRUS, 1969–1976, vol. 6: *Vietnam, January 1969–July 1970*, 170.

16. Ibid., 179–80; Willbanks, *Abandoning Vietnam*, 14–15.

17. Brigham, *Reckless*, 30–32.

18. Bui Diem, *In the Jaws of History*, with David Chanoff (Boston: Houghton Mifflin, 1987), 258.

19. FRUS, 1969–1976, vol. 6: *Vietnam, January 1969–July 1970*, 264.

20. Ibid.

21. Ibid., 266.

22. Ibid., 262.

23. Quoted in Willbanks, *Abandoning Vietnam*, 57.

24. Ibid.

25. Clarke, *Advice and Support*, 301.

26. Bui Diem, *In the Jaws of History*, 261.

27. Ibid., 259.

28. Richard Nixon, "Remarks Following Initial Meeting with President Thieu at Midway Island," June 8, 1969, PPP, https://www.presidency.ucsb.edu/node/239376; Richard Nixon, "Remarks at the Conclusion of Discussions with President Thieu," June 8, 1969, PPP, https://www.presidency.ucsb.edu/node/239388.

29. Bui Diem, *In the Jaws of History*, 262.

30. Nguyen Tien Hung and Jerrold L. Schecter, *The Palace File* (New York: Harper & Row, 1986), 33–34.

31. Truong Nhu Tang, *Vietcong Memoir: An Inside Account of the Vietnam War and Its Aftermath*, with David Chanoff and Doan Van Toai (San Diego, CA: Harcourt Brace Jovanovich, 1985), 146.

32. Robert K. Brigham, *Guerrilla Diplomacy: The NLF's Foreign Relations and the Vietnam War* (Ithaca, NY: Cornell University Press, 1999), 87; Truong, *Vietcong Memoir*, 147.

33. Bui Diem, *In the Jaws of History*, 262; Kimball, *Nixon's Vietnam War*, 64–65; Ellsworth Bunker, *The Bunker Papers: Reports to the President from Vietnam, 1967–1973*, ed. Douglas Pike, vol. 3 (Berkeley: University of California Institute of East Asian Studies, 1990), 696.

34. FRUS, 1969–1976, vol. 6: *Vietnam, January 1969–July 1970*, 378.

35. Bunker, *Bunker Papers*, 687.

36. Brigham, *Reckless*, 47–59.

37. Asselin, *Vietnam's American War*, 177–81.

38. Brigham, *Reckless*, 61–67; Jeremy Suri, *Henry Kissinger and the American Century* (Cambridge, MA: Harvard University Press, 2007), 227.

39. Richard Nixon, "Informal Remarks in Guam with Newsmen," July 25, 1969, PPP, https://www.presidency.ucsb.edu/node/239667; FRUS 1969–1976, vol. 6: *Vietnam, January 1969–July 1970*, 248–52.

3. MACV IMPLEMENTS VIETNAMIZATION

1. Bunker, *Bunker Papers*, 803. See also Daddis, *Withdrawal*, 89.
2. Clarke, *Advice and Support*, 344.
3. Ibid., 341, 344.
4. Ibid., 347.
5. Ibid., 349.
6. Ibid., 350; Willbanks, *Abandoning Vietnam*, 21–22.
7. Clarke, *Advice and Support*, 351.
8. "Special National Intelligence Estimate (SNIE) 14.3-70," *Estimative Products on Vietnam, 1948–1975* (Washington, DC: National Intelligence Council, 2005), 514.
9. Ibid., 514–15.
10. Clarke, *Advice and Support*, 351–53.
11. Webb, *The Joint Chiefs of Staff and the War in Vietnam, 1969–1970*, 118.
12. Clarke, *Advice and Support*, 354–56.
13. Ibid., 357–59.
14. Daddis, *Withdrawal*, 75.
15. Willbanks, *Abandoning Vietnam*, 50–56.
16. Ibid., 29–32.
17. Sorley, *Better War*, 195, emphasis in the original.
18. Ibid., 222, emphasis in the original.
19. Gregory A. Daddis, *No Sure Victory: Measuring U.S. Army Effectiveness and Progress in the Vietnam War* (New York: Oxford University Press, 2011), 171–72. See also Clarke, *Advice and Support*, 388; Douglas Kinnard, *The War Managers: American Generals Reflect on Vietnam* (Hanover, NH: University Press of New England for the University of Vermont, 1977), 145–47.
20. Quoted in Christian Appy, *Patriots: The Vietnam War Remembered from All Sides* (New York: Penguin, 2003), 442.
21. Clarke, *Advice and Support*, 400.
22. Boylan, *Losing Long Binh*, 58.
23. Quoted in ibid., 269.
24. Ibid.
25. Ibid., 279; Daddis, *No Sure Victory*, 209.
26. Clarke, *Advice and Support*, 402.
27. Ibid.
28. Ibid.
29. Quoted in Willbanks, *Abandoning Vietnam*, 55.
30. Ibid., 40–42.
31. Hinh, *Vietnamization*, 183.
32. Nathalie Huynh Chau Nguyen, *South Vietnamese Soldiers: Memories of the Vietnam War and After* (Santa Barbara, CA: Praeger, 2016), 39. See also Clarke, *Advice and Support*, 428–35.
33. Clarke, *Advice and Support*, 436–38.
34. Ibid., 441–43.
35. Michael A. Eggleston, *Exiting Vietnam: The Era of Vietnamization and American Withdrawal Revealed in First-Person Accounts* (Jefferson, NC: McFarland, 2014), Kindle loc. 2153.
36. Ibid., Kindle loc. 2172.
37. Clarke, *Advice and Support*, 438; "A History of the 1st Signal Brigade," *The Jagged Sword*, Special Issue (US Army 1st Signal Brigade Magazine, 1970).

38. John D. Bergen, *Military Communication: A Test for Technology* (Washington, DC: US Army Center of Military History, 1986), 341–43.

39. Thomas Matthew Rienzi, *Communications-Electronics, 1962–1970* (Washington, DC: US Department of the Army, 1985), 145; See also Bergen, *Military Communication*, 347–48.

40. William Moore, interview, December 17, 2001, 6, Vietnam Center and Archive, Texas Tech University, Lubbock, Texas, https://www.vietnam.ttu.edu/reports/images.php?img=/OH/OH0202/OH0202.pdf.

41. Ibid.

42. Clarke, *Advice and Support*, 440.

43. Rienzi, *Communications-Electronics,* 172. See also Clarke, *Advice and Support*, 438–41; Bergen, *Military* Communication, 351–56.

44. Collins, *Development and Training*, 75.

45. Clarke, *Advice and Support*, 498–99, 518.

4. BUYING TIME FOR VIETNAMIZATION

1. FRUS, 1969–1976, vol. 6: *Vietnam, January 1969–July 1970,* 377.

2. Kissinger, *White House Years*, 1481n11.

3. FRUS, 1969–1976, vol. 6: *Vietnam, January 1969–July 1970,* 388, emphasis in the original.

4. Ibid., 376–90.

5. Ibid., 456. See also William Burr and Jeffrey Kimball, *Nixon's Nuclear Specter: The Secret Alert of 1969, Madman Diplomacy, and the Vietnam War* (Lawrence: University Press of Kansas, 2015), 260; Lien-Hang T. Nguyen, *Hanoi's War: An International History of the War for Peace in Vietnam* (Chapel Hill: University of North Carolina Press, 2012), 147; David L. Prentice, "Choosing 'the Long Road': Henry Kissinger, Melvin Laird, Vietnamization, and the War over Nixon's Vietnam Strategy," *Diplomatic History* 40 (June 2016): 445–74.

6. Van Atta, *With Honor*, 477–78.

7. Burr and Kimball, *Nixon's Nuclear Specter*, 260.

8. Ibid., 4–5, 265–309.

9. Kimball, *Nixon's Vietnam War*, 173; Brigham, *Reckless*, 76–77.

10. Schmitz, *Richard Nixon*, 66–67.

11. Richard Nixon, "Address to the Nation on the War in Vietnam," November 3, 1969, PPP, https://www.presidency.ucsb.edu/node/240027.

12. Ibid.

13. Ibid.

14. Ibid. See also Davidson, *Vietnam at War*, 599; Kimball, *Nixon's Vietnam War*, 174.

15. Kimball, *Nixon's Vietnam War*, 175.

16. Richard Nixon, *No More Vietnams* (New York: Arbor House, 1985), 105.

17. Clarke, *Advice and Support*, 359.

18. Brigham, *Reckless*, 86–88.

19. Quoted in ibid., 99.

20. Ibid., 97–99.

21. Kenton Clymer, *Troubled Relations: The United States and Cambodia since 1870* (De-Kalb: Northern Illinois University Press, 2007), 105–6; Clarke, *Advice and Support*, 420.

22. Quoted in Daddis, *Withdrawal*, 121.

23. Kimball, *Nixon's Vietnam War*, 202.

24. Clarke, *Advice and Support*, 406–17; John M. Shaw, *The Cambodian Campaign: The 1970 Offensive and America's Vietnam War* (Lawrence: University Press of Kansas, 2005), 49–51.

25. Clarke, *Advice and Support*, 415–18; Shaw, *Cambodian Campaign,* 63, 93, 169.

26. Richard Nixon, "Address to the Nation on the Situation in Southeast Asia," April 30, 1970, PPP, https://www.presidency.ucsb.edu/node/239701.

27. Ibid.

28. Clarke, *Advice and Support*, 420–21; Daddis, *Withdrawal*, 126; Melvin Small, *Antiwarriors: The Vietnam War and the Battle for America's Hearts and Minds* (Wilmington, DE: Scholarly Resources, 2002), 123–33.

29. David L. Anderson, *The Vietnam War* (Basingstoke, UK: Palgrave Macmillan, 2005), 94–95; Kimball, *Nixon's Vietnam War*, 224.

30. Richard M. Nixon, *The Real War* (New York: Warner Books, 1980), 109. See also Shaw, *Cambodian Campaign*, 169–70.

31. Khoa Tran, interview, September 22, 2018, West Point Center for Oral History, US Military Academy, West Point, NY, http://www.westpointcoh.org/interviews/we-fought-with-our-hearts-and-minds-a-vietnamese-veteran-achieves-the-american-dream.

32. Davidson, *Vietnam at War*, 630–31.

33. Quoted in Clarke, *Advice and Support,* 421.

34. Daddis, *Withdrawal,* 128, 130–31.

35. Graham A. Cosmas and Terrance P. Murray, *US Marines in Vietnam: Vietnamization and Redeployment, 1970–1971* (Washington, DC: US Marine Corps History and Museums Division, 1986), 180–82.

36. Ibid., 181.

37. Ibid.

38. Ibid., 184.

39. Daddis, *Withdrawal*, 164.

5. VIETNAMIZATION

1. Bergen, *Military Communications*, 305.

2. Ibid., 291.

3. Clarke, *Advice and Support*, 349.

4. Bergen, *Military Communications*, 303–04.

5. Operational Report—Lessons Learned (ORLL), Headquarters 12th Signal Group for Period Ending 31 July 1970, dated August 13, 1970, Box 51, Records of US Forces in Southeast Asia, 1950–1975 (RG 472), National Archives, College Park, Maryland.

6. ORLL, 12th Signal Group, August 13, 1970; ORLL, Headquarters 12th Signal Group for Period Ending 31 October 1970, dated November 10, 1970, Box 51, RG 472, National Archives.

7. "SNIE 14.3-70," *Estimative Products on Vietnam*, 515.

8. Eggleston, *Exiting Vietnam*, Kindle loc. 2207-18.

9. Douglas Shivers, interview, October 4, 2002, 33, Vietnam Center and Archive, https://www.vietnam.ttu.edu/reports/images.php?img=/OH/OH0225/OH0225.pdf.

10. Collins, *Development and Training*, 99; Bergen, *Military Communications*, 345.

11. Clarke, *Advice and Support*, 440.

12. Ralph Blumenthal, "On a Delta River, a Test for Vietnamization," *New York Times*, February 17, 1970.

13. Eggleston, *Exiting Vietnam*, Kindle loc. 2163.

14. Ibid., Kindle loc. 2172.

15. Webb, *Joint Chiefs of Staff and the War in Vietnam, 1969–1970*, 121.

6. VIETNAMIZATION TESTED

1. Richard Nixon, "Address to the Nation on the Cambodian Sanctuary Operation," June 3, 1970, PPP, https://www.presidency.ucsb.edu/node/239816.

2. Ibid.

3. FRUS, 1969–1976, vol. 6: *Vietnam, January 1969–July 1970*, 1019.

4. Ibid., 1020.

5. Sorley, *Better War*, 228.

6. FRUS, 1969–1976, vol. 6: *Vietnam, January 1969–July 1970*, 1000.

7. Clarke, *Advice and Support*, 450, 524; Anderson, *Columbia Guide to the Vietnam War*, 288.

8. Andrew Wiest, *Vietnam's Forgotten Army: Heroism and Betrayal in the ARVN* (New York: New York University Press, 2007), 6.

9. Robert K. Brigham, *ARVN: Life and Death in the South Vietnamese Army* (Lawrence: University Press of Kansas, 2006), 99.

10. Robert K. Brigham, "Vietnamese Society at War," in *The Columbia History of the Vietnam War*, ed. David L. Anderson (New York: Columbia University Press, 2011), 329.

11. Juris Jurjevics, interview, July 12, 2012, West Point Center for Oral History, http://www.westpointcoh.org/interviews/a-level-of-absurdity-war-and-corruption-in-vietnam.

12. Neil Sheehan, *A Bright Shining Lie: John Paul Vann and America in Vietnam* (New York: Random House, 1988), 742.

13. Ibid., 742–44.

14. Asselin, *Vietnam's American War*, 184.

15. Hinh, *Vietnamization*, 191. See also Daddis, *Withdrawal*, 170–71.

16. Clarke, *Advice and Support*, 472–73; FRUS, 1969–1976, vol. 7: *Vietnam, July 1970–January 1972*, 377.

17. Davidson, *Vietnam at* War, 637–38; Daddis, *Withdrawal*, 170–71.

18. Clarke, *Advice and Support*, 473–74; Nguyen, *Hanoi's* War, 201–2; Sorley, *Better War*, 243–45; Bergen, *Military Communications*, 356–57.

19. Larry Berman, *Perfect Spy: The Incredible Double Life of Pham Xuan An, Time Magazine Reporter and Vietnamese Communist Agent* (New York: HarperCollins e-books, 2007), Kindle loc. 2464.

20. Willbanks, *Abandoning Vietnam*, 99–106.

21. Clarke, *Advice and Support*, 474–77; Sorley, *Better War*, 253–59.

22. Clarke, *Advice and Support*, 474; Davidson, *Vietnam at War*, 652–54.

23. Ernie Sylvester, interview, November 12 and 19, 2002, 84, Vietnam Center and Archive, https://www.vietnam.ttu.edu/reports/images.php?img=/OH/OH0240/OH0240.pdf.

24. Ibid.

25. Ibid., 86.

26. Ibid., 81.

27. Eggleston, *Exiting Vietnam*, Kindle loc. 2661.

28. Ibid., Kindle loc. 2661–70.

29. Willard J. Webb and Walter S. Poole, *The Joint Chiefs of Staff and the War in Vietnam, 1971–1973* (Washington, DC: Office of the Chairman of the Joint Chiefs of Staff, 2007), 16–17.

30. Nguyen Duy Hinh, *Lam Son 719* (Washington, DC: US Army Center of Military History, 1979), 100, 103.

31. Sorley, *Better War*, 249–60, quote on 255. See also Clarke, *Advice and Support*, 475; Nguyen, *Hanoi's War*, 203.

32. FRUS, 1969–1976, vol. 7: *Vietnam, July 1970–January 1972*, 467.

33. Ibid.

34. Ibid., 476.

35. Ibid., 487.

36. Ibid., 488.

37. Hinh, *Lam Son 719*, 152.

38. Richard Nixon, "Address to the Nation on the Situation in Southeast Asia," April 7, 1971, PPP, https://www.presidency.ucsb.edu/node/241224.

39. Davidson, *Vietnam at War*, 660.

40. Ibid., 654.

41. Quoted in Cosmas and Murray, *US Marines in Vietnam*, 210.

42. Ibid., 392.

43. Ibid., 210.

44. Webb and Poole, *Joint Chiefs of Staff and the War in Vietnam, 1971–1973*, 15.

45. Appy, *Patriots*, 409.

46. James H. Willbanks, *A Raid Too Far: Operation Lam Son 719 and Vietnamization in Laos* (College Station: Texas A&M University Press, 2014), 176–77.

47. "National Intelligence Estimate (NIE) 53-71," *Estimative Products on Vietnam*, 576.

48. Ibid., 578–79.

49. Ibid., 579.

50. Quoted in Jeffrey Kimball, *The Vietnam War Files: Uncovering the Secret History of Nixon-Era Strategy* (Lawrence: University Press of Kansas, 2004), 187. See also Brigham, *Reckless*, 147.

51. Quoted in Jussi Hanhimäki, *The Flawed Architect: Henry Kissinger and American Foreign Policy* (Oxford, UK: Oxford University Press, 2004), 232, emphasis added. See also Ken Hughes, "Fatal Politics: Nixon's Political Timetable for Withdrawing from Vietnam," *Diplomatic History* 34 (June 2010): 497–506.

52. Van Atta, *With Honor*, 339.

53. Ibid., 386; FRUS, 1969–1976, vol. 7: *Vietnam, July 1970–January 1972*, 919.

54. FRUS, 1969–1976, vol. 7: *Vietnam, July 1970–January 1972*, 918.

55. Ibid.

56. Ibid.

57. Ibid., 921.

58. Ibid., 925.

59. Ibid., 943.

60. Ibid., 945-46.

61. Ibid., 946. See also Schmitz, *Richard Nixon*, 145.

62. Bui Diem, *In the Jaws of History*, 293.

63. William J. Shkurti, *Soldiering On in a Dying War : The True Story of the Firebase Pace Incident and the Vietnam Drawdown* (Lawrence: University Press of Kansas, 2011), 241.

64. FRUS, 1969–1976, vol. 7: *Vietnam, July 1970–January 1972*, 975.

65. Richard Nixon, "The President's News Conference," November 12, 1971, PPP, https://www.presidency.ucsb.edu/node/241238.

66. Nguyen, *Hanoi's War*, 223–28, 232–34.

67. The Military Institute of Vietnam, *Victory in Vietnam: The Official History of the People's Army of Vietnam, 1954–1975,* trans. Merle L Pribbenow (Lawrence: University Press of Kansas, 2002), 283.

68. Dale Andradé, *Trial by Fire: The 1972 Easter Offensive, America's Last Vietnam Battle* (New York: Hippocrene Books, 1995), 38.

69. FRUS, 1969–1976, vol. 8: *Vietnam, January–October 1972*, 9.

70. Ibid., 11.

71. Richard Nixon, "Address to the Nation, Making Public a Plan for Peace in Vietnam," January 25, 1972, PPP, https://www.presidency.ucsb.edu/node/254597.

72. Ibid.

73. Ibid. See also Brigham, *Reckless*, 165–66.

74. Troung, *Vietcong Memoir*, 201.

75. Clarke, *Advice and Support*, 481.

76. Yasutsune "Tony" Hirashiki, *On the Frontlines of the Television War*, ed. Terry Irving (Philadelphia: Casemate Publishers, 2017), Kindle loc. 3340.

77. Nguyen, *South Vietnamese Soldiers*, 39.

78. Andradé, *Trial by Fire*, 47.

79. Brigham, *Reckless*, 169–70.

80. Quoted in Brigham, *Reckless*, 171.

81. Brigham, *Reckless*, 172.

82. Ibid., 174–75.

83. Webb and Poole, *Joint Chiefs of Staff and the War in Vietnam, 1971-1973*, 364.

84. Ibid.

85. Ibid.

86. Clarke, *Advice and Support*, 483–86; Webb and Poole, *Joint Chiefs of Staff and the War in Vietnam, 1971–1973*, 159; Frankum, *Like Rolling Thunder*, 156–58.

87. Andradé, *Trial by Fire*, 174.

88. Ibid., 175.

89. Victor Joseph Hugo Jr., interview, November 9, 2018, West Point Center for Oral History, http://www.westpointcoh.org/interviews/vietnamese-influencing-vietnamese-a-be-hind-the-scenes-look-at-counterinsurgency-at-the-birth-of-the-republic-of-vietnam.

90. Clarke, *Advice and Support*, 487; Webb and Poole, *Joint Chiefs of Staff and the War in Vietnam, 1971–1973*, 365.

91. Clarke, *Advice and Support*, 488.

92. Ibid.; Davidson, *Vietnam at War*, 715.

7. VIETNAMIZATION'S FINAL, FAILED TEST, 1973–1975

1. Asselin, *Vietnam's American War*, 207.

2. Brigham, *Reckless*, 199–203.

3. Ibid., 203–4.

4. Ibid., 213.

5. Ibid., 215.

6. Ibid., 218.

7. Ibid., 224.

8. FRUS, 1969–1976, vol. 9: *Vietnam, October 1972–January 1973*, 305–6.

9. Nguyen, *Hanoi's War*, 120.

10. FRUS, 1969–1976, vol. 9: *Vietnam, October 1972–January 1973*, 654.

11. Ibid.

12. Ibid., 650.

13. Quoted in Kimball, *Vietnam War Files*, 274.

14. Richard M. Nixon, *RN: The Memoirs of Richard Nixon* (New York: Grosset and Dunlap, 1978), 734.

15. Brigham, *Reckless*, 238–40.

16. Ibid., 242.

17. Willbanks, *Abandoning Vietnam*, 188.

18. Nguyen and Schecter, *Palace File*, 392.

19. Larry Berman, *No Peace, No Honor: Nixon, Kissinger, and Betrayal in Vietnam* (New York: The Free Press, 2001), 261.

20. Quoted in Webb and Poole, *Joint Chiefs of Staff and the War in Vietnam, 1971–1973*, 362.

21. Bunker, *Bunker Papers*, 3:858–59.

22. Willbanks, *Abandoning Vietnam*, 191–98; Asselin, *Vietnam's American War*, 211–21.

23. Willbanks, *Abandoning Vietnam*, 202–03.

24. Gary R. Hess, *Vietnam and the United States: Origins and Legacy of War* (Boston: Twayne, 1990), 137.

25. Willbanks, *Abandoning Vietnam*, 204–7.

26. Nixon, "Informal Remarks in Guam with Newsman," July 25, 1969, PPP.

27. Clarke, *Advice and Support*, 359.

28. David L. Anderson, "Gerald R. Ford and the Presidents' War in Vietnam," in *Shadow on the White House: Presidents and the Vietnam War, 1945–1975*, ed. David L. Anderson (Lawrence: University Press of Kansas, 1993), 186–88.

29. Nguyen and Schecter, *Palace File*, 234–35.

30. Gerard J. DeGroot, *A Noble Cause? America and the Vietnam War* (Essex, UK: Longman, 2000), 252–53; Marc Jason Gilbert, "The Cost of Losing the 'Other War' in Vietnam," in *Why the North Won the Vietnam War,* ed. Marc Jason Gilbert (New York: Palgrave, 2002), 187.

31. Bui Diem, *In the Jaws of History*, 341–42.

32. Cao Van Vien, *The Final Collapse* (Washington, DC: US Army Center of Military History, 1983), 155. See also Schmitz, *Richard Nixon*, 147.

33. Guenter Lewy, *America in Vietnam* (New York: Oxford University Press, 1978), 216–17.

34. Asselin, *Vietnam's American War*, 224–26; Berman, *Perfect Spy*, Kindle loc. 2536.

35. Harry G. Summers Jr., *Historical Atlas of the Vietnam War,* introduction and epilogue by Stanley Karnow (Boston: Houghton Mifflin, 1995), 192.

36. Asselin, *Vietnam's American War,* 227–28.

37. Summers, *Historical Atlas of the Vietnam War*, 200.

38. Hon Nguyen, interview, February 24, 2018, West Point Center for Oral History, http://www.westpointcoh.org/interviews/even-though-we-fight-side-by-side-i-don-t-want-you-to-destroy-my-country-a-vietnamese-perspective-on-wars-in-south-east-asia.

39. William E. Le Gro, *Vietnam from Cease-Fire to Capitulation* (Washington, DC: US Center of Military History, 1981), 179. See also Fred L. Borch, "Hall of Honor: Cau Le," *Vietnam* 31 (April 2019): 64.

40. Le Gro, *Vietnam from Cease-Fire to Capitulation,* 179.

41. Nguyen and Schecter, *Palace File*, 240.

42. Quoted in Anderson, "Gerald R. Ford," 199.

43. Asselin, *Vietnam's American War,* 23; Nguyen, *Hanoi's War*, 300.

8. VIETNAMIZATION AND THE END OF THE REPUBLIC OF VIETNAM

1. Hinh, *Vietnamization*, 189–90.

2. Sorley, *Better War*, 217.

3. Ibid.

4. Ibid., 263.

5. Ibid., 373.

6. Schmitz, *Richard Nixon*, 148.

7. Daddis, *Withdrawal*, 9–13, 131.

8. Willbanks, *Abandoning Vietnam*, 280.

9. Ibid.

10. Quoted in Thomas B. Morgan, "Reporters of the Lost War," *Esquire*, July 1, 1984, 52, https://classic.esquire.com/article/1984/7/1/reporters-of-the-lost-war.

11. Dulles memorandum of conversation with M. Faure, May 11, 1955, box 9, Subject series, John Foster Dulles Papers, Dwight D. Eisenhower Library, Abilene, Kansas.

12. Anderson, *Trapped by Success*, 114–19.

13. Edward Miller, *Misalliance: Ngo Dinh Diem, the United States, and the Fate of South Vietnam* (Cambridge, MA: Harvard University Press, 2013); Jessica M. Chapman, *Cauldron of Resistance: Ngo Dinh Diem, the United States, and 1950s Southern Vietnam* (Ithaca, NY: Cornell University Press, 2013); Geoffrey C. Stewart, *Vietnam's Lost Revolution: Ngo Dinh Diem's Failure to Build an Independent Nation, 1955–1963* (Cambridge, UK: Cambridge University Press, 2017).

14. Frances Fitzgerald, *Fire in the Lake: The Vietnamese and the Americans in Vietnam* (New York: Vintage Books, 1973), 316–18.

15. Mark Twain, Directory of Mark Twain's Maxims, Quotations, and Various Opinions, accessed March 11, 2019, http://www.twainquotes.com/Success.html.

16. Quoted in Fitzgerald, *Fire in the Lake*, 335.

17. Ibid., 337.

18. FRUS, 1964–1968, vol. 2: *Vietnam, January–June, 1965*, 741, emphasis in the original.

19. Quoted in Herring, *America's Longest War*, 151.

20. Sean Fear, "Saigon Goes Global: South Vietnam's Quest for International Legitimacy in the Age of Détente," *Diplomatic History* 42 (June 2018): 447.

21. Ibid., 451.

22. Sorley, *Better War,* 385.

23. Boylan, *Losing Binh Dinh,* 264. See also Kinnard, *War Managers,* 144, 153.

24. Shkurti, *Soldiering On in a Dying War,* 237–38.

25. Arnold R. Isaacs, *Without Honor: Defeat in Vietnam and Cambodia* (Baltimore: Johns Hopkins University Press, 1983), 121.

26. Martin Windrow, *The Last Valley: Dien Bien Phu and the French Defeat in Vietnam* (Boston: Da Capo, 2006), 156–57.

27. Ibid.

28. Cosmas and Murray, *US Marines in Vietnam,* 392.

29. Clarke, *Advice and Support,* 518.

30. Collins, *Development and Training,* 128–30; Mara Karlin, "Why Military Assistance Programs Disappoint: Minor Tools Can't Solve Major Problems," *Foreign Affairs* 96 (November/December 2017): 112.

31. Collins, *Development and Training,* 76.

32. Stanley Karnow, interview, n.d., West Point Center for Oral History, http://www.westpointcoh.org/interviews/a-front-seat-to-history-a-veteran-reporter-remembers-vietnam.

33. Gibson, *Perfect War,* 400–1; Cao Van Vien, *Leadership* (Washington, DC: US Army Center of Military History, 1981), 12–13; Windrow, *Last Valley,* 61.

34. Karnow interview.

35. Windrow, *Last Valley,* 191.

36. *Know Your Enemy: The Viet Cong,* Armed Forces Information and Education, Department of Defense, 1966, Combined Arms Digital Research Library, http://cgsc.cdmhost.com/cdm/singleitem/collection/p4013coll9/id/694/rec/1. See also Shkurti, *Soldiering On,* 241.

37. Sylvester interview, 84.

38. Douglas Womack, interview, February 6, 2006, 30, Vietnam Center and Archive, https://www.vietnam.ttu.edu/reports/images.php?img=/OH/OH0123/OH0123.pdf.

39. Boylan, *Losing Binh Dinh,* 291.

40. This recollection is from the author's conversation with a historian colleague about his Vietnam experiences.

41. Boylan, *Losing Binh Dinh,* 297.

42. Ibid.

43. Quoted in ibid., 298.

44. Vien, *Leadership,* 162–69.

45. Boylan, *Losing Binh Dinh,* 297.

46. David Elliott, "Official History, Revisionist History, and Wild History," in *Making Sense of the Vietnam Wars: Local, National, and Transnational Perspectives,* ed. Mark Philip Bradley and Marilyn B. Young (Oxford, UK: Oxford University Press, 2008), 292.

9. VIETNAMIZATION'S POSTWAR COUNTERINSURGENCY LEGACY

1. Craig R. Whitney, "Tunnel Vision: Watching Iraq, Seeing Vietnam," *New York Times,* November 9, 2003. For the debate over these comparisons, see David Elliott, "Parallel Wars? Can 'Lessons of Vietnam' Be Applied to Iraq?" in *Iraq and the Lessons of Vietnam: Or, How Not to Learn from the Past,* ed. Lloyd C. Gardner and Marilyn B. Young (New York: The New Press, 2007), 20–21; Jeffrey Record, "Leaving Vietnam: Insights for Iraq?" *Diplomatic History* 34 (June 2010): 567–76.

2. George C. Herring, "The Vietnam Syndrome," in Anderson, *Columbia History of the Vietnam War,* 409–29; Nixon, *No More Vietnams,* 13–14; Jeffrey Kimball, "Out of Primordial Cultural Ooze: Inventing Political and Policy Legacies about the US Exit from Vietnam," *Diplomatic History* 34 (June 2010): 577–87.

3. Birtle, *US Army Counterinsurgency*, 477.

4. Ibid., 480–81; Thomas E. Ricks, *Fiasco: The Military Adventure in Iraq* (New York: Penguin, 2006), 133.

5. Allan E. Goodman, "The Dual-Track Strategy of Vietnamization and Negotiation," in *The Second Indochina War: Proceedings of a Symposium Held at Airlie, Virginia, 7–9 November 1984*, ed. John Schlight (Washington, DC: Center of Military History, 1986), 150.

6. Ibid., emphasis in the original.

7. See, for example, D. Michael Shafer, *Deadly Paradigms: The Failure of US Counterinsurgency Policy* (Princeton, NJ: Princeton University Press, 1988).

8. Caspar W. Weinberger, "The Uses of Military Power," *Frontline*, PBS, November 28, 1984, https://www.pbs.org/wgbh/pages/frontline/shows/military/force/weinberger.html.

9. George C. Herring, *From Colony to Super Power: US Foreign Relations since 1776* (New York: Oxford University Press, 2008), 875.

10. George H. W. Bush, "Remarks to the American Legislative Exchange Council," March 1, 1991, PPP, https://www.presidency.ucsb.edu/node/265226.

11. Colin L. Powell, *My American Journey*, with Joseph E. Persico (New York: Random House, 1995), 502.

12. Elliot, "Parallel Wars?," 27.

13. Harry C. Summers Jr., *On Strategy: A Critical Analysis of the Vietnam War* (Novato, CA: Presidio Press, 1982).

14. Sinno, "Partisan Intervention," 1811–12. See also Terry H. Anderson, *Bush's Wars* (New York: Oxford University Press, 2011), 76–92.

15. Anderson, *Bush's Wars*, 93–101, quote on 101.

16. Ahsan I. Butt, "Why Did the United States Invade Iraq in 2003?" *Security Studies*, January 4, 2019, https://doi.org/10.1080/09636412.2019.1551567.

17. Glenn P. Hastedt, *American Foreign Policy*, 9th ed. (Boston: Pearson, 2011), 93–94; Ricks, *Fiasco*, 125–26.

18. Gary R. Hess, *Presidential Decisions for War: Korea, Vietnam, the Persian Gulf, and Iraq*, 2nd ed. (Baltimore: Johns Hopkins University Press, 2009), 286; James Mann, *Rise of the Vulcans: The History of Bush's War Cabinet* (New York: Viking, 2004), 351–53, 359–72.

19. Ricks, *Fiasco*, 394.

20. Hastedt, *American Foreign Policy*, 96; Anderson, *Bush's Wars*, 195–97.

21. Quoted in Ricks, *Fiasco*, 362. See also Anderson, *Bush's Wars*, 172–78.

22. Quotation from the preface of the 2002 edition in Max Boot, *Savage Wars of Peace: Small Wars and the Rise of American Power*, rev. ed. (New York: Basic Books, 2014), xxiii. See also Lind, *Vietnam*, 102–05.

23. John Nagl, "Learning to Eat Soup with a Knife: British and American Army Counterinsurgency Learning during the Malayan Emergency and the Vietnam War," *World Affairs* 161 (Spring 1999): 193.

24. Brent C. Bankus and James Kievit, "Vietnam and Iraq: Learning from the Past," *Joint Force Quarterly* 63 (4th quarter, 2011): 102–09, https://ndupress.ndu.edu/portals/68/Documents/jfq/jfq-63.pdf. The authors note that *Parameters* republished Petraeus's 1986 article in 2010.

25. Quoted from the dissertation in Rachel Dry, "Petraeus on Vietnam's Legacy," *Washington Post*, January 14, 2007.

26. Peter Maas, "Professor Nagl's War," *New York Times Magazine*, January 11, 2004.

27. Melvin R. Laird, "Iraq: Learning the Lessons of Vietnam," *Foreign Affairs* (November/December 2005), https://www.foreignaffairs.com/articles/vietnam/2005-10-01/iraq-learning-lessons-vietnam.

28. Ibid.

29. Robert Jervis, "The Politics of Troop Withdrawal: Salted Peanuts, the Commitment Trap, and Buying Time," *Diplomatic History* 34 (June 2010): 509.

30. Quoted in Robert Brigham, *Iraq, Vietnam, and the Limits of American Power* (New York: Public Affairs, 2008), 88. See also, Elliott, "Parallel Wars?," 33–37.

31. National Security Council, "National Strategy for Victory in Iraq," November 2005, Homeland Security Digital Library, https://www.hsdl.org/?view&did=457955, 1.

32. Ibid., 8.

33. Melvin Small, "Bring the Boys Home Now! Antiwar Activism and Withdrawal from Vietnam—and Iraq," *Diplomatic History* 34 (June 2010): 546.

34. Hess, *Presidential Decisions*, 272–75.

35. Nicholas J. Schlosser, *The Surge, 2007–2008* (Washington, DC: US Army Center of Military History, 2017).

36. US Department of the Army, Field Manual 3-24, *Counterinsurgency* (Washington, DC: 2006).

37. Douglas Porch, *Counterinsurgency: Exposing the Myths of the New Way of War* (Cambridge, UK: Cambridge University Press, 2013), 2. See also Karlin, "Why Military Assistance Programs Disappoint," 119.

38. Freedman, *Kennedy's Wars*, 291.

39. Porch, *Counterinsurgency*, 21.

40. David Galula, *Counterinsurgency Warfare: Theory and Practice* (Westport, CT: Praeger, 2006); David Galula, *Pacification in Algeria, 1956–1958* (Santa Monica, CA: Rand Corporation, 2006).

41. Daddis, *Withdrawal*, 77. See also Porch, *Counterinsurgency*, 200.

42. Porch, *Counterinsurgency*, 201–7; Daddis *Withdrawal*, 7–8; Fred Kaplan, *The Insurgents: David Petraeus and the Plot to Change the American Way of War* (New York: Simon & Schuster, 2013).

43. Porch, *Counterinsurgency*, 212.

44. Bergerud, *Dynamics*, 327.

45. James H. Lebovic, *The Limits of U.S. Military Capability: Lessons from Vietnam and Iraq* (Baltimore, MD: Johns Hopkins University Press, 2010), 2–3; Porch, *Counterinsurgency*, 212, 219, 223.

46. Small, "Bring the Boys Home Now!" 547.

47. Quoted in Anderson, *Bush's Wars*, 211.

48. Thomas E. Ricks, *The Gamble: General David Petraeus and the American Military Adventure in Iraq, 2006–2008* (New York: Penguin, 2009), 292.

49. Anderson, *Bush's Wars*, 217–18; Boylan, *Losing Binh Dinh*, 299; Hess, *Presidential Decisions*, 286; Ricks, *Gamble*, 296.

50. Anderson, *Bush's Wars*, 221.

51. Porch, *Counterinsurgency,* 331.

52. Anderson, *Bush's Wars*, 223.

53. Ibid., 224; Mark Atwood Lawrence, "Too Late or Too Soon? Debating the Withdrawal from Vietnam in the Age of Iraq," *Diplomatic History* 34 (June 2010): 589–600.

54. Sinno, "Partisan Intervention," 1812; Rajiv Chandrasekaran, "The Afghan Surge Is Over: So Did It Work?" *Foreign Policy*, September 25, 2012, https://foreignpolicy.com/2012/09/25/the-afghan-surge-is-over/.

55. Jeff Stein, "War Without End," *Newsweek*, November 2, 2018.

56. Porch, *Counterinsurgency*, 320–21.

57. Brigham, *Iraq, Vietnam, and the Limits of American Power*, 99.

58. Porch, *Counterinsurgency*, 310.

59. Quoted in Elliott, "Parallel Wars?," 42.

60. Ibid., 43.

61. George W. Bush, "Remarks at the Veterans of Foreign Wars National Convention in Kansas City, MO," August 22, 2007, PPP, https://www.presidency.ucsb.edu/node/27627.

62. Arnold Isaacs, *Without Honor,* 489.

Bibliography

Anderson, David L. *The Columbia Guide to the Vietnam War*. New York: Columbia University Press, 2002.

———. "Gerald R. Ford and the Presidents' War in Vietnam." In *Shadow on the White House: Presidents and the Vietnam War, 1945–1975*. Edited by David L. Anderson, 184–207. Lawrence: University Press of Kansas, 1993.

———. "No More Vietnams: Historians Debate the Policy Lessons of the Vietnam War." In *The War That Never Ends: New Perspectives on the Vietnam War*. Edited by David L. Anderson and John Ernst, 13–33. Lexington: University Press of Kentucky, 2007.

———. "One Vietnam War Should Be Enough and Other Reflections on Diplomatic History and the Making of Foreign Policy." *Diplomatic History* 30 (January 2006): 1–21.

———. *Trapped by Success: The Eisenhower Administration and Vietnam, 1953–1961*. New York: Columbia University Press, 1991.

———. *The Vietnam War*. Basingstoke, UK: Palgrave Macmillan, 2005.

Anderson, Terry H. *Bush's Wars*. New York: Oxford University Press, 2011.

Andradé, Dale. *Trial by Fire: The 1972 Easter Offensive, America's Last Vietnam Battle*. New York: Hippocrene Books, 1995.

Appy, Christian. *Patriots: The Vietnam War Remembered from All Sides*. New York: Penguin, 2003.

Asselin, Pierre. *Vietnam's American War*. Cambridge, UK: Cambridge University Press, 2018.

Bankus, Brent C., and James Kievit. "Vietnam and Iraq: Learning from the Past." *Joint Force Quarterly* 63 (4th quarter, 2011): 102–9. https://ndupress.ndu.edu/portals/68/Documents/jfq/jfq-63.pdf.

Bergen, John D. *Military Communications: A Test for Technology*. Washington, DC: US Army Center of Military History, 1986.

Bergerud, Eric M. *The Dynamics of Defeat: The Vietnam War in Hau Nghia Province*. Boulder, CO: Westview Press, 1990.

Berman, Larry. *No Peace, No Honor: Nixon, Kissinger, and Betrayal in Vietnam*. New York: The Free Press, 2001.

———. *Perfect Spy: The Incredible Double Life of Pham Xuan An*, Time *Magazine Reporter and Vietnamese Communist Agent*. New York: HarperCollins e-books, 2007.

Biddle, Stephen. "Seeing Baghdad, Thinking Saigon: The Perils of Refighting Vietnam in Iraq." *Foreign Affairs* 85 (March/April 2006): 2–14.

Birtle, Andrew J. "PROVN, Westmoreland, and the Historians: A Reappraisal." *Journal of Military History* 72 (October 2008): 1213–47.

———. *U.S. Army Counterinsurgency and Contingency Operations Doctrine, 1942–1976*. Washington, DC: Center of Military History, 2006.

Blumenthal, Ralph. "On a Delta River, a Test for Vietnamization." *New York Times*, February 17, 1970.

Boot, Max. *The Road Not Taken: Edward Lansdale and the American Tragedy in Vietnam.* New York: Liveright Publishing, 2018.

———. *Savage Wars of Peace: Small Wars and the Rise of American Power.* Rev. ed. New York: Basic Books, 2014.

Borch, Fred L. "Hall of Honor: Cau Le." *Vietnam* 31 (April 2019): 64.

Boylan, Kevin. *Losing Binh Dinh: Failure of Pacification and Vietnamization.* Lawrence: University Press of Kansas, 2016.

Brigham, Robert K. *ARVN: Life and Death in the South Vietnamese Army.* Lawrence: University Press of Kansas, 2006.

———. *Guerrilla Diplomacy: The NLF's Foreign Relations and the Vietnam War.* Ithaca, NY: Cornell University Press, 1999.

———. *Iraq, Vietnam, and the Limits of American Power.* New York: Public Affairs, 2008.

———. *Reckless: Henry Kissinger and the Tragedy of Vietnam.* New York: Public Affairs, 2018.

———. "Vietnamese Society at War." In *The Columbia History of the Vietnam War.* Edited by David L. Anderson. New York: Columbia University Press, 2011, 317–32.

Buffalo Springfield. "For What It's Worth." 1966. Genius. Accessed February 14, 2019. https://genius.com/Buffalo-springfield-for-what-its-worth-lyrics.

Bunker, Ellsworth. *The Bunker Papers: Reports to the President from Vietnam, 1967–1973.* Edited by Douglas Pike. Vol. 3. Berkeley, CA: University of California Institute of East Asian Studies, 1990.

Burr, William, and Jeffrey Kimball. *Nixon's Nuclear Specter: The Secret Alert of 1969, Madman Diplomacy, and the Vietnam War.* Lawrence: University Press of Kansas, 2015.

Butt, Ahsan I. "Why Did the United States Invade Iraq in 2003?" *Security Studies,* January 4, 2019. https://doi.org/10.1080/09636412.2019.1551567.

Carland, John M. *Combat Operations: Stemming the Tide, May 1965 to October 1966.* Washington, DC: US Army Center of Military History, 2000.

Chandrasekaran, Rajiv. "The Afghan Surge Is Over: So Did It Work?" *Foreign Policy,* September 25, 2012. https://foreignpolicy.com/2012/09/25/the-afghan-surge-is-over/.

Chapman, Jessica M. *Cauldron of Resistance: Ngo Dinh Diem, the United States, and 1950s Southern Vietnam.* Ithaca, NY: Cornell University Press, 2013.

Clarke, Jeffrey J. *Advice and Support: The Final Years, 1965–1973.* Washington, DC: US Army Center of Military History, 1988.

Clymer, Kenton. *Troubled Relations: The United States and Cambodia since 1870.* DeKalb: Northern Illinois University Press, 2007.

Collins, James Lawton. *The Development and Training of the South Vietnamese Army, 1950–1972.* Washington, DC: US Army Center of Military History, 1991.

Congressional Record, 88th Congress, 2d session (1964).

Cosmas, Graham A., and Terrance P. Murray. *U.S. Marines in Vietnam: Vietnamization and Redeployment, 1970–1971.* Washington, DC: US Marine Corps History and Museums Division, 1986.

Daddis, Gregory A. *No Sure Victory: Measuring U.S. Army Effectiveness and Progress in the Vietnam War.* New York: Oxford University Press, 2011.

———. *Westmoreland's War: Reassessing American Strategy in Vietnam.* New York: Oxford University Press, 2014.

———. *Withdrawal: Reassessing America's Final Years in Vietnam.* New York: Oxford University Press, 2017.

Dallek, Robert. "Lyndon Johnson and Vietnam." *Diplomatic History* 20 (Spring 1996): 147–62.

Davidson, Phillip B. *Vietnam at War: The History, 1946–1975.* New York: Oxford University Press, 1988.

DeGroot, Gerard J. *A Noble Cause? America and the Vietnam War.* Essex, UK: Longman, 2000.

Diem, Bui. *In the Jaws of History.* With David Chanoff. Boston: Houghton Mifflin, 1987.

Dry, Rachel. "Petraeus on Vietnam's Legacy." *Washington Post*, January 14, 2007.

Dulles, John Foster. Papers. Dwight D. Eisenhower Library, Abilene, Kansas.

Eggleston, Michael A. *Exiting Vietnam: The Era of Vietnamization and American Withdrawal Revealed in First-Person Accounts*. Jefferson, NC: McFarland, 2014.

Elliott, David. "Official History, Revisionist History, and Wild History." In *Making Sense of the Vietnam Wars: Local, National, and Transnational Perspectives*. Edited by Mark Philip Bradley and Marilyn B. Young, 277–304. Oxford, UK: Oxford University Press, 2008.

———. "Parallel Wars? Can 'Lessons of Vietnam' Be Applied to Iraq?" In *Iraq and the Lessons of Vietnam: Or How Not to Learn from the Past*. Edited by Lloyd C. Gardner and Marilyn B. Young, 17–44. New York: The New Press, 2007.

Estimative Products on Vietnam, 1948–1975. Washington, DC: National Intelligence Council, 2005.

Fear, Sean. "Saigon Goes Global: South Vietnam's Quest for International Legitimacy in the Age of Détente." *Diplomatic History* 42 (June 2018): 428–55.

Fitzgerald, Frances. *Fire in the Lake: The Vietnamese and the Americans in Vietnam*. New York: Vintage Books, 1973.

Frankum, Ronald B., Jr. *Like Rolling Thunder: The Air War in Vietnam, 1964–1975*. Lanham, MD: Rowman & Littlefield, 2005.

Freedman, Lawrence. *Kennedy's Wars: Berlin, Cuba, Laos, and Vietnam*. Oxford, UK: Oxford University Press, 2000.

Galula, David. *Counterinsurgency Warfare: Theory and Practice*. Westport, CT: Praeger, 2006.

———. *Pacification in Algeria, 1956–1958*. Santa Monica, CA: Rand Corporation, 2006.

Gibson, James William. *The Perfect War: The War We Couldn't Lose and How We Did*. New York: Vintage Books, 1988.

Gilbert, Marc Jason. "The Cost of Losing the 'Other War' in Vietnam." In *Why the North Won the Vietnam War*. Edited by Marc Jason Gilbert, 153–99. New York: Palgrave, 2002.

Goodman, Allan E. "The Dual-Track Strategy of Vietnamization and Negotiation," In *The Second Indochina War: Proceedings of a Symposium Held at Airlie, Virginia, 7–9 November 1984*. Edited by John Schlight, 143–52. Washington, DC: US Army Center of Military History, 1986.

Haldeman, H. R. *The Ends of Power*. New York: Times Books, 1978.

Hanhimäki, Jussi. *The Flawed Architect: Henry Kissinger and American Foreign Policy*. Oxford, UK: Oxford University Press, 2004.

Hastedt, Glenn P. *American Foreign Policy*. 9th ed. Boston: Pearson, 2011.

Herring, George C. *America's Longest War: The United States and Vietnam, 1950–1975*. 4th ed. New York: McGraw-Hill, 2002.

———. *From Colony to Super Power: U.S. Foreign Relations since 1776*. New York: Oxford University Press, 2008.

———. "The Vietnam Syndrome." In *The Columbia History of the Vietnam War*. Edited by David L. Anderson, 409–29. New York: Columbia University Press, 2011.

Hess, Gary R. *Presidential Decisions for War: Korea, Vietnam, the Persian Gulf, and Iraq*. 2nd ed. Baltimore: Johns Hopkins University Press, 2009.

———. *Vietnam and the United States: Origins and Legacy of War*. Boston: Twayne, 1990.

Hinh, Nguyen Duy. *Lam Son 719*. Washington, DC: US Army Center of Military History, 1979.

———. *Vietnamization and the Cease-Fire*. Washington, DC: US Army Center of Military History, 1980.

Hirashiki, Yasutsune "Tony." *On the Frontlines of the Television War*. Edited by Terry Irving. Philadelphia: Casemate Publishers, 2017.

"A History of the 1st Signal Brigade." *The Jagged Sword*. Special Issue. US Army 1st Signal Brigade Magazine, 1970.

Hughes, Ken. "Fatal Politics: Nixon's Political Timetable for Withdrawing from Vietnam." *Diplomatic History* 34 (June 2010): 497–506.

Isaacs, Arnold R. *Without Honor: Defeat in Vietnam and Cambodia*. Baltimore: Johns Hopkins University Press, 1983.

Jervis, Robert. "The Politics of Troop Withdrawal: Salted Peanuts, the Commitment Trap, and Buying Time." *Diplomatic History* 34 (June 2010): 507–16.

Johnson, Lyndon Baines. *The Vantage Point: Perspectives on the Presidency, 1963–1969.* New York: Popular Library, 1971.

Kagan, Frederick. "Iraq Is Not Vietnam." *Policy Review* 134 (December 2005–January 2006): 3–14.

Kaplan, Fred. *The Insurgents: David Petraeus and the Plot to Change the American Way of War.* New York: Simon & Schuster, 2013.

Karlin, Mara E. "Why Military Assistance Programs Disappoint: Minor Tools Can't Solve Major Problems," *Foreign Affairs* 96 (November/December 2017): 111–20.

Kimball, Jeffrey. *Nixon's Vietnam War.* Lawrence: University Press of Kansas, 1998.

———. "Out of Primordial Cultural Ooze: Inventing Political and Policy Legacies about the U.S. Exit from Vietnam." *Diplomatic History* 34 (June 2010): 577–87.

———. *The Vietnam War Files: Uncovering the Secret History of Nixon-Era Strategy.* Lawrence: University Press of Kansas, 2004.

Kinnard, Douglas. *The War Managers: American Generals Reflect on Vietnam.* Hanover, NH: University Press of New England for the University of Vermont, 1977.

Kissinger, Henry. *White House Years.* Boston: Little, Brown, 1979.

Know Your Enemy: The Viet Cong. Armed Forces Information and Education, Department of Defense, 1966. Combined Arms Digital Research Library. http://cgsc.cdmhost.com/cdm/singleitem/collection/p4013coll9/id/694/rec/1.

LaFeber, Walter. *The Deadly Bet: LBJ, Vietnam, and the 1968 Election.* Lanham, MD: Rowman & Littlefield, 2005.

Laird, Melvin R. "Iraq: Learning the Lessons of Vietnam." *Foreign Affairs* (November/December 2005). https://www.foreignaffairs.com/articles/vietnam/2005-10-01/iraq-learning-lessons-vietnam.

Lawrence, Mark Atwood. "Too Late or Too Soon? Debating the Withdrawal from Vietnam in the Age of Iraq." *Diplomatic History* 34 (June 2010): 589–600.

Lebovic, James H. *The Limits of U.S. Military Capability: Lessons from Vietnam and Iraq.* Baltimore, MD: Johns Hopkins University Press, 2010.

Lederer, William J., and Eugene Burdick. *The Ugly American.* Greenwich, CT: Fawcett Publications, 1962.

Le Gro, William E. *Vietnam from Cease-Fire to Capitulation.* Washington, DC: US Center of Military History, 1981.

Lewy, Guenter. *America in Vietnam.* New York: Oxford University Press, 1978.

Lind, Michael. *Vietnam: The Necessary War.* New York: The Free Press, 1999.

Maas, Peter. "Professor Nagl's War." *New York Times Magazine,* January 11, 2004.

Mann, James. *Rise of the Vulcans: The History of Bush's War Cabinet.* New York: Viking, 2004.

The Military Institute of Vietnam. *Victory in Vietnam: The Official History of the People's Army of Vietnam, 1954–1975.* Translated by Merle L. Pribbenow. Lawrence: University Press of Kansas, 2002.

Miller, Edward. *Misalliance: Ngo Dinh Diem, the United States, and the Fate of South Vietnam.* Cambridge, MA: Harvard University Press, 2013.

Morgan, Thomas B. "Reporters of the Lost War." *Esquire,* July 1, 1984, 49–60. https://classic.esquire.com/article/1984/7/1/reporters-of-the-lost-war.

Moyar, Mark, Donald Kagan, and Frederick Kagan. *A Question of Command: Counterinsurgency from the Civil War to Iraq.* New Haven, CT: Yale University Press, 2009.

Nagl, John. "Learning to Eat Soup with a Knife: British and American Army Counterinsurgency Learning during the Malayan Emergency and the Vietnam War." *World Affairs* 161 (Spring 1999): 193–99.

National Security Council. "National Strategy for Victory in Iraq." November 2005. Homeland Security Digital Library. https://www.hsdl.org/?view&did=457955.

Nguyen, Lien-Hang T. *Hanoi's War: An International History of the War for Peace in Vietnam.* Chapel Hill: University of North Carolina Press, 2012.

Nguyen, Nathalie Huynh Chau. *South Vietnamese Soldiers: Memories of the Vietnam War and After*. Santa Barbara, CA: Praeger, 2016.
Nguyen, Tien Hung, and Jerrold L. Schecter. *The Palace File*. New York: Harper & Row, 1986.
Nixon, Richard M. *No More Vietnams*. New York: Arbor House, 1985.
———. *The Real War*. New York: Warner Books, 1980.
———. *RN: The Memoirs of Richard Nixon*. New York: Grosset and Dunlap, 1978.
The Pentagon Papers: The Defense Department History of United States Decisionmaking on Vietnam. Senator Grave Edition. Vol. 2. Boston: Beacon Press, 1971.
Porch, Douglas. *Counterinsurgency: Exposing the Myths of the New Way of War*. Cambridge, UK: Cambridge University Press, 2013.
Powell, Colin L. *My American Journey*. With Joseph E. Persico. New York: Random House, 1995.
Prados, John, "Introduction to Roundtable XX-13 on Gregory A. Daddis, *Withdrawal: Reassessing America's Final Years in Vietnam*." H-Diplo. November 12, 2018. http://www.tiny.cc/Roundtable-XX-13.
———. *Vietnam: The History of an Unwinnable War, 1945–1975*. Lawrence: University Press of Kansas, 2009.
Prentice, David L. "Choosing 'the Long Road': Henry Kissinger, Melvin Laird, Vietnamization, and the War over Nixon's Vietnam Strategy." *Diplomatic History* 40 (June 2016): 445–74.
Public Papers of the Presidents (PPP). The American Presidency Project. http://www.presidency.ucsb.edu/.
Record, Jeffrey. "Leaving Vietnam: Insights for Iraq?" *Diplomatic History* 34 (June 2010): 567–76.
Records of US Forces in Southeast Asia, 1950–1975 (RG 472). National Archives, College Park, Maryland.
Ricks, Thomas E. *Fiasco: The Military Adventure in Iraq*. New York: Penguin, 2006.
———. *The Gamble: General David Petraeus and the American Military Adventure in Iraq, 2006–2008*. New York: Penguin, 2009.
Rienzi, Thomas Matthew. *Communications-Electronics, 1962–1970*. Washington, DC: US Department of the Army, 1985.
Saal, Harve, and Spencer Tucker. "Counterinsurgency Warfare." In *Encyclopedia of the Vietnam War*. Edited by Spencer Tucker, 136–39. Santa Barbara, CA: ABC-Clio, 1998.
Sadat, Kosh, and Stan McChrystal. "Staying the Course in Afghanistan: How to Fight the Longest War," *Foreign Affairs* 96 (November/December 2017): 2–8.
Schlosser, Nicholas J. *The Surge, 2007–2008*. Washington, DC: US Army Center of Military History, 2017.
Schmitz, David F. *Richard Nixon and the Vietnam War: The End of the American Century*. Lanham, MD: Rowman & Littlefield, 2014.
Schulzinger, Robert D. *A Time for War: The United States and Vietnam, 1941–1975*. New York: Oxford University Press, 1997.
Shafer, D. Michael. *Deadly Paradigms: The Failure of U.S. Counterinsurgency Policy*. Princeton, NJ: Princeton University Press, 1988.
Shaw, John M. *The Cambodian Campaign: The 1970 Offensive and America's Vietnam War*. Lawrence: University Press of Kansas, 2005.
Sheehan, Neil. *A Bright Shining Lie: John Paul Vann and America in Vietnam*. New York: Random House, 1988.
Shkurti, William J. *Soldiering On in a Dying War: The True Story of the Firebase Pace Incident and the Vietnam Drawdown*. Lawrence: University Press of Kansas, 2011.
Sinno, Abdulkader. "Partisan Intervention and the Transformation of Afghanistan's Civil War." *American Historical Review* 120 (December 2015): 1811–28.
Sky, Emma. "Mission Still Not Accomplished in Iraq: Why the United States Should Not Leave." *Foreign Affairs* 96 (November/December 2017): 9–15.
Small, Melvin. *Antiwarriors: The Vietnam War and the Battle for America's Hearts and Minds*. Wilmington, DE: Scholarly Resources, 2002.

———. "Bring the Boys Home Now! Antiwar Activism and Withdrawal from Vietnam—and Iraq." *Diplomatic History* 34 (June 2010): 543–53.

Sorley, Lewis A. *A Better War: The Unexamined Victories and Final Tragedy of America's Last Years in Vietnam.* New York: Harcourt, 1999.

———. *Thunderbolt: General Creighton Abrams and the Army of His Times.* New York: Simon & Schuster, 1992.

———. *Westmoreland: The General Who Lost Vietnam.* Boston: Houghton Mifflin Harcourt, 2011.

Spector, Ronald H. *Advice and Support: The Early Years, 1941–1960.* Washington, DC: US Army Center of Military History, 1983.

Stein, Jeff. "War Without End." *Newsweek*, November 2, 2018.

Stewart, Geoffrey C. *Vietnam's Lost Revolution: Ngo Dinh Diem's Failure to Build an Independent Nation, 1955–1963.* Cambridge, UK: Cambridge University Press, 2017.

Summers, Harry C., Jr. *Historical Atlas of the Vietnam War.* Introduction and Epilogue by Stanley Karnow. Boston: Houghton Mifflin, 1995.

———. *On Strategy: A Critical Analysis of the Vietnam War.* Novato, CA: Presidio Press, 1982.

Suri, Jeremy. *Henry Kissinger and the American Century.* Cambridge, MA: Harvard University Press, 2007.

Truong Nhu Tang. *Vietcong Memoir: An Inside Account of the Vietnam War and Its Aftermath.* With David Chanoff and Doan Van Toai. San Diego, CA: Harcourt Brace Jovanovich, 1985.

Twain, Mark. Directory of Mark Twain's Maxims, Quotations, and Various Opinions. Accessed March 11, 2019. http://www.twainquotes.com/Success.html.

US Department of State. *Foreign Relations of the United States* (FRUS), *1961–1975.* Washington, DC: US Government Printing Office, 1991–2010.

US Department of the Army. Field Manual 3–24. *Counterinsurgency Operations.* Washington, DC, 2006.

Van Atta, Dale. *With Honor: Melvin Laird in War, Peace and Politics.* Madison: University of Wisconsin Press, 2008.

VanDeMark, Brian. *Into the Quagmire: Lyndon Johnson and the Escalation of the Vietnam War.* New York: Oxford University Press, 1991.

Vien, Cao Van. *The Final Collapse.* Washington, DC: US Army Center of Military History, 1983.

———. *Leadership.* Washington, DC: US Army Center of Military History, 1981.

Vietnam Center and Archive. Texas Tech University, Lubbock, Texas. www.vietnam.ttu.edu.

Webb, Willard J. *The Joint Chiefs of Staff and the War in Vietnam, 1969–1970.* Washington, DC: Office of the Chairman of the Joint Chiefs of Staff, 2002.

Webb, Willard J., and Walter S. Poole. *The Joint Chiefs of Staff and the War in Vietnam, 1971–1973.* Washington, DC: Office of the Chairman of the Joint Chiefs of Staff, 2007.

Weinberger, Caspar W. "The Uses of Military Power." *Frontline*, PBS, November 28, 1984. https://www.pbs.org/wgbh/pages/frontline/shows/military/force/weinberger.html.

Westmoreland, William C. *A Soldier Reports.* New York: Dell, 1980.

West Point Center for Oral History. US Military Academy, West Point, New York. www.westpointcoh.org.

Whitney, Craig R. "Tunnel Vision: Watching Iraq, Seeing Vietnam." *New York Times,* November 9, 2003.

Wiest, Andrew. *Vietnam's Forgotten Army: Heroism and Betrayal in the ARVN.* New York: New York University Press, 2007.

Willbanks, James H. *Abandoning Vietnam: How America Left and South Vietnam Lost Its War.* Lawrence: University Press of Kansas, 2004.

———. *A Raid Too Far: Operation Lam Son 719 and Vietnamization in Laos.* College Station, TX: Texas A&M University Press, 2014.

Windrow, Martin. *The Last Valley: Dien Bien Phu and the French Defeat in Vietnam.* Boston: Da Capo Press, 2006.

Index

Abrams, Creighton W., 16, 19, 32, 34, 40, 72, 107, 137; combat support and, 38, 57; engineering and, 39; Laird and, 83; M1 Abrams tank, 127; Nixon and, 56; Nixon exit strategy and, 115; "one-war" concept, 25, 35, 35–36, 36; RVNAF, assessment of RVNAF operations by, 80; Westmoreland and, 18, 115

Abu Ghraib, 132

Accelerated Pacification Campaign (APC), 7–8, 25

advanced individual training (AIT), 59, 70, 127

AFB. *See* McChord Air Force Base

Afghanistan, 139, 139–140, 141

"Agreement Ending the War and Restoring Peace in Vietnam", 97

aircraft transferred to VNAF, 40

Air Force, US, 120

airmobile tactics, 39; overreliance on, 80

AIT. *See* advanced individual training

Algeria, 135

American Friends Service Committee, 121

American Vietnam veterans, 126

Amos (Captain), 64

An Loc, 88, 90

antiaircraft fire, 78

anticolonialist emotions, 1

antiwar movement, 45

antiwar pressure, 28

antiwar protests, 53, 75

APC. *See* Accelerated Pacification Campaign

Apollo 11 (spaceflight), 29

Armed Forces Council, 112

Armed Forces Radio and Television, 71

L'Armeé Nationale Vietnamienne (AVN), 119

Army and Marine Corps Field Manual (FM), 135

Army Center of Military History, 127

Army Chief of Staff, 94

Army of the Republic of Vietnam (ARVN), 8, 26, 39, 53, 78, 103; coup by, 13; defending ARVN divisions, 88; education requirement in, 69; Laird on, 51; little combat experience of, 52; living conditions of ARVN soldiers, 33; motivation of enlisted men in, 121; NCOs and, 68; pacification and, 17–18, 118; Parrot's Beak and, 99; 620th Signal Battalion, 71; top command of, 116; upgrading, 18; US training of, 107–108

Army Signal School, 42

Army War College, 129

ARVN. *See* Army of the Republic of Vietnam

automated digital network (AUTODIN), 64

AVN. *See* L'Armeé Nationale Vietnamienne

B-52s, 78, 89, 96
Baathist Party, 131
Baghdad, 134, 135, 137
Ban Me Thuot, 104
Bao Dai, 109
basic training, 59
Basra, 137
Beijing, 83, 94
Bergerud, Eric, ix, 137
A Better War (Sorley), 133, 136
Binh Dinh, ix, 36, 114
bin Laden, Osama, 130
black market, 99
Bolshevik Revolution, 119
bombing, 14, 96; Cambodia, Nixon
    bombing of, 23; Hanoi and, 50;
    Operation Linebacker, 89; suicide
    bombers, 138
Boot, Max, 18, 133
Boylan, Kevin, ix, 6, 18, 37, 106, 114, 122
Brigham, Robert, 50, 74, 140
Buddies Together (*Cung Than Thien*), 63
Bui Diem, 24, 26, 28, 85, 101, 104
Bundy, McGeorge, 14
Bundy, William, 113
Bunker, Ellsworth, 5, 23, 28, 31, 51, 107;
    Kissinger and, 80; Nixon and, 98
Burdick, Eugene, 11
Bush, George H. W., 126, 129
Bush, George W., 125, 130, 134, 138, 141
Bush Doctrine, 130

CA. *See* combat assault
Cambodia, 8, 12, 50–51, 74, 82; Abrams
    assessment of RVNAF operations in,
    80; cross-border operations in, 73, 75;
    ground raids in, 76; Nixon bombing of,
    23; Nixon lying about, 53;
    RVN–Cambodia border, 47; war
    expanded to, 54
Camp Carroll, 68
Camp Eagle, 66, 67
Camp Evans, 67
Cam Ranh, 60, 62
Cam Ranh Bay, 68
Cao Van Vien, 77, 101, 122
Carver, George, 112
Cau (Colonel), 103
cease-fire, 87, 94, 97

Central Command, 133
Central Highlands, 97
Central Intelligence Agency (CIA), 5, 12,
    32, 84
Central Military Commission, 86
Central Office for South Vietnam
    (COSVN), 23, 53
Champion, John, 63
Chennault, Anna, 113
Chiang Kai-shek, 27, 108
China, 12, 85, 110
Chinese Communist Party, 117
Chinese Revolution, 119
Chu Lai, 69
CIA. *See* Central Intelligence Agency
CINCPAC. *See* Commander in Chief,
    Pacific
civic action, 7, 128
Civil Affairs and Security Assistance
    School, 128
civilian workforce, 99
civil-military relations, 128
Civil Operations and Revolutionary
    Development Support (CORDS), 31
Clifford, Clark, 18, 19
Coalition Provisional Authority (CPA),
    131, 132, 134
COIN. *See* counterinsurgency
Colby, William, 5, 36
Cold War, viii, 3, 10, 126; early, 114;
    patriotism, 58; Vietnam War and, 5
Collins, Arthur S., Jr., 37
colonialism, 4, 16, 57; neocolonialism,
    110, 114
combat assault (CA), 79
combat support, ix, 38, 39, 40, 42, 57;
    deficiencies, 88; RVNAF and, 101
Commander in Chief, Pacific (CINCPAC),
    34
communications-electronics, ix, 59
Communications Standards Branch, 62, 63
communism, ix, 3, 4, 109, 110, 111;
    nationalism and, 120
Communist Party of Vietnam, 112
Congress, US, 14, 100, 101, 107
Consolidated RVN Improvement Plan
    (CRIMP), 34, 35
Cooper-Church Amendment, 74

CORDS. *See* Civil Operations and
  Revolutionary Development Support
corruption, 6, 8, 99, 101, 118; Ngo Dinh
  Diem and, 121; RVNAF and, 122;
  Saigon and, 75
cost of living, 99
COSVN. *See* Central Office for South
  Vietnam
counterinsurgency (COIN), ix, x, 7, 10,
  107, 123, 139; classic
  counterinsurgency formula, 106; COIN
  theory, 15; contemporary COIN
  practitioners, 136; counterinsurgency
  warfare, 2; doctrine, 127; formula for,
  1, 134; Kennedy, Counterinsurgency
  Plan of, 11; Lansdale and, 12; myths of,
  128; pacification and, 1; scaling up of
  COIN tactics, 16; tactics, 133; theory,
  viii–ix
coups, 13, 110; against Ngo Dinh Diem,
  84, 107; against Sihanouk, 51
CPA. *See* Coalition Provisional Authority
CRIMP. *See* Consolidated RVN
  Improvement Plan
Cung Than Thien (Buddies Together), 63

Daddis, Gregory, 6, 19, 36, 56, 106; on Tet
  Offensive, 107
Da Nang x, 55, 62, 63, 65, 66, 70, 71, 80,
  91, 103
Da Nang Air Force Base, 70
DAO. *See* Defense Attaché Office
date of estimated return from overseas
  (DEROS), 62, 67
Davidson, Phillip, 18, 80
Defense Attaché Office (DAO), 97
Democratic Party, 95, 135
Democratic People's Republic of Korea,
  109
Democratic Republic of Vietnam (DRV),
  1, 2, 9, 45, 83, 97, 105; Central Military
  Commission of, 86; defender against
  imperialism, 6; diplomats from, 84;
  Kissinger and, 22; negotiations and, 29,
  87; triumph of, 101
Department of Defense, 25, 42, 47
Department of State, 47
DEROS. *See* date of estimated return from
  overseas

Dien Bien Phu, 9, 117, 119
diplomatic concessions, 116
diplomats, 84
Dobrynin, Anatoly, 29
Do Cao Tri, 52
Dong Tien (Progress Together), 52
DRV. *See* Democratic Republic of
  Vietnam
Duck Hook, 26, 47
Dulles, John Foster, 108
Duong Van Minh, 84, 104, 111
Duquemin, Gordon J., 37
Durbrow, Elbridge, 12

Easter Offensive, 87, 88, 90, 96, 118
education, 1
Eggleston, Michael, 71, 72
Eisenhower, Dwight, 3, 19, 109, 110, 115
Elliott, David, 141
Ely, Paul, 9
engineering, 39
Ewell, Julian, 52

F-5A fighter-bombers, 35
Fallujah, 132
fascism, 112
favoritism, 118
Federal Electric, 42
Fire Support Bases (FSBs), 119
1st Cavalry, 52, 122
1st Logistical Command, 39
1st Signal Brigade, 41, 42, 61, 62, 63, 64,
  69, 77
First Indochina War, 2, 119
fixed fire bases, 78
Flying Tigers, 60
FM. *See* Army and Marine Corps Field
  Manual
Ford, Gerald, 100, 101, 104
Foreign Affairs (magazine), 134
foreign policy, vii
Fort Bragg, 128
Fort Huachuca, 59, 61, 62
43rd Signal Battalion, 60, 71
fragging, 67
Franco–Viet Minh War, 110
Franks, Tommy, 131
French colonization, 2, 108, 109
French Expeditionary Corps, 2, 109, 114

FSBs. *See* Fire Support Bases

Galula, David, 136
Geneva, Switzerland, 2
Geneva Agreements, 110
Geneva Conference, 7, 10, 109, 110
Giai (Brigadier General), 90
Gibson, James William, ix, 120
global communist containment, ix
Goodman, Allan, 128
Goodpaster, Andrew, 24
Gorbachev, Mikhail, 126
Great Society, 19
Guam, 29, 48
Guardian (newspaper), 113
guerrilla attacks, 11
guerrilla war, 17
Gulf of Tonkin Resolution, 14
GVN. *See* South Vietnamese government

Haig, Alexander, 80, 95
Haiphong Harbor, 46, 90
Halberstam, David, 108
Haldeman, H. R., 22, 23
Hamlet Evaluation System (HES), 35
Hanoi, x, 6, 33, 48, 101; antiwar protests
    and, 75; bombing and, 50; Kissinger
    and, 28, 83; peace talks and, 21;
    stockpiling supplies, 76
Harris poll, 82
Hau Nghia, ix, 7
Headquarters, Headquarters Detachment
    (HHD), 62
health care, 1
Heiser, Joseph M., Jr., 39
helicopter support, 40
heroin, 67
HES. *See* Hamlet Evaluation System
Heston, Charlton, 129
HHD. *See* Headquarters, Headquarters
    Detachment
Hilsman, Roger, 11, 13
Hoang Duc Ninh, 75
Hoang Xuan Lam, 55, 77, 78, 79, 81, 91
Ho Chi Minh, x, 2, 29
Ho Chi Minh Trail, 51, 52, 76, 77
Hue 2, 18, 65, 68, 69, 88, 103, 111
Humphrey, Hubert H., 19, 20
Hussein, Saddam, 125, 129, 131, 132

Ia Drang, 119
ICS, SEA. *See* Integrated Communication
    System, Southeast Asia
IEDs. *See* improvised explosive devises
IMP. *See* improvement and modernization
    program
imperialism, 3, 6
improvement and modernization program
    (IMP), 31; Phase III RVNAF IMP, 34,
    47
improvised explosive devises (IEDs), 138
income, 1
Independence Palace, 102
Indochina, 109
Indochina War, 2, 6, 108, 113, 117, 118,
    119
insurgency, 1, 133; armed, 2
Integrated Communication System,
    Southeast Asia (ICS, SEA), 41, 42, 63
integrated tactics, 17
integrated wideband communications
    system (IWCS), 41, 61
International Telephone and Telegraph, 42
Iraqi Army, 135
Iraqification, 125, 132, 134, 138
Iraqi Freedom, 136
Iraq Study Group (ISG), 135
Iraq War, viii, 125, 132
Isaacs, Arnold, 116, 141
ISG. *See* Iraq Study Group
ISIS. *See* Islamic State in Iraq and Syria
Islamic fundamentalists, 130
Islamic State in Iraq and Syria (ISIS), 138
IWCS. *See* integrated wideband
    communications system

Jackson State University, 53
JAG. *See* Naval Judge Advocate General
Japan, 110
JCS. *See* Joint Chiefs of Staff
JGS. *See* Joint General Staff
John F. Kennedy Institute for Military
    Assistance, 127
Johnson, Lyndon, 13–14, 90, 114, 132;
    changes in command made by, 19;
    escalation by, 15; Nguyen Van Thieu
    and, 16; peace talks and, 21; Tet
    Offensive and, 18, 135

Joint Chiefs of Staff (JCS), 22, 34, 96, 139; Nixon and, 46; Readiness Test, 47
Joint General Staff (JGS), 77, 122

Karnow, Stanley, 119, 120
Karzai, Hamid, 130, 138, 139
Kattenburg, Paul, 12, 136
Kennedy, John, 10, 48, 115, 132, 140; assassination of, 13; Counterinsurgency Plan, 11; John F. Kennedy Institute for Military Assistance, 127
Kent State University, 53
Kerwin, Walter T., Jr., 32
Khe Sanh, 77
Khmer Rouge, 51, 53, 102
Khrushchev, Nikita, 10
King, Martin Luther, Jr., 19
Kinnard, Douglas, 114
Kissinger, Henry, 21, 22, 23, 25, 87, 113, 122; analysis for Nixon by, 84; Brigham on, 50; Bunker and, 80; DRV and, 22; failed negotiations of, 95; Hanoi and, 28, 83; Le Duc Tho and, 94; Nixon and, 24; RVNAF and, 74; troop withdrawal and, 45–46
Know Your Enemy: The Viet Cong (pamphlet), 120–121
Komer, Robert, 26
Kontum, 88
Korean War, 120, 140
Kurds, 132, 139
Kuwait, 126

Laird, Melvin, 9, 22, 23, 24, 46, 85, 93, 134, 141; Abrams and, 83; antiwar movement and, 45; on ARVN, 51; Nixon and, 91; on Nixon Doctrine, 49; Saigon and, 22; Wheeler and, 32; on withdrawal, 25
Lam Son 719, 77, 78, 81, 91, 119; Harris poll on, 82; Marine Corps and, 117
Lansdale, Edward, 11, 12
Lao Dong (Vietnamese Communist Party), 10, 112, 119, 120
Laos, 74, 80, 81, 120
Laotian frontier, 12
large-unit operations, 18
Lawrence, T. E., 116

"Learning to Eat Soup with a Knife: British and American Counterinsurgency Learning during the Malayan Emergency and the Vietnam War" (Nagl), 133
Lederer, William J., 11
Le Duan, 29, 49, 50, 76, 94, 96, 98, 102, 126
Le Duc Tho, 49, 94
Lenin, Vladimir, 119
Leninism, 119
Limited War Task Force, 11
Lind, Michael, 133
Lodge, Henry Cabot, 23
logistics buildup, 85
logistics officers, 39
Long Binh, 62
long-range communication, 62
long-road option, 46
Lon Nol, 50, 51
Losing Binh Dinh: The Failure of Pacification and Vietnamization, 1969–1971 (Boylan), ix

MAAG. *See* Military Assistance Advisory Group
Machiavelli, Niccolò, 1
MACV. *See* Military Assistance Command, Vietnam
al-Maliki, Nouri, 132, 137
Mansfield, Mike, 113
Maoism, 119
Mao Zedong, 27, 119
marijuana, 66, 67
Marine Corps, 117, 120
Marine Corps Combined Action Programs, 137
marine deployment, 15
MARS. *See* Military Affiliate Radio System
Martin, Graham, 104
Marxism-Leninism, 3, 119, 140
massive airpower, 93
materiel aid, 101
McCaffrey, William J., 90
McCain, John, 23, 34, 51, 138
McCarthy, Eugene, 19, 48
McChord Air Force Base (AFB), 60
McCutcheon, Keith B., 55

McGarr, Lionel W., 11, 17
McGovern, George, 94
McMaster, H. R., 138
McNamara, Robert, 13
mechanized warfare drills, 127
Megger Earth Tester, 65
Mekong Delta, 50, 70, 75
Middle East, viii, 99, 141
Midway Island, 26, 33
militarism, 112
Military Affiliate Radio System (MARS),
    60
Military Assistance Advisory Group
    (MAAG), 7, 112; Geneva Conference
    and, 10; phased out, 13
Military Assistance Command, Vietnam
    (MACV), 5, 6, 15, 32, 50, 82, 89, 117;
    APC and, 25–26; created, 13; Duck
    Hook and, 47; redeployment directives
    and, 33; residual force desired by, 34;
    special schools set up by, 31; strategy
    of, 36; technical personnel and, 38; Tet
    Offensive and, 16
military avoidance, 58
military occupation specialty (MOS), 59,
    61
military threat, 1
Milwaukee Journal (newspaper), 22
modernization, 1
Modern Military Records of the National
    Archives, 65
Moorer (Admiral), 96
Moratorium Day, 48
MOS. *See* military occupation specialty
Moscow, 3, 26, 48, 89, 94, 102
Mosul, 137
My Tho, 121

Nagl, John, 133, 134, 136
Na San, 119
National Intelligence Estimate (NIE), 82
nationalism, 1, 2, 120
National Liberation Front (NLF), 10, 24,
    27, 111, 115
National Security Council (NSC), 11, 24,
    45, 85
National Security Decision Memorandum
    9 (NSDM 9), 24, 25

National Security Study Memorandum 1
    (NSSM 1), 21, 32
National Security Study Memorandum 36
    (NSSM 36), 25, 32
National Security Study Memorandum 37
    (NSSM 37), 25
"National Strategy for Victory in Iraq"
    (brochure), 134
nation building, 8
NATO. *See* North Atlantic Treaty
    Organization
Naval Judge Advocate General (JAG), 58
Naval Postgraduate School in Monterey,
    California, viii
Navy, US, 14
NCO. *See* non-commissioned officer
negotiations, 22, 84, 93, 135; DRV and, 29,
    87; Kissinger, failed negotiations of,
    95; Kissinger bilateral negotiations with
    Hanoi, 28
neocolonialism, 110, 114
Never Again Club, 11
Newsweek (magazine), 40
New York Times (newspaper), 49, 70, 113,
    125, 133
Ngo Dinh Diem, 3, 4, 13, 84, 104, 107,
    110; corruption and, 121; lack of
    popular allegiance to, 8; Lansdale and,
    11; Nixon and, 26; RVN and, 3
Ngo Dinh Nhu, 13, 122
Nguyen Cao Ky, 83, 113, 120
Nguyen Duy Hinh, 18, 80, 105, 106
Nguyen Khan, 111–112
Nguyen Van Hieu, 74
Nguyen Van Thieu, x, 4, 75, 90–91, 98,
    112; Johnson and, 16; lack of popular
    allegiance to, 8; Nixon and, 20;
    presidency, stability and survivability
    of, 83; Reagan and, 85; removal of, 84;
    resignation of, 87, 104; so-called
    reelection of, 86; survival of Thieu
    government, 43
NIE. *See* National Intelligence Estimate
9th Infantry Division, 52
Nixon, Richard, viii, 6, 9, 16, 54, 73, 80,
    105; Abrams and, 56; *Apollo 11* and,
    29; in Beijing, 83, 94; Bunker and, 98;
    Cambodia, bombed by, 23; Cambodia,
    lying about, 53; cease-fire and, 97;

Easter Offensive and, 88; election of, 21; exit strategy of, 115; failure of, 104; JCS and, 46; Kissinger analysis for, 84; Kissinger and, 24; Laird and, 91; long-road option and, 46; "madman" idea of, 45; narrow election victory in 1968, 115; negotiations and, 22; Ngo Dinh Diem and, 26; Nguyen Van Thieu and, 20; Nixon Doctrine, 29, 34, 48, 49, 100; personal insecurities, 141; policy in Vietnam of, 19; resignation of, 100; Silent Majority speech by, 47, 49, 134; troop withdrawal and, 8, 38, 81

NLF. *See* National Liberation Front

non-commissioned officer (NCO), ix, 57, 63, 68, 72

North Atlantic Treaty Organization (NATO), 109, 130, 138, 139

North Korea, 12, 110

North Vietnam, 51, 65, 93

November Moratorium, 48

NSC. *See* National Security Council

NSDM 9. *See* National Security Decision Memorandum 9

NSSM 1. *See* National Security Study Memorandum 1

NSSM 36. *See* National Security Study Memorandum 36

Obama, Barack, 138, 139

OCS. *See* officer candidate school

O'Daniel, John W., 7, 9

officer candidate school (OCS), 58

officer in charge (OIC), 63, 66

Ogden, D. W., Jr., 63

OIC. *See* officer in charge

oil embargo, 99

OJT. *See* on-the-job training

173rd Airborne Brigade, 36, 37

"one-war" concept, 17, 25, 35

On Strategy: A Critical Analysis of the Vietnam War (Summers), 129

on-the-job training (OJT), 39

On War (von Clausewitz), 129

Operational Report—Lessons Learned (ORLL), 64–65

Operation Desert Storm, 127, 129

Operation Linebacker, 89, 90

Operation Linebacker II, 96

Operation Rolling Thunder, 15

ORLL. *See* Operational Report—Lessons Learned

orthodox–revisionist argument, 6

Ottoman Turks, 116

Pacific Architects and Engineering, 39

pacification, viii, x, 17, 26, 114, 136; ARVN and, 17–18, 118; COIN and, 1; CORDS and, 31; VC harassing efforts of, 76

Parrot's Beak, 99

patriotic revolutionary nationalism, 1

PAVN. *See* People's Army of Vietnam

peace, 141

peace talks, 21

peasants, 99

Peers, William R., 36, 37

Pentagon, 9, 25, 32, 89, 130

People's Army of Vietnam (PAVN), 5, 6, 7, 15, 18, 24, 37, 50, 140; black market and, 99; numbers of, 74; pressure from, 32; reserve divisions of, 86; RVN, PAVN combat troops in, 97; South Vietnam, forces in, 99; Soviet Union and, 89; tanks of, 90; top command of, 116–117, 118; triumph of, 122; troop withdrawal, 21

People's Liberation Armed Forces, 50

People's Republic of China (PRC), 86, 88, 108, 126

performative war, 131

Petraeus, David, viii, 132, 133, 135, 136–139

PFs. *See* popular forces

Pham Xuan An, 78, 102

Phan Huy Quat, 113

Phnom Penh, 50

Phu Bai, 18, 62–63, 65, 66, 67, 68, 70, 71

Phuoc Long, 102

Platoon (1986), 126

Policy Planning Council, 11

Politburo, 6, 29, 75, 96, 98, 101, 126; military commission of, 88; Moscow and, 102; on offensive, 86; political control of, 112

popular forces (PFs), 37, 102

Porch, Douglas, 135, 140

postcolonial world, 10

Powell, Colin, viii, 128
Prados, John, 12
PRC. *See* People's Republic of China
presidential election, 1972, 47
PRG. *See* Provisional Revolutionary
   Government
prisoners of war (POWs), 4, 86, 87, 96
"A Program for Pacification and Long-
   Term Development of Vietnam"
   (PROVN), 16, 17, 18, 35
Progress Together (*Dong Tien*), 52
Provisional Revolutionary Government
   (PRG), 28, 87–88, 97
PROVN. *See* "A Program for Pacification
   and Long-Term Development of
   Vietnam"
public policy, vii
public safety, 1

al-Qaeda, 130, 132
Quang Da Special Zone (QDSZ), 55
Quang Tri, 65, 77, 90
Quang Tri City, 88
Qui Nhon, 77

radar-guided surface-to-air missiles, 78
Radio Saigon, 112
RC4 campaign, 117
Readiness Test, JCS, 47
Reagan, Ronald, 85, 101, 129
The Real War (Nixon), 54
redeployment directives, 33
redeployment schedule, 74
regional forces (RFs), 37, 102
Republican Party, 135
Republic of China, 108
Republic of Korea (ROK), 62
Republic of Vietnam (RVN), ix, 1, 7, 97,
   104; ability to survive, 32; basic social
   condition in, 54; combat operations in,
   9; corruption and, 6, 8, 18, 75, 86, 91,
   98, 99, 101, 103, 111, 118, 121, 122;
   deficiencies of, 53; Diem and, 3;
   economic lifeline of, 100; effectiveness
   of RVN forces, 33; funding of, 113;
   material aid to, 47; PAVN combat
   troops in, 97; repression by, 12;
   RVN–Cambodia border, 47; structural
   weaknesses of, 72; threats to, 4

Republic of Vietnam Armed Forces
   (RVNAF),. *See* RVN Armed Forces
revisionist historians, 5
RFs. *See* regional forces
Rienzi, Thomas M., 41, 42
Robbins (Master Sergeant), 61
Rogers, William, 23, 28, 51, 85
ROK. *See* Republic of Korea
Rostow, Walt W., 11, 12
Route 9, 77
RVN. *See* Republic of Vietnam
RVNAF. *See* RVN Armed Forces
RVN Air Force (VNAF), 35, 39; aircraft
   transferred to, 40; helicopter support
   and, 40; signal sites for, 41
RVN Armed Forces (RVNAF), 5, 8, 10,
   21, 50, 54, 114, 140; Abrams
   assessment of RVNAF operations, 80;
   combat support and, 101; complete and
   final collapse of, 102–103; corruption
   and, 122; Easter Offensive and, 88–91;
   expanded, 31; expanding in size, 38,
   43; flaws of, 88; increased supplies to,
   29; Kissinger and, 74; Lam Son 719
   and 77–83; language differences and,
   72; leadership of, 25, 116–123; major
   breakdown in RVNAF command and
   control, 79; modernizing, 134; Phase III
   RVNAF IMP, 34, 47; regular forces of,
   36; self-sufficient, 100; senior military
   leadership of, 118; strength of, 16;
   tactical air support for, 85; training and
   equipping of, 15; training of, 11;
   transfer of effort to, 23; use of
   ammunition and supplies by, 99
RVN Navy (VNN), 35

Saigon, x, 32; corruption and, 75; demise
   of government in, 102–103; lack of
   public support, 15; Laird and, 22;
   legitimacy problems of, 76; national
   revolt against, 38; political ineptitude
   of, 13; politically chaotic, 107; Reagan
   and, 85; rich provinces around, 111;
   support for, 4
Sainteny, Jean, 29
sappers, 66
satcom, 41
Schlesinger, James, 106

Schulzinger, Robert, 4
SEATO. *See* Southeast Asia Treaty Organization
Second Indochina War, 6, 117, 119
sectarian violence, 133
security, 6
SEER. *See* System for Evaluating Effectiveness of RVNAF
Selective Service System, vii
September 11, 2001, viii, 130
17th Armored Cavalry, 70
17th parallel, 7, 98
7th Infantry Division, 52
7th Marine Division, 55
Sheehan, Neil, 75
Shiites, 132
Shultz, George, 128, 129
signal sites, 41
Sihanouk, Norodom (Prince), 50, 51
Silent Majority speech (Nixon), 47, 49, 134
Sinno, Abdulkader, 130
620th Signal Battalion, 71
Sky Soldiers, 36, 37
Small, Melvin, 138
small wars, 135, 136
Socialist Republic of Vietnam (SRV), 114, 125
social reform, 74
Sorley, Lewis, 5, 18, 106, 113, 133, 136, 141; critics of, 107
Southeast Asia Treaty Organization (SEATO), 3, 110
South Korea, 110
South Vietnam, x, 2, 57, 87, 101, 116, 140; French Expeditionary Corps and, 114; independence and survival of, 25; new presidential election in, 87; PAVN forces in, 99; poor political and military leadership of, 116; scaling back US involvement in, 13; security of, 121; Southeast Asia Treaty Organization, 3; US military presence in, 5
South Vietnamese armed forces, ix
South Vietnamese government (GVN), 21, 122
South Vietnamese Signal Directorate, 69
Soviet Union, 3, 85, 88; PAVN and, 89
SRV. *See* Socialist Republic of Vietnam

stability operations, 128
staff functions, 117
Stars and Stripes (newspaper), 71
Stills, Stephen, 6
Stone, Oliver, 126
Strategic Communications Command, 63
suicide bombers, 138
Summers, Harry, 129
Sunni Muslims, 132, 139
Sun Tzu, 116, 140
survivor syndrome, vii
Sutherland, James W., 81, 120
Syngman Rhee, 108
System for Evaluating Effectiveness of RVNAF (SEER), 35

Table of Organization and Equipment (TOE), 61
tactical air support, 85
tactical area of responsibility (TAOR), 55
Tactics and Techniques of Counterinsurgent Operations (McGarr), 11
Taiwan, 110
Taliban, 139
tanks, 90, 127
Tan Son Nhut Airport, 32
TAOR. *See* tactical area of responsibility
Taylor, Maxwell, 10, 14, 140
Tchepone, 77
T-Day. *See* termination of hostilities day
TDY. *See* temporary duty
tear gas, 68
technical personnel, 38
temporary duty (TDY), 59, 64
Temporary Equipment Recovery Mission, 10
termination of hostilities day (T-Day), 32
Territorial Forces Evaluation System, 35
terrorism, viii
Tet Offensive, 7, 18, 38, 49, 103, 118; Daddis on, 107; Johnson and, 18, 135; MACV and, 16
III Marine Amphibious Force (III MAF), 55, 65
Third World conflicts, 128
Thompson, Robert, 11, 13, 55
361st Signal Battalion, 60, 61, 62, 68, 69
369th Signal Battalion, 41

Thunder Run, 131
Time (magazine), 78
TOE. *See* Table of Organization and Equipment
Tonkin–Chinese border, 117
transmitting and switching facilities, 40
troop withdrawal, x, 88; announcements of, 48; escalation and, 14; increments of, 25; Kissinger and, 45–46; mutual, 24; Nixon and, 8, 38, 81; PAVN, 21; phases of, 33; unilateral, 32, 49, 93; US, 9, 13, 20, 22, 23, 27
Truman, Harry, 114
Trump, Donald, 139
Twain, Mark, 112, 141
12th Signal Group, 63, 65, 71
25th Infantry Division, 52

The Ugly American (Lederer and Burdick), 11
unconventional warfare, 133
United States (US), 84, 94, 97, 109; aid from, 100; ARVN training by, 107–108; elections in, 87; heavy toll of Vietnam War on, 141; lack of motivation among soldiers from, 121; military and civil involvement of, 7; military presence in South Vietnam, 5; South Vietnam, scaling back US involvement in, 13; troop withdrawal, 9, 13, 20, 22, 23, 27
UT Law School, 58

Van Atta, Dale, 23
VanDeMark, Brian, 16
VC. *See* Viet Cong
VCI. *See* Viet Cong Infrastructure
Veterans of Foreign Wars, 141
Viet Cong (VC), 6, 10, 32, 103; black market and, 99; guerrilla attacks by, 11; numbers of, 74; organized VC units, 37; pacification, VC harassing efforts of, 76; triumph of, 122
Viet Cong Infrastructure (VCI), 7, 17, 31; hard-core, 37; persistent danger of, 114
Viet Minh, 2, 3, 7, 108, 119; Dien Bien Phu and, 9
Vietnamese Communist Party (Lao Dong), 10, 112, 119, 120

Vietnamese National Army (VNA), 9, 112, 119
Vietnamese nationalists, 2
Vietnam Interdepartmental Working Group, 12
Vietnam Syndrome, 127
Vietnam Veterans Memorial, 126
Vietnam War, viii, 107, 112, 125, 127; Cold War and, 5; heavy toll on US, 141
Village Voice (newspaper), 81
VNA. *See* Vietnamese National Army
VNAF. *See* RVN Air Force
VNN. *See* RVN Navy
Vogt, John W., Jr., 89
von Clausewitz, Carl, 129, 136
Vo Nguyen Giap, 116, 117

Wallace, George, 19, 21
War Powers Resolution, 98
Washington, D. C., 4; total military failure by, 103
Washington, George, 85
Watergate scandal, 95, 97–98, 99; Nixon resignation and, 100
weapons of mass destruction, 131
Weinberger, Caspar, 128
Weinberger-Powell Doctrine, 129, 137
Westmoreland, William, 6, 15, 17, 19, 35, 113, 137; Abrams and, 18, 115; airmobile tactics and, 39; large-unit operations and, 18
Weyand, Frederick C., 89, 94
Wheeler, Earle, 22, 32, 53
White House, 28
Willbanks, James, 6, 106, 107
Williams, Samuel T., 10, 17
Workers Party, 140
World Trade Center, 130
World War II, 40, 108, 112

Xuan Loc, 103, 104

Young Turks, 112, 113

Zhou Enlai, 83
Zinni, Anthony, 132

About the Author

David L. Anderson is a professor of history emeritus at California State University, Monterey Bay. From 2012 to 2019, he was a senior lecturer in the Department of National Security Affairs at the Naval Postgraduate School in Monterey, California. He is a past president of the Society for Historians of American Foreign Relations (SHAFR), and is general editor of the Vietnam: America in the War Years series, published by Rowman & Littlefield. He served in Vietnam from 1968 to 1970 as a sergeant in the US Army Signal Corps, and received the Bronze Star and Army Commendation Medals.

He is the author or editor of *Imperialism and Idealism: American Diplomats in China* (1985); *Trapped by Success: The Eisenhower Administration and Vietnam* (1991; received the Robert H. Ferrell Book Prize from SHAFR); *Shadow on the White House: Presidents and the Vietnam War* (1993); *Facing My Lai: Moving Beyond the Massacre* (1998); *The Human Tradition in the Vietnam Era* (2000); *The Columbia Guide to the Vietnam War* (2002; received a "Best of the Best" designation from the American Library Association and the American Association of University Presses); *The Human Tradition in America since 1945* (2003); *The Vietnam War* (2005); *The War That Never Ends: New Perspectives on the Vietnam War* (2007, with John Ernst); *The Columbia History of the Vietnam War* (2011); and *The Lowdown: A Short History of the Origins of the Vietnam War* (2011).

CPSIA information can be obtained
at www.ICGtesting.com
Printed in the USA
LVHW111628081120
671087LV00002B/6